D1267281

R. S. V. P.

Elsa Maxwell's Own Story

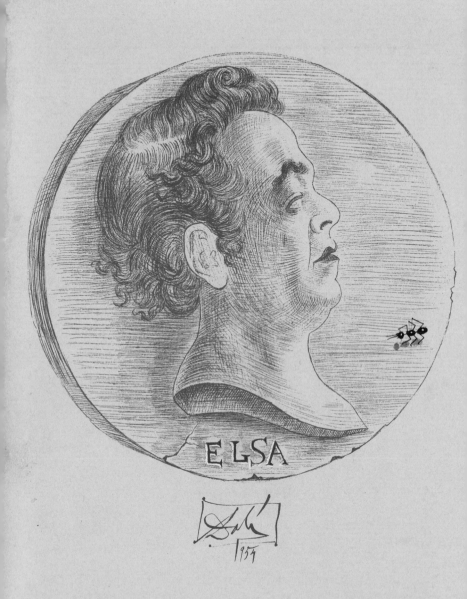

ELSA

R. S. V. P.
Elsa Maxwell's Own Story

by
ELSA MAXWELL

With Illustrations

Little, Brown and Company · Boston · Toronto

B
M465

*Published simultaneously in Canada
by Little, Brown & Company (Canada) Limited*

PRINTED IN THE UNITED STATES OF AMERICA

My grateful thanks to Salvador Dali for his frontispiece drawing, and to his wife, Gala, who has always been his inspiration.

List of Illustrations

All illustrations except the frontispiece will be found between pages 182 and 183.

R. S. V. P.

Elsa Maxwell's Own Story

Chapter 1

ON May 24, 1953, I gave a dinner party at Maxim's, in Paris, for eighteen guests. The occasion was my seventieth birthday and the party was at Maxim's because I never receive a check there. Albert, the world's greatest headwaiter, supervised the dinner, which included all the caviar and champagne his sturdiest waiters could carry, then relieved me of a heavier burden — the business of picking up the check. When I asked for the bill, Albert went through the customary byplay of murmuring, "I'm sorry, Mademoiselle, it is lost." Albert, whose soul shriveled while he was forced to serve Goering, Himmler and Von Ribbentrop during the German occupation of Paris, always adds his personal accolade to the Legion of Honor and the Medal of Resistance awarded to me by his government in recognition of my support of France during the war.

A sumptuous dinner on the house was not my only trophy of the chase that evening. Although the restaurant was crowded with beautiful women dressed to the teeth by the leading couturiers of Paris, I was wearing the most expensive and elegant gown, a red chiffon creation that would have cost anyone else 400,000 francs, the equivalent of $1100. It was made by Jean Dessès, who gives me fourteen dresses a year which, considering my figure, flout the old dictum that the artist cannot improve on nature. Perhaps that is why Dessès chose me for the most hilarious role of my career. After being known as the biggest frump in America and Europe, I am now the world's oldest and fattest mannequin. Making me a walking advertisement for his salon establishes Dessès as a masterful designer of publicity as well as clothes.

It was just two years ago that Dessès said to me: "I'd like to make some dresses for you." I replied that I couldn't afford so much as a Dessès scarf.

"Oh, no, I want to make you clothes for nothing," said the great Dessès. "Only you must let me make *enough* — at least twelve dresses a year."

"You must have a hole in your head," I cried. "Look at me!" I had never paid any attention at all to how I looked. But what woman could turn down the offer? When I returned to the States I appeared on television, spoke at public meetings, had parties, and all the columnists spoke of my transformation. Last year when I was in Paris, Dessès took me by the arm and said with a wry smile: "You told me I have a hole in my head. Now whose name did they mention — the Duchess of Windsor, Mrs. Byron Foy? Any of the other ten best-dressed? No. It was Elsa Maxwell."

Prince Aly Khan, a guest at the dinner, gave me a handsome diamond-studded comb for my birthday. I had the comb in my bag a few days later when I went to the birthday party for Senator Jacqueline Patenotre, who admired it so much that I gave it to her. I wish I could say I'm in the habit of presenting friends with costly gifts, but I do like to remember one gesture

I made a quarter of a century before on another birthday.

Early one May in the late 1920's, the secretary to Ralph Beaver Strassburger, the publisher of the Norristown, Pennsylvania, *Times Herald*, phoned me in Paris to say there was a credit of $5000 for me at Cartier's. Strassburger, who was wealthy in his own right, had further feathered his nest by marrying May Bourne, daughter of the president of the Singer Sewing Machine Company. When the Strassburgers were in Paris I had invited them to some of my parties. The secretary explained that the Strassburgers were sailing for America before my birthday but wanted to show their appreciation for my kindness.

Then, as now, there was nothing I cared for less than expensive jewelry. On an impulse I asked the secretary, "Would Mr. Strassburger mind if I use the money to get Kreisler?"

The question threw the girl off beam. "I'll have to ask Mr. Strassburger," she said. "Will you please hold on?"

"What kind of a Chrysler do you want?" Strassburger boomed. "An Imperial? I can get you fast delivery. Walter is my friend."

"I don't want an automobile," I told him. "I want Kreisler, the violinist, to play at my party."

"Five thousand dollars for a fiddler!" Strassburger cried incredulously.

It was the fourth time in one week I had heard that identical phrase, and it raised my blood pressure to the boiling point. The same supercilious crack had been made by the Barons Maurice, Robert and Henri de Rothschild, who had been thinking of engaging Kreisler to play at a private party before his public concert at the Paris Opera later in the month. Maurice got the idea first, but there was such terrific jealousy among the Rothschilds that his sisters-in-law, Kitty and Nellie, decided to beat him to the punch in pulling a social coup.

The Rothschilds came to me separately to ask if I could contact Kreisler, whom I had known in London before the First World War. So I wired to Kreisler in Berlin asking what his fee would be. He answered that he hated to play at parties but would do it for $5000, a price deliberately designed to discourage offers. He succeeded in cooling the musical ardor of the Rothschilds.

"Five thousand dollars for a fiddler!" each exclaimed. "Ridiculous."

Music has been the one passion of my life and the cavalier attitude of the immensely rich Rothschilds toward a great artist annoyed me. I'd never had $5000 in one piece before, of course, but I promptly decided to engage Kreisler for my party with Strassburger's present. The principal guests at the party were the Big Three of popular music — Cole Porter, George Gershwin and Irving Berlin — and, as an amusing afterthought, I invited the three Barons de Rothschild and their wives. I wanted to see their reaction when Kreisler played for an unknown American whose belongings had been put on the street for failure to pay her rent a few months earlier. The Rothschilds' performance was eminently satisfactory. They appeared to be on the verge of heart attacks, as they eyed me suspiciously — wondering how I had done it.

Kreisler played like an angel, amused that I, of all people, had met his price. His contempt for snobs is equalled only by mine. An American woman whose undistinguished French title was traceable in a direct line to her father's money once invited Kreisler to a party and added casually, "Of course, you'll bring your violin."

"In that case, my fee will be fifty thousand francs," Kreisler replied.

"In that case, I'll have to ask you not to mingle with my guests," the woman said haughtily.

Kreisler bowed. "In that case, my fee will be only ten thousand francs."

The Kreisler incident brought me a nice little dividend soon afterward. I was on the Riviera when Lloyd Osborne, Robert Louis Stevenson's stepson, phoned and said George Bernard Shaw wanted to meet me. I was both flattered and curious.

"Why does Shaw want to see *me?*" I asked.

"I haven't the foggiest notion," Osborne answered. "The old boy calls you the eighth wonder of the world."

A meeting was arranged and I put the question to Shaw myself. "I read about your party in the London newspapers," he said, "and I was amused by a woman who preferred Kreisler to a valuable jewel."

The Rothschild angle had not been covered in the newspapers. When I told Shaw of their chagrin, he laughed lustily, and said: "Everyone was happy except the barons, who couldn't afford Kreisler while *you* could — mistaken sense of values, that was all."

The great Shaw was a stingy man *and* a socialist. "Mr. Shaw," I asked, "would you have paid five thousand dollars to hear Kreisler?"

"I wouldn't have to," Shaw twinkled, "he'd play for me for nothing."

He'll play for me for nothing one day, too, I said to myself
— and he *did*.

Shaw, who began his literary career as a music critic, would
have been more captivated had he been at my fortieth-birth-
day party at Monte Carlo in 1923. My friend Serge Diaghilev,
the famous impresario, celebrated the occasion by staging the
premières of two new ballets, with Ernest Ansermet conducting the orchestra. Diaghilev asked me whether a young pianist
who had just escaped from Russia could play during the inter-
mission. I told him I would not think of inflicting an unknown on the distinguished audience, but Diaghilev was so
insistent that I finally consented to let his protégé play one
selection. I apologized to the Aga Khan, the most cultivated
man I know, for the punishment about to be inflicted on us.
He shrugged and murmured politely that he always was happy
to encourage young talent.

A slim, dark-haired young man of nineteen came out on the
stage, and began to play Lizst's Mephisto Waltz — and gave
me the most electrifying experience of my life. He was Vladimir
Horowitz, the most brilliant piano virtuoso of this generation,
whose first public performance in Western Europe was at my
party.

These, and a thousand other incidents involving fascinating
people and places, are wonderful and improbable things to
have happened to a fat, unattractive woman who was born in
Keokuk, Iowa, and was reared in San Francisco without money,
family position or even a grammar-school diploma. It is wildly
amusing to me — and a wry commentary on our times — that
I am recognized as an arbiter of international society and the
world's most famous hostess, distinctions calling for advantages

and attributes I lacked completely when I first barged into what is known as high society.

How, then, did Elsie (my real name) Maxwell, daughter of an unsuccessful insurance man, become the public utility of society? Walt Whitman said that democracy stimulates "the never-ending audacity of elected persons." Paraphrasing that statement to make it read the audacity of "self-elected persons" is the explanation of the reputation I have attained.

I won my title strictly by default. I realize it sounds as banal as a soap opera to say that any woman could have accomplished what I have done, yet it's perfectly true. Anyone with enough energy and imagination would have had a similarly vivid impact on the wealthy, who live in marble mausoleums surrounded by the suspicions and neuroses that have replaced the medieval moats which once isolated so-called aristocrats from reality.

Most rich people are the poorest people I know. Guilt complexes stemming from the way they made, married or inherited their money warp their normal outlets of warmth and vitality. I brought to them a capacity for friendship and gaiety that offered escape from plush-lined boredom, casual sex without passion and excessive gambling without excitement. I have been called a parasite for accepting the largesse of the wealthy, but I contributed as much, at least, as I received. I had imagination and they had money, a fair exchange of the commodity possessed by each side in greatest abundance.

I'm not being coy — a pose as ridiculous to me as a grass skirt on the Venus de Milo — when I say I got staggering mileage from a little imagination. Although I'm usually associated with lavish costume balls, the parties that established me as a personality in the monkey cage of society were based on a simple formula. Amusing, interesting people make successful parties. The first party I ever gave for royalty cost seven dollars for a dozen guests. Princess Helena Victoria, Queen Victoria's daughter, sat on the floor of my tiny two-room apartment in a converted stable in London, ate hard-boiled eggs and sausages and had the time of her life laughing at the antics of four young music-hall troupers named Noel Coward, Bea Lillie, Gertrude Lawrence, and Ivor Novello.

You protest that such entertainment cannot be produced by the average hostess? Granted. Any gimmick or glimmer of an amusing idea is a suitable substitute for professional talent. Once, when I was stuck with a covey of dull bankers and other assorted bores, I dreamed up a variation of an age-old game children play. The only props were corks tied to pieces of string and a large saucepan. The corks were pooled in the center of a table and the object of the game was to avoid having the corks trapped when the player brandishing the saucepan brought it down suddenly. The players who were caught had to pay a small forfeit; those who got away were paid double by the holder of the saucepan. The stakes were dimes, but my guests had a bigger kick playing that idiotic game than they got from gambling thousands of dollars in casinos on the Riviera.

Some of my ideas were so corny that I'm ashamed to repeat them. About fifteen years ago I was confronted with the bleak prospect of giving what was advertised as a bright, sophisticated lecture to several hundred clubwomen in the auditorium of a Cleveland department store at eleven o'clock in the morning. I already had run through my stock of carefully rehearsed ad libs in a previous lecture in Cleveland that season and the chances were splendid that I would lay an imposing egg with an audience that resented the fancy price charged for tickets by a charity organization. The thought of whipping up new material was too depressing to consider. In desperation, I bought a batch of paper mustaches and told the ushers to hand them out at the door. The mustaches were accepted as though they were dead mice, but a woman finally put on one and a chorus of giggles swept the auditorium as others followed suit. By the time I walked out on the stage wearing an outsize pair of handlebars, the place was in an uproar. I said nothing smart or significant that morning, but a few dollars spent on a silly gag won the most responsive audience I've ever faced.

There were elaborate parties and balls that cost enough to support comfortably the average family for ten years, but I'll leave the details for another chapter. I know there is greater curiosity in how I have managed to give lavish affairs and live in apparent luxury without money or sources of income for the last forty years. I have been a target for slander, half-truths and vicious gossip all my mature life, and I've finally decided to answer the ugly rumors and acknowledge publicly my indebtedness to friends who have carried me over the rough spots.

It has been said that I receive regular handouts from people — notably Mrs. Millicent Hearst and Cole Porter — that I exploit friends, that I charge heavy fees for sponsoring social climbers, that I blackmail people for keeping scandal out of the newspapers and that I collect kickbacks from caterers. The only shred of truth in all this is the assistance Mrs. Hearst has given me. All the other charges are utterly false.

In the last forty years, I have asked a small group of old friends to bail me out of jams from time to time by advancing me modest loans, and they have practically all been paid back. Such loans have totaled less than $20,000 in forty years.

Malicious rumormongers ignore one rather important detail. I have been working constantly since 1906. I have been a pianist in a nickelodeon, an accompanist for a vaudeville star in America, Europe and South Africa, a songwriter, a partner in two Paris night clubs, a consultant to a dressmaker, a press agent for Monte Carlo, an enthusiastic — if completely talentless — actress in the movies, theater, radio and television, a script-writer, a newspaper columnist, a contributor to magazines and a lecturer. I have earned an adequate income since 1938, although I'm the first to concede it is hardly sufficient for the social pattern I maintain.

Four old friends — Mrs. Hearst, Mrs. Jessie Donohue, Mrs. Eleanor Loder and Mrs. Margaret Emerson — who know I'm always strapped for ready money give me substantial checks at Christmas or on my birthday. The late Mrs. Evelyn Walsh McLean asked me to go to Hollywood with her in 1943 and gave me a check to cover $4000 worth of radio commitments I could not afford to pass up. The fabulously wealthy Mrs. McLean had such a wonderful time meeting the movie celebrities whom I introduced to her that she threw a mink coat into the bargain.

Such occasional windfalls do not explain, though, how I have been able to follow the social sun to Paris, London, Venice, Rome, Vienna, Biarritz, the Riviera, New York, Washington and Hollywood for nearly half a century.

Just to show how success seduces the memory, years ago I

reproached the late Prince Christopher of Greece for staying with a New York family notorious for what Thorsten Veblen called conspicuous consumption. "Where would poor royalty get three meals a day if not for the snobs?" he answered. I was properly squelched.

Frankly I could not make my headquarters in the three most expensive spots on earth without some sort of special angle or arrangement with hotels and restaurants eager to capitalize on the publicity I bring them.

The nearest approach to a home I've had since leaving San Francisco in 1907 is the Waldorf Astoria Hotel in New York, where I have been living from October through April, on and off, since 1931. I moved into the Waldorf for the very good reason that I was given a rent-free suite. The Waldorf opened in October 1931, in the depths of the depression, and Lucius Boomer, the president, made the offer thinking my presence in his hotel might bring other more-desirable guests. Boomer was right; the Towers filled up with friends. In 1946, when I resumed my globe-trotting after the war, I became self-conscious tying up badly needed space and made a deal to pay the Waldorf $350 a month for a two-room suite, about one third the regular rental.

In Paris I always have paid full rates for the suite I occupy at the Ritz. The famous Ritz operates on the sensible principle that it doesn't need promotion by me, but the management make a concession by letting me run up bills. The bookkeeping charges for carrying my account have been repaid a thousandfold by epic parties given for me by well-heeled friends. On one occasion, a derrick was needed to pick up a bill for $20,000 dropped on Jay O'Brien.

The former husband and dancing partner of Mae Murray, the movie star, O'Brien had married the ex-Mrs. Julius Fleischmann after her divorce and huge settlement from the yeast heir. I adopted Jay and Dolly, a gay, handsome couple who were a great addition to my parties, when they came to France in the mid-1920's. Old gallants recaptured their lost youth, if only briefly, flirting with Dolly, and Jay charmed the tiaras off the dowagers by dancing with them. Jay asked Cole Porter what he could give me for my birthday and Cole told him there was nothing I adored more than a party, so Jay gave me the green light. Serge Diaghilev was in Paris and that meant, of course, that I must have his ballet company perform at the party. I had the Ritz build a stage in the garden and sent out 300 invitations to a buffet supper. In the vast confusion, however, I neglected to tell Jay the magnitude his nice little gesture was assuming. The day before the party, Jay was walking through the Ritz and saw dozens of workmen scurrying around a five-story scaffolding.

"Building a new addition to the hotel?" he inquired.

"No, we're just preparing for Miss Maxwell's gala," he was told.

Jay was revived by the concierge, who kept brandy and smelling salts handy for such emergencies.

After Paris, my schedule takes me to the Riviera for four months, with brief excursions to Biarritz and Venice. I have standing invitations to be a guest at the most magnificent showplaces on the Côte d'Azur, but I prefer to stay with Dorothy "Dickie" Gordon, my oldest friend, who owns an unpretentious farm at Auribeau, a small village in the hills about a dozen miles from Cannes. Dickie's farmhouse, built in 1841, is chiefly distinguished for a lovely view, a waterfall and a huge millstone converted into an outdoor table. The millstone is set so low on a pedestal that it is decidedly uncomfortable, yet literally hundreds of people who command headlines throughout the world have driven over narrow, back-country roads to cramp their legs under the millstone at dinner parties. At one typical affair a few years ago there were the Duke and Duchess of Windsor — when I was friendly with the duchess — Clark Gable, Dolly O'Brien, Tyrone Power and Linda Christian, the Darryl Zanucks, the Jack Warners, the Charles Feldmans and Lord Milford-Haven.

Why did they come? Surely, it wasn't my beauty, wit or even the dinner, excellent as it was. It may sound immodest to the point of arrogance, but I honestly believe they were attracted by the gaiety I radiate as naturally as I breathe. As far back as I can remember, I've always been like a little girl on Christmas morning. I wake up every day with the unshakable — call it idiotic, if you will — conviction that something wonderfully exciting is about to happen. The ability to communicate that sense of anticipation was the quality that first drew people to me.

If I had all the money I've spent out of my own pocket on parties, I wouldn't have to be scrambling for a living at the age of seventy. I must confess, though, that some of my elaborate costume balls and memorable revels were given with the help of others. Friends turned their houses and staffs of servants over to me or hired hotel facilities, provided the food and liquor, just to make certain they were in on the fun. I suppose it's incomprehensible to a rational reader that people could become so jaded that they needed a social director to show

them how to enjoy themselves. It was analogous to backing a
revival of *Tobacco Road* on Broadway to be sure of a seat on
opening night.

The whole thing still doesn't make sense to me, but
the merry cycle snowballed as Elsa Maxwell's scavenger
hunts, murder parties, and fancy-dress affairs became all
the rage in Paris, London and New York. Guests who had
been the beneficiaries of other people's hospitality recip-
rocated by giving me carte blanche to organize lavish
shindigs.

I want to make several points clear. I never arranged a party
for a stranger. I never charged a fee for my services, although
some of the parties took weeks of careful planning. I never exploited friends for personal gain. My social whirl was purely a
labor of love in pursuit of pleasure.

Money never has interested me for the material possessions
it can buy. The example set by my father stifled my acquisitive
impulse, and I saw so many vulgar abuses of money as I grew
older that I developed a positive disdain for the ostentatious
symbols of wealth. I did not own a car until I was past fifty,
and then it was a secondhand jalopy. The only piece of jewelry
I own is a plain ring set with an emerald, my birthstone. When
I returned to Paris after the war, a clerk at Cartier's phoned to
tell me he had held in safekeeping during the German occupation a package I had left with the company in 1939. It contained two diamond rings worth several thousand dollars
apiece, given to me by Baroness Eugene de Rothschild for
Christmas nearly twenty years earlier. I had worn the rings so
infrequently that I had completely forgotten about them. Six
months later, I donated the rings to a New York charity at a

time when I was afflicted with the most plebeian of all ailments, severe anemia of the bank account.

In 1927, I was paid a retainer of $6000 to promote Monte Carlo as a summer resort. I lost it at the roulette tables as fast as I received the quarterly installments. In May, 1953, I was given a $5000 advance for this story. I immediately sent it to help stimulate a fund-raising campaign for the New York City Center, a nonprofit cultural organization that had previously honored me with an appointment to the board of directors.

Had I taken advantage of opportunities dumped in my lap, I'd be a rich woman today. Back in 1915, I spent a week end in Short Hills, New Jersey, at the home of Louis G. Kaufman, president of the Chatham Phenix National Bank and a big wheel in several industrial empires. Kaufman and William C. Durant, a pioneer automobile tycoon, passed the entire week end talking about the reorganization of General Motors. I couldn't help overhearing them; it was their only topic of conversation. Some twenty years later I met Kaufman again. He smiled at me benignly.

"Well, Elsa, you should have a tidy fortune now," he said.

It struck me as a bad joke because I was flatter than usual at the time. "Maybe I don't move in the right circles," I snapped. "Your humor is lost on me."

"Don't you remember when Durant and I spoke of General Motors?"

"I didn't listen. Business always bores me stiff."

Kaufman looked at me in amazement. "You'd be a millionairess if you had bought a few shares of stock. Anyone would have given his right arm to have heard our conversation."

I didn't bother to tell Kaufman I had other uses for my right arm, such as playing the piano, a more satisfactory pastime to me than clipping coupons.

The identical routine was repeated in 1922 when I was visiting Harold E. Talbott and his pretty wife Peggy on Long Island. Talbott, now the dynamic secretary of the air force, was organizing the Auto-Lite Corporation with Royce G. Martin, chairman of the board. Again I heard how a new company would revolutionize the automobile industry and again I turned a deaf ear. Auto-Lite stock was put on the market at a few cents a share. At the 1953 Automobile Show, Martin casually mentioned his company's stock was selling for something like $78 a share.

Wealth never interested me because I did not need it as a key to doors always open to me. I admire artists and creative geniuses above all other people, and I have associated with them all my life. I have known seven Presidents of the United States, entertained a dozen kings and have been on a first-name basis with half the titleholders in the *Almanach de Gotha*, but I'd trade places with anyone who knows a man I never have seen. He is Albert Schweitzer, musician, doctor and humanitarian, who isolated himself from the world to care for the natives in Africa.

I've been told a psychiatrist could have a field day with me, but I'm inclined to doubt it. My analysis would be completed in one quick session because I know, almost to the minute, the two incidents that freed me of the complications that clutter up the lives of most people — money and sex.

I never had a sexual experience, nor did I ever want one. I realize that sex is the most important drive in the world, that women should marry and bear children for their emotional fulfillment, that sex is the natural manifestation of love. Only I had a peculiar pride that prevented even curiosity about sex matters or allowing any person to *know* me intimately. I was fascinated by the passionate love affairs of my friends and helped their problems with an equally passionate devotion. I loved love but never loved a lover. I discovered when I was sixteen that I could not permit myself even to be kissed by a man. A traumatic shock did not inhibit my reaction; the man was charming and gentle. We were engaged and planning for the future, yet a psychological block made me reject the physical aspect of marriage.

Maybe egotism, or false idealism, prevented me from letting any man know me well enough for such intimacy. Maybe I expected too much of a man. I have been attracted by two men in my life — Cole Porter for his wit and musical genius and Aly Khan for his masculine appeal — but I was much too old when I met them to consider a romantic attachment. It was just as well. That thought never crossed their minds.

As I matured, I could not help wondering whether I was missing an enriching relationship. It is entirely possible my attitude would have changed had I seen the sex drive sublimated by love of family. I moved in a moral climate, however, where sex practically was an obsession. I was appalled that women bounced from pillow to four-poster without delicacy or discrimination, that repeated exposures to shoddy crises sabotaged their sensitivity and dignity. Maybe my perspective was distorted, but I saw so much unhappiness in the marriages of friends that I was content to have chosen music and laughter as substitutes for husbands and lovers.

At least one authority gave me a passing grade in emotional development. In 1931, I met the great Sigmund Freud in Vienna. He must have been amused by my talk, for he engaged me in conversation for fully a half hour. Freud asked me about my background. When I told him, he nodded and murmured: "A healthy woman who will never suffer from neuroses . . . " I didn't know then what neuroses were.

Instead of concentrating my affection on a family, I was free to lavish it on a hundred friends and establish accord with vibrant personalities. My emotional release might have been vicarious, but I was satisfied to have a front-row seat at some of the most romantic episodes of our time.

A contrived plot never had a happier or more charming ending than the Duchesse de Grammont story. The duchesse was the beautiful Princess Maria Ruspoli, from an old but impoverished Italian family, who was the third wife of the old duc, one of the wealthiest nobles in France. The de Grammonts gave the first great, glittering ball in Paris after World War I, at their mansion near the Etoile, and as Lady Alex Colebrooke and I were leaving we saw a young man walking off with his coat collar turned up against the rain. He was George Cuevas, a young man who literally danced for his suppers. Cuevas didn't have taxi fare to protect his dress suit — really his working uniform — and gratefully accepted our offer of a lift.

When the duc died, leaving her a modest fortune, Maria married Jean Hugo, the novelist's son, and restored the Castle di Vigoleno, a magnificent medieval fortress on a mountain peak at Salsomaggiore, near Milan. Maria had a flair for the dramatic that made Vigoleno one of the most imposing showplaces in Europe. Once when I took a group including the Princess Winnie de Polignac, Artur Rubinstein and a string quartet to visit her in a raging storm, she gave us a guiding beacon by illuminating the entire outline of the castle with torches set in the battlements and towers, a sight that put to shame the electric displays of Broadway and Piccadilly.

Maria lost the castle and all her money during World War II. She went to work in New York for a famous beauty salon. She kept the job for six years, until poor health forced her to quit in 1951. In the meantime, Cuevas had married Margaret Strong, who inherited more than fifty million dollars from John D. Rockefeller, her grandfather. Unlike many who hit the jackpot, Cuevas does not forget past favors. In September, 1953, Cuevas gave an elegant gala at Biarritz featuring the ballet company he subsidizes. The guest of honor was the Duchesse de Grammont, his former benefactress, whom Cuevas now supports in gracious style in a villa he bought for her at Aix-en-Provence.

Then there was Laura Corrigan, the principal in a little gem of a human-interest story. Laura, a telephone operator at a hotel in Cleveland, made a blind date with a guest who was drinking heavily, married him the following morning and acquired her husband's entire estate when he died six months later. Among other properties bequeathed to Laura were steel holdings she subsequently sold for eighty million dollars, in cash. Europe in the 1920's was awash with rich Americans who used money as a springboard for high dives into society, and no one made a bigger, cruder splash than Laura. She gave dinner guests diamond-studded cigarette cases and bracelets as favors. She chartered a yacht, invited a boatload of people on a Caribbean cruise and at each port handed everyone $200 apiece for spending money.

Ridiculing Laura's gaucheries and malapropisms was a favorite indoor pastime in the smart set. Laura, about to go on a Mediterranean cruise, was asked whether she intended to see the Dardanelles. "I have letters to them," she said airily, "but I won't have time to drop in on them."

Elsie Mendl took Laura on a tour of her exquisite villa at Versailles soon after Wendell, the Austrian decorator, had installed indirect lighting. Laura was properly impressed. "I just love this invisible lighting," she gushed.

Laura was a parvenu, all right, but she had more character and social conscience in her little finger than all the phony patricians who sneered at her. When the Germans overran France in 1940, Laura refused to take refuge in the United States. She remained in France and sold her fabulous jewels at sacrificial prices to Hermann Goering, the repulsive monster whose arms, it was said, were covered from wrist to elbow under his uniforms with bracelets he had bought from Laura. She spent the proceeds feeding French prisoners of war held by the Nazis. France lost a gallant champion when Laura died in 1948.

What makes Elsie run? I believe my major motivation can be traced to my first exposure to snobbery when I was twelve years old. My parents lived on Nob Hill in San Francisco, across the street from Senator James G. Fair, whose fortune came from the legendary Virginia Lode in Nevada. He was giving a party for his oldest daughter, Theresa, and I assumed we would get an invitation from our neighbors. Today, almost sixty years later, I can still feel my burning resentment when my mother told me we were too poor to be asked to the party. It was the first time I ever realized money was a social weapon. I swore to myself I would give great parties all over the world — I didn't know how or when — to which everyone would want to come, but the rich would be invited only if they had something more important to offer than money. Subconsciously, I suppose, I have been trying ever since to prove my social equality with the Fairs.

It wasn't easy for a woman who couldn't have looked chic wearing a Molyneux creation at an Amish prayer meeting. In straining to gain my objective, I adopted temporarily the attitude I now despise. I was an insufferable musical and intellectual snob. The loudest psalm singer in the congregation always is a reformed sinner. I offer one defense in pleading guilty to the charge. When I became aware of the phony airs I was affecting, which hurt no one but myself, I attacked hypocrites who used their power and prestige to harm a great many people.

Enemies I made deliberately — I still do. Important enemies to me are the *sauce piquante* to my dish of life! They are generally people I either dislike or disapprove of. The first was Lady Maude (Emerald) Cunard, who ruled London society with an iron hand for three decades. She operated on a far loftier level than mine, but I resented her because she, adopted by a rich man named Carpentier after she was left an orphan in California, was utterly contemptuous of America and her countrymen. Lady Cunard had room in her brilliant salons only for arrived successes who could dress up her guest lists in the newspapers and for sycophants willing to fawn on her. When Queen Mother Elizabeth, then the Duchess of York, became queen she was asked whether she was ever invited to Lady Cunard's social functions.

"Oh, no," she answered grimly. "Bertie and I weren't chic enough for her."

Several other well-publicized feuds — notably with the Duchess of Windsor — might have given the impression that I snapped constantly at transgressors as the self-appointed watchdog of public ethics. It's a notion that should be corrected. Between two world wars I suffered from the worst case of delayed maturity on record. I liked too many people and was too busy having fun to be concerned with feuds. Further, I was so intrigued watching history written by the chief figures on the world stage that I did not join the spear carriers until it was my journalistic job to add a few minor footnotes. I'm not superstitious, but I can't help wondering whether I was born under a galaxy of lucky stars. There is no other explanation for the fantastic breaks I've had.

For example, I was the first American without official status to hear the inside story of the Rudolph Hess affair from Winston Churchill himself. It will be remembered that Hess, Hitler's chief deputy, caused a terrific sensation by parachuting from a German plane and landing on the Duke of Hamilton's estate in Scotland, shortly before the Nazis invaded Russia in 1941. The British immediately clapped Hess in solitary confinement and refused to issue a statement on his flight, measures which served to increase wild speculation on the bizarre incident.

When Churchill came to the United States for conferences with President Roosevelt a few weeks after America's entry into the war, reporters pulled wires like crazy trying to get the lowdown on Hess from Churchill. After his business with Roosevelt was concluded, however, Churchill gave the press the slip and went to a secret hideout at Edward Stettinius's home in Palm Beach for a much-needed rest.

I was in Palm Beach for the first time in twenty years and didn't know Churchill was in the same city, much less the same hemisphere, until the Jacques Balsans, the friends with whom I was staying, gave a small dinner party. I had just driven back from a radio broadcast in Miami and I was depressed by the war news from the Philippines, but the Balsans promised a rare surprise. They were not guilty of overstatement.

When I recovered from the astonishment of seeing Churchill, I strained slightly an acquaintanceship of thirty years' standing by asking his opinion of General Charles De Gaulle, my idol, who was rallying French resistance against the Nazi conquerors. "My greatest cross is the Croix de Lorraine," Churchill muttered, referring to De Gaulle's symbol. For once, I kept a discreet tongue in my head — Churchill's estimate of De Gaulle was correct, I later learned — and mentioned the Hess affair. Churchill, always fond of a good story, laughed and began to talk freely.

"The Hun is such a fool he believes everything he reads," Churchill said. "Someone showed Hitler an old magazine in which the Duke of Hamilton was identified as the king's steward. A child knows that's purely an honorary title, but Hitler, the idiot, thought Hamilton actually served dinner to the king. He sent Hess to Hamilton to get to the king behind my back and negotiate a separate peace before he attacked Russia. What fools! The Huns even believed me when I said we would fight them on the beaches and in the streets. They thought we had the arms to beat them back."

Churchill went on to recount the Duke of Hamilton's embarrassment that he was selected as the pipeline to George VI, giving rise to rumors that he was pro-Nazi. "It's like taking your wife to a restaurant and meeting your mistress," Hamilton told Churchill. The prime minister chuckled when he described the pink polish Hess wore on his toenails. Then he clenched his famous bulldog jaw and murmured grimly, "The Nazis will lose."

My most fantastic break came on the night of November 8, 1932. I hardly expect anyone to believe it, but I was the first person to congratulate Franklin D. Roosevelt on his election to the presidency.

A chain of pure coincidences was touched off when I received a cable from Count Stanislaus de la Rochefecauld to the effect that he was arriving in New York that day and needed my help urgently. It developed that the count had been assigned to write a series of articles for *Figaro*, a leading newspaper in Paris, and wanted me to arrange interviews with important candidates.

"You know everyone," he said blandly. "I shall be most grateful for any small assistance you can give me."

I didn't want to disillusion the count by admitting that a candidate for county clerk wouldn't know me from Adam's off ox, so I made an appointment to meet him later that evening. I phoned Elisabeth Marbury, an old friend, to ask whether she had any bright ideas. Elisabeth, a contributor to the Democratic campaign fund, was ill and said she would give me her tickets to the anticipated celebration at party headquarters in the Biltmore Hotel. That was better than parking the count in front of a radio to hear the returns, my only alternative, and I accepted her offer.

To kill time, I took the count to Times Square to observe the quaint customs of the natives on election night, then went to the Biltmore. When I showed my tickets at the door of headquarters, the guards went into a huddle and gave us an escort to another floor. Elisabeth Marbury was a *heavy* campaign contributor and her tickets were for the inner sanctum. Big Jim Farley, Mrs. Millicent Hearst and the Vincent Astors were the only people in the room. Farley, whom I knew slightly, nodded and told me to go through the door.

"Go in and meet the boss," he said.

"But I've never met him and this hardly seems the proper time to introduce myself," I protested.

"There'll never be a better time," Farley said laughing. "He's up in the clouds tonight."

I opened the door, with the count in tow, and saw Roosevelt, surrounded by a battery of teletype machines, cradling a phone with his shoulder. At that precise instant he got the flash of a return that insured his victory. He threw back his massive head and the famous magnetic grin that was to revitalize the hopes of millions flooded his features.

"It's all over," he announced to no one in particular. "We're in."

There were two or three aides in the room, but I was nearest Roosevelt and was the first to grasp his hand. I don't remember what I said, and I'm sure Roosevelt didn't hear it. But I do recall, as vividly as though it happened ten minutes ago, my feeling of exhilaration at witnessing that decisive turning point of history.

My life has been a modern American version of the Cinderella story — and midnight has not struck yet.

Chapter 2

MOST people climb the ladder of success rung by rung. I made it note by note, on the piano. My one genuine — if undisciplined — talent is for music, and it was demonstrated at the earliest possible moment. I broke up a performance of *Mignon* by being born in a theater box in Keokuk, Iowa, just as a road-company prima donna was struggling through her big aria.

It never was established whether the whole thing was due to my father's love of music or my mother's inability to count by the calendar. Like a decorous young woman of the Victorian era, she had gone back to Keokuk to have her first, and only, baby in her parents' home. She was mortified by the commotion my first public appearance caused. So was my father, although for another reason.

"If you had to be born in the middle of an opera," he always said, "you might've shown more taste and chosen something better than a mediocre mess like *Mignon*. You did redeem yourself, though," he added reflectively, "by yelling louder than that dreadful mezzo soprano who was desecrating 'Connais-tu le pays.' Your birth cry was the only true note that came out of a female throat the entire evening."

My parents were so different temperamentally that they supplemented each other perfectly. My mother, the former

Laura Wyman, the daughter of a doctor, derived a double dose of down-to-earth qualities from her French-Dutch ancestry. She was practical, economical, a meticulous housekeeper and a bit of a fanatic on keeping up appearances. When company was expected, I was not permitted to sit down in a freshly starched dress until the visitors arrived and I passed inspection. She was a stiff disciplinarian, but I suppose it was necessary to counterbalance the easygoing attitude of my indulgent father.

James David Maxwell was the rarest of all nonconformists — a Scotsman who had absolutely no interest in money. He casually went through the motions of selling insurance to earn a living, but his major attention was wrapped up in a job that barely paid his expenses. He was the Pacific Coast correspondent for the New York *Dramatic Mirror*, a newspaper devoted to the theater, music and the performing arts. He got $10 for a weekly column of news and comment, but, if the truth were known, he would have paid the paper for the privilege of living and breathing the same air with the artists he admired.

My mother's sense of propriety must have been outraged constantly by the odd assortment of people my father cultivated. Once he brought home a sailor, and a pet monkey which, to my mother's horror, was a present for me. I dearly loved Max, the monkey. Max was my first, and most appreciative, audience when I began training for a career as the life of the party.

Another exotic addition to our household was Hi Foo, an amiable Chinese thug my father engaged as my nurse. My mother would have preferred a proper French governess, but she was quick to recognize Hi Foo's recommendations. He was pleasant, efficient and, above all, cheap. Hi Foo took care of me for three years, until an untoward incident led to his dismissal. He was walking me in Golden Gate Park when a bunch of Chinese armed with knives attempted to carve their initials on him. My father heard of the rumpus and reported it to the police, who suspected, quite correctly, that Hi Foo was mixed up in the tong wars that erupted periodically in San Francisco. A few years after he left us, Hi Foo was hanged for murder.

When my father did bring home a guest who met with my mother's approval, the chances were splendid that my bratty behavior would ruin the occasion. One day, when I was five years old, my father excitedly announced that Adelina Patti, the greatest opera star of the age, was coming for lunch the following afternoon. I was in raptures waiting for the glamorous creature, but I felt that I was the victim of a cruel joke when Patti's carriage stopped at our door. Instead of a dazzling beauty, I saw a frail woman who appeared as old and prosaic as my grandmother. Patti was only forty-five that summer, but to me she looked positively ancient.

I sulked during lunch while the fraud of a celebrity told of her travels and triumphs. Not a word was said about my voice. I decided a person guilty of such bad manners had to be put in her place. I carefully moved out of range of my mother's foot.

"I sing too," I declared.

"Ah, that is nice," Patti said. "What is your favorite song, darling?"

" 'Comin' Thro' the Rye.' "

"It is one of my favorites too. Would you like me to sing it for you?"

Patti closed her eyes and began to sing softly, but she didn't even know the words. When she finished, my parents' praise infuriated me. They never told me I had a divine voice, and I knew two verses.

"Did you like the way I sang your song?" Patti asked me.

"No," I blurted. "I can sing it better." Before my mother could throttle me, I plunged into my version, bellowing at the top of my lungs to show up the impostor. Patti applauded politely and murmured that interpretations of music varied with individual artists.

The next day, while my father was agreeing with my mother, for once, that something would have to be done about "that child," a special messenger delivered a package for me. It contained a little gold bracelet and a note: "To my best and only singing teacher — Adelina Patti."

The tribute from Patti was not the only triumph of my childhood. When I was sixteen months old, I won a beauty contest in competition with 4000 babies at Mechanics Pavilion in San Francisco. I am well aware that this revelation is a severe strain on anyone's credulity, but I still have the gold medal to prove it. I mention this merely to prepare doting parents for the shocks the future may hold.

To paraphrase one of F. Scott Fitzgerald's observations, I was a faded beauty by the time I was four years old, but I was cultivating a more enduring natural endowment. I discovered music, my meal ticket and chief social grace. My father took me to a performance of *Lohengrin*, a profoundly moving experience.

The morning after I heard *Lohengrin* I played the Wedding March with one finger on our piano. By the afternoon, I was improvising simple chords to go with the melody. Within the week I could play any tune or operatic excerpt my father whistled or my mother hummed. My father, who played a little by ear, showed me the proper positions for my fingers on the keyboard, but that was the full extent of any instruction I've ever been given.

The one regret of my life is that I did not develop my extraordinary musical talent. I have perfect pitch, which enables me to play any classical or popular selection in any key after hearing it once. Dozens of great musicians, including Caruso, Gershwin, Rubinstein and Kreisler, have put me through rigorous exercises testing my infallible ear, and have wound up admitting it was impossible for me to strike a false note. I toured America, Europe and South Africa as accompanist for Dorothy Toye, a vaudeville star of forty years ago, who had a trick voice that ranged from baritone to soprano. She would switch keys without warning in the middle of a number, but she never caught me off guard. I never learned to read music, yet I've written some forty songs, and at least a half dozen were big hits.

That 1887 performance of *Lohengrin* had two other lasting effects on me, both for the good. I changed my name from Elsie to Elsa, after the heroine of the opera. And I made a resolution that later saved me from boring celebrities. My father had given me a synopsis of the opera and Elsa annoyed me to distraction with the interminable questions she asked. Whenever something exciting was about to happen on the stage, Elsa threw a monkey wrench into the works with her inane questions, which Lohengrin could not answer without giving away the whole plot. I made up my mind then that I never would pester people with irritating questions. Since that day, I deliberately broke the rule just once. I could not resist the opportunity of asking Albert Einstein to explain the theory of relativity in words of one syllable.

It was at a small party in London in 1927, soon after Einstein presented scientific proof of the time-space concepts he first advanced in 1905. It was said that only eight people in the world were capable of understanding Einstein's theory, although that didn't stop everyone from discussing it as though he knew what he was talking abo . There was at least one she who could give it a once-over-lightly with a smattering of authoritative ignorance. Me. From sketchy newspaper accounts of Einstein's work, I gathered that his conclusions were strikingly similar to the theory propounded by Henri Bergson, the French philosopher, in 1908. How did I know? I had studied briefly with Bergson at the Sorbonne in Paris years before.

Before approaching Einstein, I told Lord Haldane, the famous English statesman who had brought him to the party, of my background with Bergson, so that I would not get the quick brush off that is an intellectual's only protection against a gushing female. I'd be transfixed by a bolt of lightning for telling a whopping lie if I said that Einstein was enthralled by my conversation, which was relayed to him by an interpreter. He flattered me by expressing interest in my studies with Bergson. But when I asked him to explain the practical application of the theory of relativity, he laughed and said it was much too complicated. Einstein was so charming that I did

not realize until our chat was finished that he had given a
gushing female a very adroit brush off.

I next met Einstein at Charlie Chaplin's home in Hollywood six years later. Einstein remembered our previous meeting and smilingly addressed me as "the Disciple of Bergson."
With such a distinguished guest present, everyone took his
cue from Einstein and the affair gave promise of a memorable
evening, as he seemed to be enjoying himself hugely. His
spirits rose higher than ever when a first-rate string quartet
engaged by Chaplin came in to play during dinner. Einstein's
mood changed, suddenly and inexplicably, while the quartet
was playing the first movement of a Mozart quartet. He was
restless and inattentive to the talk at the table. I thought
someone had offended him until Frau Einstein leaned across
the table and whispered to me, "He would like to be playing
himself. This quartet is one of his great favorites."

I should have had the permission of Chaplin, my host, but
I was so eager to please Einstein that I went up to the first
violinist in the quartet and asked whether the great scientist
could borrow his instrument. The musician almost fell off his
chair begging me to give his violin to Einstein. The beatific
smile that flooded Einstein's face was a wonderful reward for
a thoughtful gesture. Einstein played very well and I was dying to accompany him. I didn't have the heart, though, to ask
the pianist to relinquish his place. He, too, must have been
a Jewish refugee from Germany. The pride and adoration that
beamed from him as Einstein joined in the sonata were inspired by something more emotional than music.

It was characteristic of the catch-as-catch-can pattern of my
life that I took a philosophy course with Bergson at the

Sorbonne but never was graduated from grammar school. My father had many unorthodox ideas, and one of them was his prejudice against formal education. He was convinced that he was a better teacher than any employee on the San Francisco payroll. He taught me to read and write at home when I was five years old, then turned me loose in his library, which ran heavily to poetry and the classics. I never saw McGuffey's Reader, but I was familiar with Browning, Keats and Plato and I had struggled through Herbert Spencer's philosophy by the time I was eleven. And I was familiar with Aristotle. I particularly liked Aristotle's definition of happiness as "a gentle stirring of the soul." Another quotation that had a profound impression on me was Socrates's last prayer: "Grant me an inward beauty of the soul. May I count the wise only as wealthy and have just as much gold as a modest man can carry." My father's opposition to the classroom probably was a complex stemming from his own sketchy schooling, yet he was a cultured, sensitive man. He believed knowledge and aesthetic appreciation were acquired by a process of osmosis, and I suspect he was right.

Since I don't want to spend the rest of life fighting off educators and Parent-Teacher Associations, I hesitate to recommend similar methods for children. All I know is that the system worked for me. While I do not move in circles cluttered up with long-hair intellectuals, the majority of the people I meet have had the alleged advantages of top prep and finishing schools and the best universities in America and Europe. I can more than hold my own in any discussion of literature, music or art. Unhampered by regimentation, I never had "culture" rammed down my unwilling throat, a forced feeding that makes educational refinements indigestible to too many children.

Had there been truant officers in San Francisco in the early 1890's, my father would have been hauled into court every other week for keeping me out of school. As it was, he had a running battle in his own home with my mother, who was scandalized by the free rein he gave me. She finally wore down his resistance when I was eight and entered me in public school, but her triumph was short-lived. A month later, my father calmly took me with him on a business trip to Japan. I doubt that he did it to spite my mother; he didn't have a vindictive bone in his body. He simply was an advocate of learning-through-doing long before the term was invented by progressive education.

Time has dimmed my memories of the trip to Japan, but I do recall that my childish curiosity was intrigued by the tiny houses, the dwarf trees and the miniature scale of the country. It all came back to me in June, 1953, at a dinner party given by Lady Deterding in Paris. I was seated next to Nishimura, the Japanese Ambassador to France, and to keep the conversational ball rolling I mentioned that I had visited his country before he was born. Nishimura asked what impression Japan made on me.

"Everything was so small it was just like a toy," I replied.

Nishimura didn't like my description — and neither did I when I remembered the death and destruction that "toy" brought to Pearl Harbor and Bataan.

What with staying out of school until I was eight and batting off to Japan for four months, my educational routine was so helplessly balled up that my mother made only one more effort to reform me. When I was twelve, I was enrolled in Miss Denham's private school, but that lasted only six months. I couldn't take the discipline of the school, or maybe it was the other way around. In all, I had less than two years of formal education.

While other youngsters were confined to the classroom, I had a wonderful time prowling around Nob Hill in San Francisco, where we lived in a four-room flat. Although there were more millionaires to the square mile there in those days than in any other city in America, a caste system founded on wealth had not yet crystallized. San Francisco was a neighborly town and I assumed everyone was my friend. I took it for granted that the Maxwells would be invited to the party given for Theresa, the oldest daughter of Senator James G. Fair, whose fine mansion was just across the street from our ramshackle house. The Fair girls were older than I was, but I knew them well enough to have free run of their spacious grounds and drop into the kitchen for a handout of cookies and cocoa.

The party Senator Fair was giving for Theresa, who later married Herman Oelrichs and was a social bigwig of Fifth Avenue and Newport, promised to be a glittering affair. On the morning of the great day, the street was jammed with delivery wagons from florists, confectioners, bakers, butchers and fish markets. A boy on one of the wagons told me that Fair was even bringing an orchestra all the way from New York to play at the party. I rushed home to tell my mother the latest bulletin from fairyland.

"What are we going to wear?" I asked breathlessly.

My mother looked at me gravely. "You don't have to worry about that," she said quietly. "We haven't been invited."

I couldn't have been more stunned if she had slapped me across the face. "Not invited! Why?"

"We're too poor to be asked," my mother said bitterly.

I sat at the window that night, too proud to cry, watching a procession of carriages deliver gorgeously dressed women and well-tailored men at the Fair mansion. The incident must have made an indelible impression on me. Whenever I achieve a small social triumph today, my memory invariably darts back to that first exposure to snobbery and the feeling of resentment that choked me.

In a sense, my first party created more of a furore than Fair's. Although it was a fiasco, it had one thing in common with some of my later jamborees. People talked about it for days. It happened on my thirteenth birthday at Belvedere, a small island in San Francisco Bay where my parents had rented a cottage. The day began with the promise of high adventure. My father gave me a whole dollar for my birthday. And our next-door neighbor, George Cameron, now my oldest living friend, the present publisher of the San Francisco *Chronicle*, went to work leaving his fourteen-foot gasoline launch *La Perle* tied up at the dock. *La Perle*, to me the last word in luxury, had an engine that was as temperamental as a prima-donna between love affairs. It had to be cajoled to start and threatened with a sledge hammer before it would stop. Cameron spent most of his spare time wrestling with *La Perle's* balky engine, but I was sure I could master its mysteries.

Fortified with sublime confidence, which at the moment was a suitable substitute for my total ignorance of navigation, I climbed aboard *La Perle*. I tinkered with a few gadgets and *La Perle* purred gently. It was three o'clock in the afternoon and the prisoners had just been released from the Belvedere grammar school. Their wide-eyed respect when they saw me at the wheel made me feel more expansive than ever.

"Want to go to San Francisco, kids?" I yelled. "I'll treat to ice-cream sodas at Maskey's." In those days, a dollar bought twenty sodas.

My guests scrambled aboard and *La Perle*, still in a docile mood, bore a resolute course for San Francisco across the bay. Everything was fine for about five minutes, and then the engine, reconsidering its unusual cooperation, decided to act up. It sputtered violently and the boat, under my inept handling, caught the backwash of a passing freighter.

"Bail out the boat!" I ordered the crew. I hadn't read Herman Melville for nothing. The kids, who had thoughtfully emptied Cameron's biscuit tins, went to work with commendable zeal, but a new menace loomed ahead. A ferryboat was charging at us with terrifying speed. The captain was gesticulating wildly and next to him a woman, whom I recognized as the mother of one of my passengers, was screaming loud enough to be heard above the piercing blasts of the ferry's whistle. *La Perle*, intimidated by the frightful racket, suddenly quit its shenanigans and meekly followed the course I steered back to the dock.

I heard plenty about my seamanship during the next few days while my father was placating the delegations of irate parents who descended on our cottage. The parents, all of whom had total recall, further reminded my father of my previous depredations on their windows, lawns and orchards. The chief of police also dropped in and made some pointed references to a local gang of ruffians who, it was rumored, were

led by a plump, dark-haired girl. The *La Perle* escapade was
the last straw for my mother.

"If you're going to act like a tomboy," she said, "you'll look
like one." She cropped my hair and made me wear pants, a
punishment that undoubtedly will give modern parents the
leaping fantods. With applied child psychology a dubious refinement of the distant future, however, my mother's forth-
right measures were not considered unduly harsh. I suppose
my enforced impersonation of a boy will give curbstone psychiatrists all sorts of clues to my later attitudes, but as far as
I'm concerned the whole thing is nonsense. I didn't mind the
penalty at all. I didn't have to comb my hair and the pants
gave me more freedom of motion. I was too young and too
busy with other mischiefs to have any awareness of sex.

That complication involved me for the first, and last, time
when I was sixteen. I had gone shopping for my mother and on
my way home up Nob Hill I noticed that the curtains in the
mansion belonging to the von Schroeders, a prominent banking family, had been taken down for spring cleaning. Unable
to resist the temptation to peek, I looked through the windows
and was so absorbed in rubbernecking that I lost my balance
and fell flat on my face. The paper bags I was carrying broke
and sent tomatoes, potatoes and apples rolling down the hill.
I scurried to retrieve them and did not hear a man open the
gate of the house.

"May I help you, *Fräulein?*" a voice asked.

Fräulein? I looked up and saw a handsome young man with
a deep scar on his right cheek. Rather absurdly, he clicked his
heels before rounding up my fruits and vegetables, then formally introduced himself. He was Alexander von Schroeder,

the banker's younger brother. He insisted on walking me home, and on the way he said that he had just been graduated from the University of Bonn and was visiting his brother before getting his commission in the German army, on the crown prince's staff. When we reached my house, he asked whether he could call on me. I forgot the maidenly reserve I was supposed to maintain and urged him to come the next day. Although Alex was only six years older than I, his continental manners and air of sophistication made him a man of the world compared to the other boys I knew. He was handsome and rich — and I had read enough romantic novels to realize that a girl could not afford to be too coy under the circumstances.

Alex came the next day, and every day thereafter for several weeks. We discovered we had common interests in poetry and music and the theater. Since he knew no other young people in San Francisco, Alex spent practically all of his time with me, reading poetry aloud, singing in his rich baritone to my piano accompaniment and taking me to the theater. It first dawned on me that our friendship was taking a serious turn when we ran into Alex's brother, a pompous, cold fish, at the theater one evening. Alex was embarrassed, and I was annoyed, by the brusque, almost contemptuous "How-do-you-do" the elder von Schroeder gave me when Alex introduced us.

On the way home that night, Alex suddenly said: "I think, *Liebchen*, you should wear an evening dress occasionally."

The implied criticism of my appearance hurt me. Looking back, I can see Alex's point. I had an inexpensive black velvet suit that didn't fit too well to begin with, and constant wear had not improved its style. At the moment, though, I was too humiliated to be objective. I had no money to buy a new dress and, besides, I thought Alex was too civilized to be concerned with mere clothes. Alex knew my folks didn't have much money and, sensing he had offended me, tried to make amends. He merely succeeded in aggravating the wound.

"I will take you shopping tomorrow," he said, "and buy you a beautiful décolleté gown."

That was too much. I left him without saying good night, and burst into the house sobbing convulsively. My father, who had not seen me cry since I was a little girl, listened sympathetically while I told him what had happened. Then he patted me gently on the shoulder and gave me a twenty-dollar bill, probably the only one he had to his name.

The following morning I was up at the crack of dawn and went downtown. I window-shopped for two hours before the stores opened at nine o'clock. At 9:05 A.M. I bought a black chiffon evening frock with a pink velvet belt, reduced from $35 to $18.75. I never had any illusions about my looks, but when I saw myself in the mirror I knew that dress certainly did things for me. The dress had the same effect on Alex. When he saw me that evening, he took me in his arms and kissed me on the mouth. It's difficult to describe the feeling of revulsion that swept over me. I gave Alex a violent shove.

"How can you be such a brute!" I screamed. "You've ruined everything!"

I dashed to my bedroom, tore off the black chiffon dress I now hated and changed to my old velvet suit. When I regained control of myself, I went back to Alex in the parlor. He apologized profusely and carefully sat on a sofa on the opposite side of the room. He said he was sorry he had offended me, but he wanted me to know he was in love with me. It was only fair to tell me, he went on, that his parents had "arranged" for him to marry the daughter of an aristocratic German family, but we would work things out so that we could be married.

"I don't want to hear about it!" I cried. "I'm not in love with you. Besides, I never intend to get married. That spoils everything."

What I said didn't make sense, especially to a methodical German. "Do you want me to go away, *Liebchen?*" Alex asked.

I shook my head. I wasn't sure what I wanted, but I knew I needed his friendship. I said we could continue seeing each other if he promised never to kiss me again. He sighed and promised — and I was sufficiently feminine to be piqued when he kept his word. I further confused Alex by flirting with him pretty outrageously. I can't imagine myself playing the coquette now, but my technique must have been effective. One night after the theater he took me to the Poodle Dog, a notorious restaurant in San Francisco. That precipitated another row. What would my family's friends think if they saw me in such a disgusting place? They would have every reason to jump to the worst conclusions.

Now Alex was too angry to apologize. What did I mean by "the worst"? What was wrong with going to the Poodle Dog with a man who loved you? Alex proceeded to give me a stern lecture on the physical basis of true love. He made me feel like such a stupid prude that I realized it was my turn to make a concession.

"You're right," I said. "I will marry you."

Alex took me in his arms passionately, declared his love for me in German. I understood only *"Ich liebe dich,"* a phrase from a song by Grieg he had taught me. Alex took the family signet ring he was wearing and put it on my finger to make our engagement official.

During the month that followed, we were engrossed in plans for the future. Since I was to be his *"Gnädige Frau"* and supervise a large staff of servants, Alex began to teach me German. After a stiff session of declining irregular verbs, we read Goethe and Schiller aloud for relaxation. The courtship of Miles Standish was a wild orgy compared to our chaste romance.

One day Alex said quite casually that he had to go to New York on business for about a month. I sensed something was wrong, but his fervent promise to write me every day was slightly reassuring. He did send me seven letters the first week he was away, but the following week I received only three. By the end of the month, Alex had stopped writing. I had not heard from him for several weeks when he called at my home at the usual time. The moment I saw him I knew that our relationship had ended. He gave himself away by rising when I entered the room and clicking his heels, something he had not done since our first meeting. After a few minutes of strained conversation, I asked him point-blank whether he had reconsidered marrying me. He nodded slowly.

"Is there another woman?" I asked, trying hard not to make it sound melodramatic.

"When you say another woman," Alex answered gravely, "you imply there are two women in my life. That is wrong. There is only one woman, but she is not you. You are a fine person, but there is something in you that will always stop you from becoming a real woman."

There was nothing I could say, for I knew he was right. I broke down and wept unashamedly. Alex wanted to comfort me, but I refused to let him come near me.

"I did not mean to be unnecessarily blunt," he said gently, "but I had to tell you before you were hurt deeply in learning the truth about yourself. I am sorry, but I cannot help it any more than you can."

Alex bowed formally, clicked his heels and left. As he walked out, I knew I was losing something I would never find again, but, as he had said, I couldn't help it.

I saw Alex in Berlin years later, before World War I. By that time, he had a palatial home in the Tiergartenstrasse and I was playing the piano in a music hall. Alex introduced me to his *gnädige Frau*, a lovely, charming woman who was most cordial, but we moved in such different spheres that we no longer had common interests. Alex, an aide-de-camp on the kaiser's staff, took me to Potsdam for a military review and presented me to Wilhelm II, the first royalty I ever had met. I think I embarrassed Alex by the inept curtsy I gave the kaiser and the pro-British cracks I made to his fellow officers. Both of us were relieved when we said good-by for the last time.

Late in 1916, I saw a short paragraph in a New York newspaper reporting that Baron Alexander von Schroeder, brother of the well-known San Francisco banker, had been killed in action on the Western Front. I still have the signet ring he gave me, but I stopped dwelling on the bittersweet uses of what might have been long ago. Deep down, I know nothing would have changed. I was not meant to marry Alex or any other man.

Chapter 3

AN adolescent girl trying to forget a blighted romance could not have chosen a better place for it than San Francisco at the turn of the century. Even a recluse living in a cave would have been infected with the excitement and animation that were in the air. The city had the vitality of a boom town and an urbane tradition that made it the cultural center of the United States second only to New York.

The recent annexation of the Philippines and Hawaii and the Alaska gold rush gave tremendous impetus to the city's commerce and shipping. The new millionaires who popped up daily copied, as always, the established plutocrats and generously supported the theater, music and the arts. Fees were so lucrative that musical giants of the stature of Paderewski, Caruso and Kubelik made the long, uncomfortable trip across the continent to perform in San Francisco. Broadway hits with the original casts played to sellout performances. The liberal spirit of the cosmopolitan metropolis attracted and stimulated the largest concentration of young writers west of Chicago.

My father's connection with the influential New York *Dramatic Mirror* gave me easy entree to San Francisco's cultural activities. My omnivorous reading qualified me for all the literary societies and little-theater groups in sight, and the fact that I was the daughter of a critic with a direct pipeline to Eastern impresarios wasn't exactly a handicap. I became a leading member of amateur theatrical organizations that introduced the plays of Ibsen, Strindberg and Hauptmann on the Pacific Coast. I hate to think of the friendships I abused palming off tickets to recitals and exhibitions given by obscure musicians and artists who were struggling for recognition.

The best dividend I drew as J. D. Maxwell's daughter was meeting most of the celebrities who came to San Francisco. My father was one of the first members of the Bohemian Club, the headquarters for notable visitors, and he brought to our small flat practically everyone who was passing through town. The most volatile personality I met was Luisa Tetrazzini, the greatest of all coloraturas and a figure flamboyant enough to attract attention in a city with a full quota of people studying to be characters.

Tetrazzini was a short, enormously fat woman with a simple outlook on life. She held all indoor and outdoor records for collecting love affairs. Ten seconds after we were introduced, Tetrazzini asked me who my fiancé was. She flew into a tizzy when I said I didn't have one.

"Sensa l'amore, ecco la morte!" she screamed, shaking her finger under my nose. No knowledge of Italian was required to understand that, as far as she was concerned, there was nothing but death in the absence of love. A Senor Urriburro with her was striking proof of Tetrazzini's determination to stay alive.

It seemed that Tetrazzini had picked up Senor Urriburro, the president of Peru's nephew, in Italy, and promptly decided her husband of the moment was an intolerable encumbrance. Ignoring other legal restraints, such as a full season of singing commitments, Tetrazzini fled to America with her Peruvian admirer. She came to San Francisco to put more distance between herself and the husband, but much to her annoyance he followed her and challenged Senor Urriburro to a duel. The senor picked up the gauntlet and a spot near Oakland was selected for the mortal combat, at sunrise, with pistols at twenty paces.

At eight o'clock on the morning of the duel, the ferry dock in San Francisco was jammed with a delegation waiting to welcome the survivor. Neither the husband nor the senor disembarked. Three more ferries arrived and still there was no sign of either contestant. Could it be that the jealous lovers had done each other in? A posse was sent across the bay to investigate. It returned several hours later reporting no evidence of bloodletting had been found. The crowd dispersed for lunch, but the curiosity that consumed me was more urgent than the pangs of hunger. I rushed to Tetrazzini's hotel and found her in near hysterics, although not with grief.

The husband and the senor were playing cards and drinking toasts to each other's health. Tetrazzini was furious and made caustic remarks about people who didn't know the meaning of honor, but the gentlemen paid no attention and serenely continued their card game, and toasts. When I left, they were so relaxed they could hardly move. The crushing humiliation befell Tetrazzini a week later. Senor Urriburro invited the husband to go to Lima with him, and they sailed off, leaving the livid Tetrazzini to compete with the Golden Gate's celebrated sunsets.

Tetrazzini, who had no intention of doing any professional work when she came to San Francisco, accepted singing engagements for want of something better to do. She was such a great success that the Metropolitan Opera offered her a contract. Tetrazzini never saw her spouse or Senor Urriburro again, but she managed to assuage her grief with a procession of other husbands and lovers. She was past sixty and, in her own words, "tired and full of sleep" when she went through the formality of acquiring her last husband.

Apart from the puppy-love crisis with Alex, I never had experienced disappointment or tragedy. As a consequence, I was wholly unprepared for the most profound shock of my life — the death of my father, for whom I had a deeper attachment than any person I ever have known. In 1905 my father, then in his early fifties, contracted an illness doctors could not diagnose and began to fail rapidly. When he knew that he had little time left, he called me into his room and held my hand gently. Grief made my senses more acute, for I still remember distinctly every word he said.

"It won't be easy for you after I'm gone," he said quietly. "You are plain and plump and as time goes by you will get plainer and plumper. You can turn your looks into an asset because no woman will be jealous of you and no man will be suspicious of you.

"As you know, I haven't much money. What little I have, I'm leaving to your mother. I'm afraid I have nothing to give you except four rules for living, and I believe they'll work for you because you are so much like me. These are the rules, for what they're worth.

"First, never be afraid of what They say. They exist only in your fears. What you *do* is the only thing that counts. What They *say* means nothing.

"Second, the more you own, the more you are possessed. Keep free of material things and enjoy life as it comes.

"Third, take serious things highly. Take light things seriously.

"Fourth, always laugh at yourself first — before others do. There is something ridiculous about every person. Don't be afraid to admit your weaknesses and failures."

I don't know how well I have used my father's advice. But the more I see of men and women who inherited fortunes, the less anxious I am to trade my legacy for theirs. I would be a fool to do it. Mine is not in bondage to the stock market. It has survived wars, social revolutions, earthquakes and depressions. It is one of the very few trust funds in existence that never has stopped paying dividends.

Not so long ago, my father's principles were given a flattering endorsement in the Stork Club, of all places. I was lunching there and a waiter brought a note asking me to drop by the table of Madame Pandit, who was in New York as India's ranking representative to the United Nations. We chatted briefly, and then Madame Pandit bowled me over by asking:

"What are you trying to do, Elsa? Export American philosophy to India?"

It developed that I had written of my father's four rules in a column which, in some roundabout fashion, was picked up in the New Delhi newspaper owned by Nehru, India's prime minister and Madame Pandit's brother. Madame Pandit encouraged me to talk about my father, and when I finished she nodded gravely.

"Your father and my brother would have been good friends," she said. "They would have understood each other."

After the death of my father, his friends saw to it that I was not forgotten when special invitations were handed out. I was one of the favored few who had supper with Enrico Caruso on the night of April 17, 1906, a memorable date for more than one reason. The Metropolitan Opera Company opened its spring season in San Francisco with a performance of *Carmen* featuring Caruso, Antonio Scotti, Olive Fremstad and Emma Eames. San Franciscans eagerly anticipated the Met's annual visit and they were rewarded lavishly that night. Fremstad sang the Habanera so brilliantly that the applause actually drowned out the orchestra and stopped the opera. Scotti was a superb toreador, but the mounting excitement reached a tremendous crescendo in Caruso's Flower Song in the second act. The audience cheered and screamed for ten minutes, an ovation that almost exhausted Caruso with all the bows he was forced to take.

A bigger thrill was still to come. I was asked to join a small supper party for Caruso and Scotti at Zinkand's, a restaurant that specialized in Italian food. Out of costume, Caruso looked like a fat, overgrown boy, an illusion that was heightened by the gusto with which he dived into heaping platefuls of spaghetti. Between courses, he drew on the tablecloth caricatures of all those present, then pained Mr. Zinkand by cutting out the sketches and giving the pieces of cloth to us.

Caruso was a notorious ladies' man — or a wolf, as he would be called today — and could have enjoyed delectable hunting among the alluring females ready to swoon at his feet. He took an immediate shine to me, though, when I went to the piano and, without music, played his famous arias. A dyed-in-the-wool chauvinist, Caruso didn't like the name Elsa or anything that smacked of Wagner's operas and dubbed me *"mio pappone."* Several hours — and much champagne — later, Caruso took me home and asked me to have lunch with him the next day at the St. Francis Hotel.

It was three o'clock in the morning, but I was too excited to sleep. It was lucky for me that I was wide-awake. I was lying in bed, rehearsing the terribly witty stories I would tell Caruso, when there was a distant rumble and the house trembled as though a giant hand were shaking the foundations. I jumped out of bed terrified and ran to my mother's room, which she was sharing with a woman friend who was staying with us. I awakened them and the three of us managed to reach the front door before it was jammed by the walls, which were heaving crazily.

We were halfway down a flight of marble steps leading to the street when it buckled and pitched us headlong to the cracking pavement. We lay there too stunned to speak while the house collapsed behind us. We were engulfed by a roar so deafening that it seemed to well up from every point of the compass. I tried to help my mother to her feet to escape the debris raining down on us from crashing houses, but both of us were immediately knocked down by a violent jolt.

My recollection of the great San Francisco earthquake is unique in only one detail. I must have been the only one of the 600,000 victims whose first reaction was not concerned with safety or salvaging personal possessions. True to form, I thought only of keeping my luncheon appointment with Caruso (while the destroyed city was rallying to fight the fires that were spreading the devastation). At that, it took a detachment of the United States Army to stop me from going down Powell Street to the St. Francis at the bottom of the hill and meeting Caruso.

At least one San Franciscan was amused by my scatter-brained determination to keep my date with Caruso. He was Jack Barrymore, who had not yet launched his theatrical career and was working as a newspaper cartoonist. The earthquake had interrupted a gay, all-night party Barrymore had been attending and he still was dressed in white tie and tails. While we were standing on the hill watching the raging fires that had sprung up after the earthquake, Jack London, the writer, and George Sterling, the poet, came along. They told me I was insane to think of lunch at the St. Francis. The hotel was in ruins and they had heard rumors that Caruso was dead.

Caruso escaped unhurt and spent the entire day in Union Square outside the St. Francis bemoaning the loss of trunks containing his precious opera costumes. He took the earthquake as an unpardonable inconvenience and swore he would never return to a city where "that kind of disorder was permitted." To the best of my knowledge, he kept his promise.

My easy, sheltered life went up in the smoke of ruined San Francisco. While the authorities were estimating the damage to the beautiful city of my childhood, I faced the equally dis-couraging job of self-appraisal. My personal balance sheet added up to a bleak blank.

I was approaching twenty-three, I had never earned a penny and it was high time I did. My father's entire estate was a $10,000 life-insurance policy he had bought in a rare, provident moment. Medical expenses, the funeral and six months of household bills had reduced my mother's bank account to $4000. She was trying to keep up my father's insurance business, but she had no training for it and depended on the kindness of friends to sell an occasional small policy. It was obvious that I could not go on being a burden to my mother. The very least I could do was to support myself.

Came the agonizing question: How? I didn't have a single accomplishment that vaguely resembled a commercial asset. I could play the piano well enough to entertain at parties, but not well enough to make a career of it. I might have used my extensive knowledge of literature to teach English in high school, but my lack of formal education ruled out that possibility. Anyway, I wouldn't have lasted a month in such a pedestrian job. Through my connections on the fringes of San Francisco's cultural activities I might have eked out a bare living before the earthquake. But a city confronted by a staggering task of reconstruction had no time or money for my trivial talents.

The blunt truth was inescapable. I was nothing but a dilettante with no usefulness in my home town. I had to leave and earn a living somewhere, but now there were two blind alleys instead of one. Where could I go? I didn't know a soul outside of San Francisco.

Then fate intervened in the disguise of an English actress named Constance Crawley. She had a fairly good following in London, where she had co-starred with Ben Greet in Elizabethan dramas, but she was completely unknown on the Pacific Coast. To complicate matters, Constance was seized by a strange delusion. She was convinced that California was a cultural desert where the natives were thirsting for her touring

Shakespearean stock company. She was working up to San Francisco, the golden oasis, by easy stages, but her timing was as atrocious as her concept of America. She opened her grand tour in Pasadena on the night of the earthquake. Every theater on her itinerary was leveled, leaving the troupe high and dry, without money and with no immediate prospect of getting it.

Good samaritans at the University of California sent a rescue party to Pasadena and brought the stranded company to nearby Berkeley. At a reception given for Constance, someone with a perverted sense of humor played her a cruel trick. Constance was told that I was a wealthy, stage-struck heiress who would be only too ecstatic to bail her out of the jam. If she was looking for an angel, her search was ended. Constance pointed like a bird dog and fell on me with gladsome cries that assured me she had heard of my "wonderful creative work" while she still was in England. That should have alerted me. I was so overwhelmed by her attention, though, that I bit hard at the bait and accepted an invitation for an audition at Constance's hotel the next day.

When I arrived at the shabby hotel the troupe couldn't have greeted me more effusively had I been the British consul with free transportation back to England. A dog-eared script of a Shakespeare play was thrust in my hands. I read two lines and was interrupted by bravos from one and all, praising my regal poise, my mellifluous diction, my impeccable phrasing. Although it was obvious that I was a devotee of Shakespeare, they said, they would be more than willing to include modern dramas and comedies in their repertory if such was my heart's desire.

Arthur Maude, the manager of the company, requested the favor of a brief conference in his room.

"We will be delighted to have you join our company," he said, "but let me ask you a question. How much do you wish to invest in our enterprise?"

The heady wine of the last ten minutes made me feel capable of supporting the world. "Twenty thousand dollars," I said, lying in my brazen teeth.

Maude frowned. "You must realize, Miss Maxwell," he said with a tinge of asperity, "this is an unparalleled chance for a girl of your tender age and relative inexperience. It is not a privilege given to everyone to make a world tour with as distinguished an actress as Miss Crawley.

"Tell you what," Maude went on. "You can have your choice of roles. Juliet . . . Lady Macbeth . . . Ophelia. Miss Crawley is in delicate health and finds these tours rather enervating. You can be her understudy. Can you make it thirty thousand?"

"Thirty thousand it is," I said hollowly.

Maude wrung my limp, clammy hand and I was the coowner, comanager and costar of a troupe of strolling players.

On the way home, the delayed impact of the commitment I had made merely fortified my determination to go through with it as best I could. My mother and I might as well be broke as the way we were. The $4000 we had in our joint banking account would be gone within the year if it was not beefed up with fresh money. It wasn't as though I was risking the money. How could my investment possibly be a gamble? Maude had mentioned solid bookings in Texas before taking off on a glamorous world tour. The capital I advanced the company would be returned in a matter of a few weeks, and the box-office receipts thereafter would be pure velvet.

The following morning I packed the few clothes I had managed to save from the earthquake, withdrew $2000 from the bank and took the ferry to the Oakland railroad station to keep my rendezvous with Constance Crawley and destiny. Before boarding the train, I mailed a letter to my mother.

My Dearest:
    I am running away. I am not in love and I am not going to have a baby. I simply can't stand this life. I want to make my own way and I'll never amount to anything if I stay in San Francisco. I won't come back until I'm somebody.

It took me more than a quarter of a century to make good on my brash word. The hard way.

Two days later the Constance Crawley Company landed in San Antonio broke again. My $2000 had been spent for railroad fares, meals en route and freight charges for the scenery. Although there wasn't a cloud in the Texas sky, two tornadoes hit us in quick succession. The manager of the local theater had bad news. San Antonio's enthusiasm for Shakespeare was so low that he was forced to cut our engagement from two weeks to one and reduce the scale of tickets from the contracted two-dollar top. To lure enough customers into the theater to keep the ushers company, he was charging thirty cents for the orchestra, twenty cents for the first balcony and ten cents for the peanut gallery. Shakespeare's searing poetry went for Sweeney in San Antonio. The Bard was on the ten-twent'-thirty circuit, and no fooling.

The second blow fell when the railroad depot caught fire and our scenery and billboard posters went up in flames. I was too crushed by the disaster to put up a kick when Maude told me that my debut in *Romeo and Juliet* was not to be in the lead but as the Nurse. He also wasn't much of a business manager or a con man. After demoting me as an actress, he bluntly asked me to give him a check for $5000 to replace the scenery lost in the fire.

My first impulse was to invent a new, bigger lie. I lost my nerve, though, and broke down and confessed that I was a rank impostor. I was about to get hysterical, but Maude beat me to the gun. He sat down and sobbed convulsively. He could not bear the thought, he wailed, of burying Miss Crawley's triumphant world tour in a town with a thirty-cent top.

"Don't worry, we'll pull through," I said soothingly. "I don't know how, but we will. Now, if I'm going to do justice to the role of the Nurse, I must brush up on the lines."

That was another curve ball for Maude. "Why?" he asked dully.

"The opening speech is the key to the characterization." I plunged into the Nurse's first long delivery:

> Even or odd, of all days in the year,
> Come Lammas-eve at night . . .

Maude withered me with a look of utter contempt.

"You are not only a liar," he said, "but the dumbest semi-literate I ever have met. Don't you even know that a stock company never follows the original text? What you call your opening speech will be cut. You'll be lucky if we permit you to inflict two lines on the audience. You are a fool and a bloody bore. Get out. Leave me alone. I wish to God I never met you."

Chastened by Maude's outburst and my own duplicity, I was as discreet as an undertaker during the next few days while we rehearsed and improvised scenery out of cheesecloth and crepe paper. But the ham in me could not be suppressed when Maude gave me the cue for my entrance on opening night. Instead of remaining silent, I took off on a sustained lyrical flight and delivered every one of the Nurse's thirty-four lines. It was such a shock to the elderly actress playing Lady Capulet that her jaw dropped and she lost her false teeth. The audience's roars smothered my speech, but I had the satisfaction of delivering it just as it was published in the First Folio.

Constance wanted to strangle me, but she denied herself that pleasure in view of an impending crisis. I sent a telegram to my mother asking for a few hundred dollars to get us to Waco, our next stop. My mother came across with $200 and I was seen in the part of Good Deeds in *Everyman*, that hardy perennial and lifesaver of all traveling stock companies. For some reason I never could fathom, rural audiences invariably came running when we put on *Everyman*. The old chestnut always paid for our sandwiches and coach fare to the next tank town.

Our triumphant world tour lasted ten months. Maude must have studied geography in a very strange school, for our travels were confined mainly to a stupefying succession of one-night stands in Texas, Louisiana and Missouri. We held out long enough to hoard enough money to get back to New York, where the troupe disbanded, by all odds the high point of our association.

I landed in New York with nothing but three dollars in my purse to show for my $2000 investment. In all fairness to Constance Crawley and Maude, I did gain invaluable experience with them. They taught me the art of stalling off landladies and hotelkeepers. It was to be very handy in my precarious future.

Chapter 4

GEORGE ORWELL wrote in 1933 a little book with the explicit title of *Down and Out in Paris and London*. Orwell had a great gift for vivid expression, of course, but he was just a Johnny-come-lately expert on the subject. I did similar field research a quarter of a century earlier, with New York thrown in for good measure. *Down and Out*, like all of Orwell's work, had a light, tongue-in-cheek touch, but a strong undertone of bitterness ran through it. Many writers have described the deteriorating effects of privation on self-respect, but Orwell was one of the few who emphasized the point that poverty is squalid and boring. Especially boring. I'll take my chances on surviving a plague, but boredom is the one affliction that always has terrified me.

At that, I would have envied some of Orwell's advantages when I arrived in New York on a dismal, rainy day in March, 1907. He, at least, had friends and the promises of jobs — as a dishwasher in Paris and a companion to a congenital imbecile in London — which materialized. I didn't know a soul in the big, overwhelming city and I didn't have the slightest idea where I could begin to look for a job. And I had only three dollars' worth of breathing time before I discovered the answer.

I walked a mile through the downpour from Grand Central Station to a boardinghouse on West Forty-sixth Street recommended to me by a conductor on the train. The landlady looked at my soaked clothes and battered cardboard suitcase and didn't bother to show me a room.

"It's twelve dollars a month — in advance," she said. "Not that I mistrust you, dearie. It's the rule of the house. Sure, you can leave your stuff here 'til the bank opens. As long as I'm paid by three o'clock this afternoon the room's yours."

The thought of not having a place to stay made me panicky. I had one forlorn hope. My father had been West Coast correspondent for the New York *Dramatic Mirror*, published by Harrison Fiske. I found the address in the telephone directory, went to the office and ran into a formidable roadblock in Fiske's secretary. She had been on the job only a year and never had heard of my father. Besides, Mr. Fiske was very busy that morning and could see no one. When I said I would wait, the secretary suddenly remembered Mr. Fiske had left the office and would not return all day. Just then a small, dynamic woman swept majestically into the office. It was Minnie Maddern Fiske, one of America's leading actresses and the publisher's wife. Her picture appeared in the newspapers almost as often as President "Teddy" Roosevelt's, and, further, she had dined at our apartment in San Francisco several years before.

I rushed toward her. "Mrs. Fiske," I cried, "I'm the late J. D. Maxwell's daughter. He was your friend. You came to our house. I must have help. I'm tired and I need a job. I owe my landlady twelve dollars. I must pay it by three o'clock. It's the rule of the house."

Mrs. Fiske recoiled from my machine-gun outburst, then re-acted swiftly to the Lady Bountiful role I had foisted on her. She led me past the sullen secretary to her husband's office. Fiske, a mild-mannered man, must have been an old hand at listening to hard-luck stories.

"What can you do?" he asked laconically when I finished my sad recital.

"I can play the piano and act," I panted. "I can lecture on poetry and music. I compose a little."

"Can you do any of it well?" Fiske asked gently.

I was trapped. "No," I admitted, "except that I can play the piano pretty well."

"Tell me, Miss Maxwell, are you interested in earning a hundred dollars a month?"

The incredulous look in my eyes gave him his answer. "I can get you a job as a pianist in a nickelodeon. It's long, hard work and the surroundings aren't pleasant, but it pays a hundred dollars a month. All right?"

At noon, when the grubby movie house opened in a converted store front in the West Thirties, I was pounding a broken-down piano. During the first show, I watched the screen as I had been told and played music appropriate to the action. But the next time around, I began to brush up on some old personal favorites. When the good cowboys headed off the bad guys at Eagle Pass, it was to the accompaniment of a Chopin nocturne, and I rippled through the Moonlight Sonata while the thundering train bore down on the heroine left gagged and trussed on the tracks by the dastardly villain. The manager presently came down the aisle.

"Listen, girlie," he said. "You want to keep this job, keep

your eye on the screen. If you don't . . ." He jerked a thumb toward the door. "You know what I mean?"

I knew what he meant and began to develop incipient palsy in my left hand, giving out with tremolos from noon to midnight, with only a twenty-minute break for dinner, seven days a week. In my "spare" time, I composed songs and took a batch of them to Leo Feist, then the biggest publisher of popular music. Feist listened impassively while I played and sang my tunes.

"They're lousy," he said. "The one you call 'The Sum of Life' is not as lousy as the others, though. I'll give you ten dollars for it."

I rushed to tell Harrison Fiske, my benefactor, the great news. "How old are you?" he demanded. "Twenty-four? I don't believe it. Don't you know better than to sell a song outright for a paltry ten dollars without getting the usual royalty rights?"

Fiske's scorn failed to put a crimp in my elation. What did a tradesman know of the supreme satisfaction of creative effort? Feist sold 200,000 copies of "The Sum of Life," but I never regretted the deal. The thrill of seeing "Words and Music by Elsa Maxwell" on the cover of the song was all the reward I wanted. It had to last me a long time, I didn't sell another song for six years.

What with spending my morning composing songs, and pounding the piano in the nickelodeon twelve hours a day, I would have gone out of my mind if not for infrequent backstage visits to Mrs. Fiske. She was appearing at the Empire Theatre a few blocks from the nickelodeon, and one night there I met an exquisite girl who was to change the entire course of my life with a casual word. She was Marie Doro, one of the biggest and unquestionably the most beautiful of all the stars on Broadway.

"I understand you play the piano very well," she said. "How would you like to come to my house tomorrow night and help entertain a few guests? I think you'll enjoy it."

I was dying to go, but my fingers were worn down to the knuckles after a twelve-hour stretch in the nickelodeon.

Marie construed my hesitancy for shyness. "You don't have to worry about your clothes," she said gently, merely succeeding in making me conscious of them. "Just a few old friends are coming for an informal party after the theater."

Among the guests at her little party were John Drew and William Gillette, reigning matinee idols, and two fellow refugees from the San Francisco earthquake — Enrico Caruso and Jack Barrymore. Much to my delight, Caruso recognized me at once. He kept me on a treadmill all evening between the piano and the kitchen, where he was preparing one of his elaborate practical jokes that often tempered friends' admiration for his vocal virtuosity. He volunteered to cook a special Italian dish, but used face powder instead of flour. After he stopped choking on his own gag, Caruso sang, Drew did devastating imitations of show people and Barrymore, recently embarked on acting and amatory careers, told Rabelaisian stories of his adventures in both fields. Gillette did nothing. He just sat and stared at Marie.

That was the typical reaction she inspired. Marie wasn't a great actress, but only a dyspeptic critic would have mentioned it, at the risk of being invited into an alley by her army of adoring fans. Audiences were enthralled by her luminous beauty and the magnetism she generated. Charles Frohman, the top producer on Broadway, shrewdly exploited Marie's appeal. Frohman, who went down with the *Lusitania* when it was torpedoed by a German submarine in 1915, would have brained a later-day press agent who tried to build up an actress as a wife, mother or a woman with social consciousness. A star in Frohman's galaxy lived on a remote, exalted mountaintop and was seen only by customers who observed the proper ritual at the box office. He autocratically ruled the private as well as the professional lives of his attractions. Maude Adams, his Number One star, was not permitted to be seen in public. He was slightly more lenient with Marie Doro, but made her wear a heavy veil whenever she went on the street. Marie was aghast when I suggested that it was nonsense for an American girl to traipse around like a Mohammedan woman in deepest Asia.

"Why," she gasped, "C.F. would kill me if he found out that I was seen unveiled in Central Park. He has spies everywhere. He knows everything."

Marie was so exquisite that few men discovered she was one of the most-intelligent and best-read actresses on Broadway. Certainly, she was the only one I ever knew who could read an ode in the original Greek while removing her make-up. We got along so well that Marie added me to her entourage as a companion, to play the piano at parties and to balance her supper tables, which always were top-heavy with men. I loved every minute of it. Marie represented glamour and luxury; she was my introduction to the sort of people I loved. I was so naïve that I did not realize at first why Marie wanted me to be around when I wasn't chained to the piano in the nickelodeon.

After all, she didn't entertain so much that she needed an extra woman and official life of the party on tap constantly.

Unconsciously, Marie was resorting to the oldest female stratagem in the world. She took me for the identical reason that a lovely jewel is displayed against a simple black background. The contrast in our appearances set off Marie's beauty. Since I had no vanity, I didn't mind. Marie was my one avenue of escape from a miserable job and the awful loneliness of a big, strange city.

As a consequence, I jumped at the chance when Marie invited me to go on tour with her in *The Richest Girl*. She had no job for me, but there was brave talk of collaborating on writing an operetta. What really sold me was the fact that Marie was to travel in a private railroad car equipped with all comforts, including a French chef. Ever since leaving San Francisco I had gone through a routine of second-rate boardinghouses and I was fed up with that grubby existence. I was so eager to accept Marie's offer that I didn't bother to tell the manager of the nickelodeon that I was quitting, even though he owed me two weeks' salary.

We had a wonderful time on tour, but I arrived back in New York worse off than before. I couldn't ask Harrison Fiske to help me again after walking out on the job he had gotten for me. I was on the blacklist at the nickelodeon for leaving without giving notice. The most depressing aspect of the whole thing was the double life I was leading. During the day, when I wasn't in my dreary room trying to write songs, I tramped the streets looking for work half-heartedly and ate in dismal cafeterias. At night, I was in demand to liven up parties with my piano playing in luxurious surroundings that made my environment all the more difficult to bear. Rubbing shoulders with successful people merely accentuated my failure.

One evening, some people I had met through Caruso invited me to their home. I marched straight to the piano and, as usual, began to play for my supper. An extraordinary-looking woman came over to listen and, after humming along with me for a few minutes, asked whether I could play something from *Il Pagliacci*.

"Of course," I replied. "What would you like?"

"Oh, the tenor aria 'Vesti la Giubba,' " she said.

"Who's going to sing it?"

"I am," the woman said with a straight face.

"In what key do you want me to play it?"

"Exactly the way it's written. For a tenor."

I looked again at the woman, thinking she was mad, as I played the opening bars of "*Vesti la Giubba*." The woman sang one bar and I almost fell off the stool. Not only was her voice amazing but it had the quality and timbre of a pure tenor. Everyone roared at my stupefaction. I was the only one present who did not know Dorothy Toye, a veteran vaudevillian billed as The Trick Voice. She was strictly as advertised. Dorothy had a strong, true voice in any register above baritone, and her extensive repertory made her act a sure-fire hit. Dorothy evidently liked my ability to follow her, for she hired me on the spot as her accompanist.

The next few months were the happiest I had known since before the death of my father. For the first time in my life I was accepted on my own merits without the aid of another person's influence. Dorothy was a considerate boss and a thorough professional with no phony airs or pretensions. Trouping with her along the Eastern seaboard was fun, the work was steady and the pay was good. I was beginning to settle down in a comfortable groove when I was uprooted by a cablegram to Dorothy. She was offered an engagement in England that was too good to pass up. Dorothy wanted to take me along, but she always had been pretty casual about money and could not afford to pay for my transportation. I didn't have the fare for an overnight boat ride, much less a transatlantic voyage. Practically all my salary had been spent on traveling expenses and a stage wardrobe. So I waved good-by to Dorothy, then went back to my old dugout in West Forty-sixth Street to weather another storm.

Friends laugh at my childlike faith in small miracles, but there is a good deal of basis for it. Whenever I'm in a hole, something utterly unexpected turns up to pull me out. That sort of thing has been going on all my strenuous life, and one of these days my luck must desert me. Until that happens, though, I'll play one of the world's longest winning streaks for all it's worth.

Back in the spring of 1908, I was brooding with self-pity when I had a phone call from Marie Doro, whom I had not seen or heard from for some time. Marie said she was sailing for Europe within the hour and would I like to follow on the next boat?

"I'll mail you a check for your passage," she said. "When you get to London, contact the Charles Frohman office. They'll know where you can reach me. 'Bye. See you soon."

By the time I had settled some bills which could not be dodged, I had only enough money for a ticket on the S.S. *Minnetonka*, a ship with a curiously unbalanced passenger list.

She carried twelve people and enough cattle for a stampede in Cinemascope. Among those who dined at my table were Captain and Mrs. Mahon Sands, obviously members of the British hunting set. They were taking a slow boat as a rest cure.

Captain Sands wasted no time on small talk at dinner the first night out. "Do you ride?" he asked me, going straight to the heart of the matter.

It struck me as an odd question to put to a San Franciscan. How could anyone get up and down its hills without riding the cable cars? "Of course I ride," I said. "Nobody walks in San Francisco."

My *bon mot* drew a blank from the captain. He puzzled over it during the soup and fish courses, then broke into a guffaw. "But I mean, do you ride to hounds?"

"Captain Sands is an M.F.H.," his wife announced proudly. It was my turn to look blank. Mrs. Sands hastened to enlighten an illiterate colonial. "The captain is Master of Fox Hounds," she said imperiously.

I suddenly remembered a remark made by William Gillette at one of Marie Doro's parties. "If you ever go to England," he said, "observe one rigid rule. The British will condone all conceivable bad manners except ignorance of their sports. If they ask you a sports question, pretend you know all about it. Use every cliché you've ever heard and you'll be a social and conversational success."

I fixed the Sandses with a haughty look. "All Californians are born to the saddle."

The captain beamed at me. "Splendid. You must come down to Ebrington Hall, our place in Warwickshire, for our first meet."

The voyage took two weeks and the Sandses spent every waking hour discussing my hunting debut in England. I neglected to tell them two pertinent details. I never had been on a horse anywhere, any time, and I had no intention of jeopardizing my chances of surviving my approaching twenty-fifth birthday. The only "brush" the Sandses would get was the one I planned to give them when Marie met me at Southampton.

When we landed, a messenger boy was waiting for me at the gangplank with a telegram to the effect that Marie was somewhere on the Continent, and advising me to leave my address with the Frohman office in London. It was a Friday afternoon and by the time I reached London the office would be closed for the week end. I didn't have the slightest notion where Dorothy Toye was. I had the equivalent of about three English pounds in my purse. The Sandses suddenly were invested with a charm I hadn't noticed before. A broken neck was preferable to slow starvation. It was faster and tidier. I went with the Sandses to their manor in Warwickshire as though I knew what I was doing.

The following morning Captain Sands, full of that abysmal cheerfulness only the British are capable of radiating at the crack of dawn, couldn't wait to show me the "fair bit" of horse he had selected for me. The black beast had sprung full-born from a dinosaur.

Women were using sidesaddles in those days and, after a series of convulsive heaves, I made a lifesaving discovery. The seat — and all other vital parts of the body — could be maintained if the lower thigh, which jammed under the pommel, was sufficiently plump. I had just the build for a sidesaddle, and I managed to hang on to the monster. That's all I remember of the ordeal. I was too frightened and numb to acknowledge congratulations on my dashing ride. My wild beast had led the pack and practically breathed down the fox's neck during the chase.

Pleading an indisposition, an understatement if ever there was one, I rode back with a groom on a high, two-wheeled cart that followed the hunt to collect the maimed and walking wounded. The cart hit a deep rut and tipped, throwing me to the road heavily. When I came to, I was told that I had torn the ligaments in my side and would have to stay in bed with a plaster cast for a week. Captain Sands speeded my recovery by telling me I had been asked to attend a hunt ball the Duke of Beaufort was giving.

"An invitation from the duke is considered a great honor in the Shires," the captain said. "Good show, Old Girl."

The Old Girl decided to get out of there if she was to live long enough to deserve the sobriquet. I caught the next train for London and went to the Frohman office in the Globe Theater, but no one knew when Marie Doro was expected back from the Continent. And Dorothy Toye's agent said she was on tour somewhere in the provinces.

Left to my own nonexistent resources, I stumbled on a secret that has sustained more than one out-at-the-elbows opportunist. You can be broke with more dignity in London than any of the world's large cities. The British, with their beautiful manners, never ask a stranger embarrassing questions. The room clerk at a dingy hotel in Russell Square did not request the rent in advance. The chambermaid did not report me as a potential deadbeat for doing laundry in my room. Although everyone in the old firetrap must have known I was cooking over the gas burner in my room, the manager did not mention that violation of house rules. I even risked disaster by signing for meals in the restaurant, and was not presented with a bill for two weeks.

Having nothing but time to spend, I followed the example set by a long, distinguished line of dawdlers and made the British Museum my clubhouse. It was manifestly impossible to read all the books in that huge, gloomy structure, but I made a good try and accumulated a fund of useless information guaranteed to cast a pall over any dinner table.

People who have escaped from poverty are like old soldiers. In later years they recount the little, amusing incidents that happened infrequently, and conveniently forget the long, unrelieved stretches of misery and boredom. It was no fun being hungry and friendless in a foreign country, and I was near the end of my rope one night as I walked aimlessly down Oxford Street. I had not yet become accustomed to the perverse British habit of driving on the left side of the road and I looked in the wrong direction as I stepped off the curb. There was a harsh screech of brakes followed by a stream of Cockney profanity from the driver of the bus that barely had avoided running me down.

As I looked up at him, my eye caught a sign on the bus:

DOROTHY TOYE
DOUBLE-VOICE PHENOMENON
EMPIRE MUSIC HALL NOW

"Oh, thank you, thank you," I babbled to the driver. The poor man must have thought I had lost my mind.

Dorothy welcomed me with open arms and with my old job at ten pounds a week. There is no therapy like security. The first matinee at the Empire Music Hall erased all the troubles that had been weighing me down only sixteen hours earlier. Getting back into the routine of two shows and three square meals a day was a wonderful tonic, and there was the additional stimulation of new sights and experiences in Europe. Dorothy was one American vaudevillian who was not stymied by language barriers. Her act was a popular, headline attraction on the Continent as well as in the British Isles. After England and Scotland, we were booked solidly in France and Germany for more than a year and a half.

In 1909, at my urging, Dorothy reluctantly accepted an offer to appear in South Africa. There was no prestige playing so far off the beaten path, and Dorothy, a blasé trouper, had none of my curiosity in out-of-the-way places. But I was so eager to see South Africa, and a long voyage with expenses paid was such a pleasant break in our grind, that Dorothy took a month's work in Capetown and Johannesburg. As usual, another turning point for me hinged on nothing more substantial than a whim. The junket was to transform me from a professional piano player into an amateur celebrity hunter.

My first catch didn't impress Dorothy. We sailed on the S.S. *Edinburgh Castle*, an old tub, and the only live wire aboard was a glib young Irishman whose name I forget. Dorothy suspected he was a phony name dropper, and she was convinced of it when he promised to introduce me to Lord Gladstone, son of the Victorian prime minister, then the governor general of South Africa.

"That proves the guy is a fourflusher," Dorothy argued.

"What good Irishman would even want to know the son of a man who made it tough for his people?"

The day we arrived in Capetown, the young Irishman sent two invitations for a reception at the governor general's palace. Dorothy still was skeptical. She said she wasn't going to make a fool of herself by being turned away at the door, but I chose to believe my invitation was genuine. It was. My Irishman was waiting in the hall of the rambling, unprepossessing palace. A battle-ax of a dowager wearing a monocle swooped down on us and promptly identified herself.

"I'm Mrs. Dale Lace," she announced. "My husband has mining interests in Johannesburg. I know everybody. You're a new one. Who are you?"

"Maxwell. Elsa Maxwell," I said. "I'm an American."

"Doesn't mean a thing to me. What do you do? Diamonds?"

I shook my head.

"Gold?"

I shook my head again.

"Well, what do you do?" Mrs. Lace demanded impatiently.

"I'm just plain piano," I said humbly.

Mrs. Lace stared at me through her monocle. "Come meet this droll American gel," she shouted to a man in uniform.

The officer sighed but obeyed the order. He was Sir Henry Scobell, commander of the British garrison in Capetown. Sir Henry rescued me from the battle-ax and put me through the same cross-examination. He thought my "plain piano" crack was uproariously funny and introduced me to everyone as though I were an amusing freak.

"How would you like to meet General Botha?" he asked.

"The Botha? The hero of the Boer War?"

Sir Henry winced. "He wasn't a hero to us, but I'll introduce you if you like. Only I must tell you the old boy is rather gruff. Not much of a lady's man, you know."

Since I wasn't much of a gentleman's woman, Botha and I got on famously. It developed that he was fond of Viennese waltzes played with a good loud oompah, and that was right down the alley of an old nickelodeon thumper. Botha was so pleased that he invited me to dine with him and his wife. The word got around that I had made a hit with Botha, and before the evening was over I was bombarded with more invitations than I could accept.

I rushed back to the hotel, awakened Dorothy and regaled her with a full account of my triumphant impact on South African society. Dorothy was not impressed. "One more week in Capetown," she said, "and you'll be a full-fledged snob."

I had met many celebrities before, of course, but always tagging along with my father or friends. Now in Johannesburg I was the belle of the ball who attracted celebrities with my piano playing, my informality and the new crop of stories I had imported. Following the classic pattern, I concocted a glittering background. Wasn't California a lush goldfield when South Africa was an obscure outpost? Well, my father was one of the intrepid pioneers who had struck it rich beyond the dreams of avarice. My fling in vaudeville was laughed off as a typical eccentricity of a headstrong, enormously wealthy heiress. I was so brazen that I began to tell barefaced lies in front of Dorothy. She was too loyal to expose me in public, but she did rake me over the coals when we were alone together. Two days before

our engagement at the Globe Music Hall ended, I told Dorothy I wasn't returning to England with her. I was staying in
Johannesburg.

"You'll starve," she said flatly. "This country can't support
a piano player like you for more than another month."

In the first truthful statement Dorothy had heard from me
in weeks, I told her there was no prominent place for a piano
in my future. I had been invited to be the house guest of Sir
Lionel and Lady Phillips at Arcadia Farm, their estate near
Johannesburg. Sir Lionel, the head of the enormously rich
Central Mining Company, was a sardonic little man who
wasn't fooled by me for a minute. I think he took to me because he was rather amused by the bill of goods I had sold the
gullible upper crust of Johannesburg. Sir Lionel refused to take
himself or anyone else seriously. When he showed me his portrait, he repeated James Whistler's imperishable crack: "The
innate vulgarity of the subject almost exceeds that of the
painter."

The invitation to remain at Arcadia Farm as long as I liked
was extended by "Florrie," Lady Phillips. She industriously
collected people with the zeal of a stamp fancier, and her
boundless energy and lively interest in a welter of activities
made us kindred spirits. Florrie was the catalyst in most of the
civic and cultural advances made in Johannesburg during the
decade after the Boer War. She organized committees to
improve hospitals, streets and housing for natives. She was
lavish with Sir Lionel's fortune in supporting theaters, art
galleries, music and publications.

Taking my cue from Florrie, I plunged into all her projects
and found a few new ones on my own hook. I became a feature

writer of *The State*, the only illustrated magazine in Johannesburg at the time. I occasionally conducted the orchestra of the Wheeler Light Opera Company and gave weekly readings at the Browning Society. I took a course at the local university in farm irrigation and canal construction. I had a hand, and a foot, in almost everything going on. I persuaded winegrowers to put sneakers on natives who previously had been treading on the grapes with their bare feet. As a lifelong teetotaler, I don't know whether my innovation improved the end product, but it certainly was more sanitary.

The calendar says I spent the better part of a year and a half in Johannesburg, but I was so busy and happy that I hardly was aware of it. South Africa was wonderfully stimulating and I was prepared to settle there permanently until I passed a travel bureau one day. Posters in the window advertising European capitals gave me a sudden, overpowering feeling that I was isolated from the mainstream of the life I wanted. I went in and booked passage on the next ship sailing for England.

Leaving a patroness as kind and generous as Florrie was a severe wrench, but an augmented chorus of angels must have sung at my christening. On the boat I met a tall, stunning girl who was — and still is — the best and most helpful friend I ever have known. She was Dorothy ("Dickie") Fellowes-Gordon, who was traveling with her stepfather, Colonel Alexander Wylie, a wealthy coal man. Dickie was then twenty-one and already had the beauty and sharp wit that were to make her one of Europe's *femmes fatales*, a role she attained without half trying.

Although Dickie had Scottish scorn for the chi-chi pack shrilly pursuing notoriety after World War I, she was so outstanding that she was mentioned prominently in many of the personal reminiscences written during that period. A typical reference was made by Ronnie Bodley in his *Indiscretions of a Young Man:*

> She [Elsa Maxwell] was accompanied that night by an attractive girl called Dickie Fellowes-Gordon, who had one of the most lovely voices I have ever heard. I am sure she would have made her name and fortune in opera if she had not been blessed with a lazy temperament and enough money to live on without working. I once heard her sing at the same party as Mary Garden and I am not sure which of the two had the purer voice.

Bodley's description was correct in every detail but one. The opera star with whom Dickie compared favorably was Nellie Melba, not Mary Garden.

Dickie swears my first words to her were: "I'm giving a little party tonight and I'd like you to come." I don't remember saying it, but it's entirely possible I did. Lord only knows how often she was to hear that refrain.

Chapter 5

A STRANGE wind was sweeping London in 1912, a gathering gale presaging the cataclysm that was to convulse Europe two years later. There was a fatalistic acceptance of the inevitability of war that impelled people to look for excitement with a grim, almost hysterical, intensity before time ran out. Although I hardly was an authority on the London scene, I could not help but notice the radical change in the atmosphere when I returned from South Africa. In the comparatively short period I was away, most of the restraints remaining from the Victorian era had been discarded. Even the most sedate newspapers were giving a heavy play to sex and scandal.

London's quickened tempo was not entirely symptomatic of unhealthy tensions and attitudes, however. A good deal of it stemmed from the impact of vigorous, vivid American women on British society. The invasion of Europe by second-generation American heiresses looking for husbands with genuine or phony titles was in full swing, and the huntresses had no trouble bagging prime, pedigreed specimens.

Americans were, and still are, the world's biggest snobs, of course. We always have made a greater fuss over royalty and rank than Europeans. (The coronation of Queen Elizabeth in 1953 caused more of a stir in the United States than it did in England.) Conversely, European men always have been less squeamish — or more realistic — than Americans about being supported by women and consider trading their titles for money as a fine bargain. As a consequence, there was brisk activity in the marriage market, with buyers and sellers in a receptive frame of mind to do business.

Anna Gould, the unattractive daughter of a multimillionaire financier, made a spectacular catch in the Marquis Boni de Castellane, the elegant man-about-Paris and social arbiter of France. With Gould money, he built the Pink Palace in Paris, a direct copy of the Grand Trianon at Versailles. Boni once took me on a tour of the showplace. When we came to the bedroom, decorated in the rococo Louis XVI manner, he said laconically, "La chambre expiatoire" (the penance room).

Envious Europeans didn't realize they indicted themselves in ridiculing the blunders of American social climbers they courted assiduously. Mrs. Kate Moore, the wife of a midwestern tycoon, was a laughing stock for her malapropisms, yet the upper crust scrambled for invitations to her lavish salons. Once she entertained King Edward VII, who admired her sculpture. "Oh, wait until you see the lovely bust of my hands I've commissioned," Mrs. Moore said grandly.

Although most of England's great fortunes still were intact, practically anyone who dispensed food and drink with a free hand was a social success in pre-World War I London. Ethel Levey, the divorced wife of George M. Cohan, who was appearing in *Hullo Ragtime*, a revue, still is remembered as the Woman Who Fed Mayfair. She established such high standards of hospitality that more than one American later went broke in London trying to pull an Ethel Levey. Even

Elsie Janis's mother, a thrifty Ohio housewife, went overboard
in buying her way into British society. When Lord Lonsdale,
the well-known sportsman, dined at her home, Mrs. Janis was
so impressed that she told her butler, "John, dear, fetch a
seventy-five cent Corona for the noble lord."

Circumspect Britishers were blinking in astonishment at
the antics of a bombshell named Dorothy Taylor, a girl from
Watertown, New York, who had inherited some twelve million
dollars from her father's leather-goods business. She was better
known afterwards as la Contessa di Frasso, whose escapades
and racy tongue provided feature writers with good copy for
forty years, until her death on January 4, 1954. Dorothy may
have had faults — who hasn't? — but you had to love her for a
great capacity for laughing at herself. Henry Miller might have
been describing Dorothy when he wrote of one of his characters: "His frailties were human frailties and he wore them
jauntily, tauntingly, like banderillas."

I've heard celebrated wits tell funny stories, but none can
top Dorothy's own account of her screwball treasure hunt.
Dorothy was off and running on the misadventure when an
old Canadian prospector, whom she met in a bar, hopped her
up to the ears with a yarn only she would have believed. A
hundred years ago, the prospector related, a revolution was
brewing in Peru and the government asked a British sea captain
named Thompson to take the state treasury of $300,000,000 out
to sea until the rumpus quieted down. Captain Thompson had
murky designs on the treasury, however, and murdered the
agents assigned to guard it, then buried the loot on Cocos
Island off the coast of Costa Rica. He had the only copy of a
map showing the location of the treasure and it vanished when

he died shortly afterward. The prospector, inspired by the whisky Dorothy fed him, claimed he had seen the precious document and reproduced it on the tablecloth with Dorothy's lipstick. Dorothy richly rewarded the old codger's revelation, chartered a yacht for the expedition and asked her dear friend Buggsy Siegel, the gangster, to round up a crew.

Dorothy naïvely believed Buggsy was an innocent, overgrown boy, an opinion that was hardly shared by the business associates who later liquidated him. Buggsy recruited a weird assortment of grifters, cutthroats and confederates who found it expedient to take an ocean voyage for their health. Only three members of the crew ever had been to sea before. The first day out, the yacht became a seething caldron of hatred over the division of the loot and the attentions of the ship's nurse. Mario Bello, Jean Harlow's stepfather, temporarily cooled off competition for the nurse by marrying her. On Cocos, the good companions immediately discovered why the island was uninhabited. It was touch and go whether the climate was worse than the insect life. The crew decided drinking was more to its liking than digging, especially after a few desultory stabs failed to unearth buried treasure. The return trip was enlivened by a mutiny and the breakdown of the ship's engine a few hours after the radio, the only gadget on board that was working, picked up warnings of an approaching hurricane. Fortunately, a passing tramp steamer came to the rescue and towed the floundering yacht into Acapulco, for a fee that exceeded its original cost.

Although it is difficult to select Dorothy's dizziest brainstorm, it probably came shortly after World War II. She and her husband Carlo introduced Buggsy to Italian royalty and stiff-necked Roman society as "Bart" Siegel. Exiled King Umberto II, who misinterpreted the nickname as an abbreviation for baronet, must have been baffled by the rather unconventional speech and mannerisms of Dorothy's protégé. He asked me, when dining with me at Auribeau last year, what the Baron Siegel's antecedents were.

"He acted oddly for a baron," Umberto said. "He tried to sell us dynamite."

I told His Majesty that the Baron Siegel had a good deal of experience in that line as a big shot in Murder, Incorporated. Umberto was incredulous when I explained that Murder, Incorporated was a gangster syndicate in America that controlled gambling, the vice and dope rackets and hired professional killers to keep the underworld in line.

"It's impossible to believe that your government permits such an organization to exist," Umberto said.

"Unfortunately, it did, and your countrymen from Sicily started the whole thing."

Umberto shook his head ruefully, then laughed uproariously as the audacity of Dorothy's joke dawned on him.

Dorothy always did have a peculiar sense of humor. She married Claude Graham-White, a pioneer English aviator, in 1913, and soon suspected Ethel Levey, her bosom pal, of carrying friendship too far with her husband. Dorothy hired a private detective to check on Graham-White, and startled the birds for miles around with her howls of laughter when a detailed report was submitted. The ceiling of Ethel's bedroom was painted sky-blue and depicted a plane coming through the clouds as though it were preparing to make a forced landing on the bed. Dorothy thought it was so funny that she didn't stop laughing long enough to divorce Graham-White until 1916.

"I married England's greatest aviator and the greatest gentle-man in Europe," Dorothy reflected recently, "and it's a tossup which jerk took me for more dough."

Dorothy and I had arguments over the years — including a hair-pulling match in Venice once — but I was devoted to her for one reason in particular. It was through her that I met Maxine Elliott, unquestionably the most dynamic woman in London, in 1912 when it was the social capital of the world. It seemed almost unfair that so much beauty, intelligence, talent and success were incorporated in one woman. Maxine probably was the most glamorous of all American actresses. It is signifi-cant that she and Ethel Barrymore were the only actresses for whom Broadway theaters ever have been named. Her stage earnings and friendship with J. P. Morgan, her financial adviser, made Maxine enormously wealthy, yet unhappiness and loneli-ness clouded the latter part of her life.

Maxine, who came from a small town in Maine, bitterly resented the prejudice she encountered in her native country. American social leaders were so busy making money or con-solidating their positions a half century ago that they had not yet acquired the culture to appreciate a woman of Maxine's stature. Europe's sophisticated society courted actors and musi-cians, but in America performers were treated little better than servants. Maxine, who maintained a brilliant salon at Hartsbourne Manor, in Hartfordshire, spent all her money and free time in Europe in protest against the shabby snobbery of New York. Although she was just past forty and at the height of her career when I met her, Maxine was on the verge of retiring from the stage. She loathed the monotony of repeating lines from mediocre scripts for months on end, the gaping crowds that interfered with her private life and the strain of taking plays on tour. The late Lee Shubert, her partner in the Maxine Elliott Theatre, used every conceivable argument in an effort to forestall Maxine's retirement.

"You'll miss the glamour and the glory of the stage," he predicted.

"I'll miss it about as much as the early Christian martyrs missed the man-eating lions in the arena," she snapped.

After her divorce from Nat Goodwin — an actor who had the grand total of eight wives — Maxine was besieged by proposals from England's most eligible peers and industrialists. Her most persistent suitor was Lord Curzon, the former viceroy of India and future foreign secretary, but Maxine had fallen in love with young Anthony Wilding, the Australian tennis champion. On August 4, 1914, the day England declared war on Germany, Wilding was in the United States helping Australia regain the Davis Cup. He sailed that same night to join the British Army. Maxine followed him into service organizing and underwriting the expenses of the Canteen Barges which plied the canals of Belgium feeding and clothing refugees close behind the front lines. Anthony Wilding was killed in France, but Maxine assuaged her grief by devoting all her energy to the Allied cause.

Albert I, King of the Belgians, presented Maxine with his country's highest civilian decoration. At the presentation Albert, in pinning the medal on Maxine's thin dress, pierced her breast.

"You have been wounded!" he exclaimed when he saw the blood seeping through the material.

"Yes, Sire," she responded, "but not by the enemy."

After the war, Maxine moved to France and built the Chateau de l'Horizon, the most magnificent showplace on the Riviera, near Cannes. It now is owned by the Aly Khan, who bought it in 1946. Maxine passed the last decade of her life there forgotten by the public, but England's statesmen remembered, and still responded to, the magnetism that had made Maxine London's leading hostess. Winston Churchill was a frequent guest and occupied himself with painting and writing there while England permitted his genius to lie fallow. Anthony Eden held many secret conferences with French and Italian foreign ministers at the Chateau de l'Horizon before the Ethiopian and Munich crises.

I last saw Maxine in the summer of 1939, eight months before her death the following March. As another devoted admirer who remembered Maxine as the most vibrant woman of her time, I was shocked by the change in her. She was monstrously fat and spent all her days at the side of the pool playing backgammon. Her thwarted affection was sublimated in Kiki, a filthy, bad-tempered monkey that had the run of the lovely house and bit everyone who approached Maxine. On the eve of another war, Maxine's active mind had become so dulled by reading cheap detective stories that she was not interested in the latest news. Her chief concern was finding someone with whom to play backgammon.

Maxine was listless until lunch was served, a huge meal that ran heavily to whipped cream and thick, rich sauces. She brightened up and began to eat ravenously.

"I've just received my death sentence," she said casually, between mouthfuls. "The doctor tells me I've got uremia. He says I must cut out all rich food." She motioned to the butler for another helping.

"You'll kill yourself if you don't listen to him," I cried.

She shrugged. "There's only one better way to die, and I'm too old for it," she answered.

The spark that once had burned so brightly in Maxine began to flicker and fade the day Anthony Wilding was killed on a muddy field somewhere in France.

Psychologists recognize the curious sensation that sometimes makes a person feel he is revisiting a familiar place which he knows, positively, is strange to him. I had that feeling, as though I had come home, when I returned to London from South Africa. It puzzled me for a while until I realized the cause of it. I was meeting once again artists and intellectuals, the same sort of people with whom I had mingled as a girl in San Francisco.

Arthur Rubinstein, the brilliant young Polish pianist, popped up constantly at parties, where he was in great demand for his wit and charm. Willie Maugham, who had not yet written *The Moon and Sixpence* or the other novels and stories that were to put him in the front rank of contemporary authors, was one of the town's gayest bachelors and most indefatigable dancers. One night at a party given by Mrs. Syrie Wellcome, whom he later married, Willie and I locked horns in an endurance contest. He danced and I played the piano for three hours without a break, until both of us were ready to drop from sheer exhaustion. We since have grown smarter and more sedentary and now confine our competitive drive to marathon sessions at the bridge table.

Willie was known for his sharp, sarcastic wit, and stuffy veterans in the British Foreign Office still turn nip-ups when they recall one example of it. During World War I, Willie was attached to the staff of Lord Curzon, the foreign secretary, to decode confidential messages. Just before England's ill-fated invasion of the Dardanelles, a Secret Service agent was sent to Greece to investigate rumors of widespread unrest. In due time the agent sent back a coded message reporting that conditions indeed were unsettled. The situation was so chaotic, the agent reported, that even the devout monks of Mount Athos, an old monastery, were violating their vows. In Willie's translation, though, it came out that the monks were violating their cows. When Willie showed the garbled message to his chief, Lord Curzon said dryly: "Send them a papal bull."

The social lion of London in 1913 was Serge Diaghilev, the impresario of the Russian ballet company featuring the unforgettable Nijinsky. Diaghilev, more than any man in modern times, revolutionized a classical art form with the innovations he brought to the ballet. He commissioned Stravinsky, Debussy and other noted composers to write scores for him. His sets and costumes were designed by the finest artists available. At his direction, choreographers gave the ballet a fluidity and dramatic continuity it never had known before.

Diaghilev operated on a scale that burned up money faster than the public could pour it into the box office. His company invariably played to sell-out houses, yet he constantly dodged sheriffs and lawyers brandishing judgments and lawsuits. Such actions never disturbed Diaghilev. He was sublimely confident that a millionaire would turn up to bail him out of financial difficulties, and he rarely was disappointed.

"I spent nothing on myself," he used to say with a disarming smile. "My tastes are simple. The best is good enough for me."

Money was the least of Diaghilev's troubles. His chief concern was preventing Nijinsky from slipping into the twilight zone that bordered on insanity. On the stage, Nijinsky was an exalted Greek god come to life, but between performances he was a morose, inarticulate schizophrenic. Diaghilev was the only person who could handle Nijinsky and the dancer cracked completely when he was separated from his guardian for the first time in his adult life. Nijinsky was visiting his wife's family in Budapest when World War I broke, and he was interned as an enemy alien. Four years later, when Nijinsky was reunited with Diaghilev, he was hopelessly insane.

The first time I saw Diaghilev, a young man wearing an ill-fitting brown tweed suit and shoes that squeaked followed him around the room like a faithful dog. I almost cried with disappointment when I realized that Diaghilev's shadow was the divine Nijinsky. The epitome of grace and rhythm shuffled his feet and didn't know what to do with his awkward hands when we were introduced. I tried to make conversation with him in halting French, our only common language, but it was hard going. Nijinsky stared at me with the vacant, expressionless eyes of a sleepwalker. I finally penetrated the fog when I asked him what he considered the most important asset of a great dancer. Nijinsky suddenly came to attention.

"*Les reins, mademoiselle*," he said promptly. "*Les reins.*"

Sketchy as my French was, I knew that *les reins* meant the kidneys. That really threw me for a loss. Diaghilev, who seldom left his star's side for long when they were in public, came along to solve my confusion. He explained that *les reins* also meant the lower muscles of the back. Nijinsky smiled and retreated into a brooding reverie.

"He does not talk much," Diaghilev said. "Great dancers should not be heard, anyway. They should only be seen, preferably in a theater at a distance."

I often saw Diaghilev in the decade that followed World War I, but he wasn't the same man he had been when he was creating ballets for the greatest dancer the world ever had seen. Although he produced a succession of artistic masterpieces, his mind was far away in that sanitarium in Switzerland where Nijinsky was sinking deeper into the labyrinth from which he never escaped.

The British often are lampooned for their caste system, but there was far less class consciousness in prewar London's high society than there was among New York's so-called Four Hundred at that time. In fact, the chief charm of the London social whirl was its thoroughly democratic spirit. The same people who flocked to Lady Randolph Churchill's receptions pulled wires to get an invitation from Rosa Lewis, a woman as far removed from Lady Churchill's background as the poles of the earth.

Jennie Churchill, the American-born mother of the greatest Englishman of the twentieth century, had no patience for stuffed shirts. Talent was her only criterion for appraising people and she remained a staunch admirer of Oscar Wilde despite the scandal still attached to his name more than ten years after his death. Lady Churchill loved to tell anecdotes about Wilde. Her favorite story concerned a woman who once asked Wilde if it was true he could deliver a witty, extemporaneous speech on any conceivable subject. Wilde, who never ducked a conversational challenge, drew himself up to his full height.

"Quite true," he answered. "Give me a subject."

"Queen Victoria," the woman said, believing she had Wilde trapped. He wouldn't dare make irreverent cracks about Her Majesty.

"My dear lady," Wilde snapped, "the queen is not a subject."

Rosa Lewis graduated from a kitchen in Surrey to the Cavendish Hotel in Jermyn Street, which, under her management, became one of the most fashionable salons in London. The Cavendish was a ramshackle inn, but King Edward VII once observed, rather plaintively, that it was more difficult to arrange for a dinner or accommodations there than it was to be presented at the Court of Saint James. The food was superb and the company was convivial, but the principal attraction of the Cavendish was Rosa herself. She was a lusty, volatile woman who treated peers of the realm in an offhand manner, as though they were lackeys.

The star boarder at the Cavendish was Sir William Eden, the eccentric father of England's perennial boy wonder in the Foreign Office. A newcomer to the Cavendish was accepted as a charter member in the club when Rosa: (a) Extended an invitation to stay for a dinner she cooked herself, or (b) Ordered Sir William to tell the hilarious story of James Whistler's lawsuit against him. Rosa gave me a double-barreled initiation into the lodge by having Sir William recount the incident during dinner in his room. The old gentleman balked but quickly capitulated when Rosa threatened to give the dinner to another guest.

Many years before, Sir William related, he had commissioned Whistler to paint Lady Eden's portrait. When the job was completed, Sir William refused to accept the picture because, he claimed, it was a poor likeness of his wife. Whistler, the one-time West Pointer who was almost as famous for his controversies and feuds as he was for his painting, took Sir William to court in an effort to collect his fee. At the trial, the defense lawyer asked permission to introduce in evidence Whistler's celebrated painting *Nocturne*. Permission was granted and the lawyer proceeded to turn it upside down, then asked the jury to guess what the picture was supposed to represent.

"That's unfair!" Whistler protested. "You're not displaying the picture properly."

"It should make no difference," the lawyer retorted. "According to you, this is a picture of Battersea Bridge in a fog. I am sure the gentlemen of the jury can recognize Battersea Bridge, regardless of the position of the picture, if it is a true likeness."

The jury, evidently bemused by the lawyer's devious logic, handed down a decision in favor of Sir William. Whistler, however, had the satisfaction of getting in the last dig.

"If I had not been a gentleman," he told Sir William, "I would have demanded that you display Lady Eden to the jury upside down. I wonder how many would have recognized her."

I began to circulate in London's liveliest circles, immediately after my return from South Africa, through a series of lucky windfalls. Mary Ryan, who worked for an American newspaper syndicate, paid me fifteen pounds for writing two articles on my experiences in Johannesburg. Emboldened by the sale, I moved into the Lyceum Club, a haunted house nowadays but a well-known hotel with a large clientele of writers in 1912. I made the acquaintance of Henry Arthur Jones and Sir Arthur Pinero, England's leading playwrights, the first week at the Lyceum Club. Pinero was such an easy man to talk to that I asked him what a girl with my background could do to make a living.

"Why don't you write a play?" he suggested. I think he meant well, but he should have known better. I took him seriously. In a rare burst of modesty, I told him I didn't have the vaguest notion of how to go about constructing a play.

"It's quite simple," Pinero said blandly. "Build your action around the Big Four of sex — Love, Marriage, Adultery and Divorce. It's a sure-fire formula that never misses."

Although no one in the United Kingdom who had reached the age of consent had less firsthand knowledge of Pinero's last three dramatic elements, I industriously tackled the project. Lady Diana and Sir Archibald, my protagonists, were teetering madly on the precipice of passion in Act I when a small catastrophe overtook their creator. I ran out of money. Then I went out to look for a job that would keep me in luxuries such as food and rent and, by sheer coincidence, met Dickie Gordon on the street. "And then I met" is the recurring theme that runs through my life, but my good fortune hit an all-time high the day I chanced to run into Dickie, whom I had not seen since the voyage from South Africa.

Dickie had just come from a run-in with her stepfather and was looking for someone to share a flat with her.

"Let's pool our resources and room together," she said.

"Add my share to what you've got and you'll wind up with your original stake," I said. "I'm flat broke"

She shrugged. "I get a comfortable income from my father's estate. It's enough for both of us. One of these days you'll make a strike and the shoe will be on the other foot."

Candor compels me to admit that it was a long time before our shoes were remotely interchangeable, but Dickie's confidence in me seemed to be justified right off the bat. I wrote a song, "The Tango Dream," for Grace LaRue, an American vaudeville star appearing at the London Palace, which became an overnight hit. English publishers did not drive as hard a bargain as Leo Feist, or maybe I had gotten a lot smarter than I had been when I sold "The Sum of Life" for ten dollars. At any rate, I held out for a royalty arrangement and got two hundred pounds, the equivalent of a thousand dollars, for "The Tango Dream." That was more money than I ever had earned before in one piece and Messrs. Fortnam and Mason's deluxe food establishment was given a big play by a new customer.

Instead of reading about the gay Mayfair set in second-rate novels, I began to explore it at firsthand. I had money in the bank and champagne in the icebox. Dickie and I hit it off perfectly in our flat. I was busily, and gainfully, occupied in the mornings writing special-material songs for vaudeville stars. I was busier in the afternoons and evenings making a widening circle of friends. Through my old vaudeville contacts I got to know Ethel Levey, then Maxine Elliott and the fascinating artists and intellectuals she attracted to her home. I really was living and loved every minute of it.

London's glorious sunshine in the summer of 1914 was

obliterated, abruptly and completely, by the dark clouds of war. England suffered a succession of disastrous reverses in the early weeks and among the first casualties in France were the two Grenfell boys, whom Dickie and I knew very well. The morning the newspaper reported they had been killed in action, I tried to write a letter of condolence to their father, Lord Desborough. The words were so futile that I gave up and went out of the flat to throw off my feeling of depression and uncertainty. The American embassy was urging all nationals to return to the United States immediately and I was debating whether I should take the advice while transportation still was available.

I was walking down Piccadilly, approaching the Guards' Club, when I saw an elderly gentleman come down the steps with his hat at a jaunty angle, swinging a stick and wearing a boutonniere. I recognized Lord Desborough, but he looked so chipper that I didn't believe he had heard of his sons' deaths. I didn't have the heart to confront him, but it was too late to turn away. As he strolled by, Lord Desborough raised his hat and murmured, "Lovely morning."

That was all, but in the fleeting instant our eyes met I saw something there that told me, more poignantly than any outward show of emotion, that Lord Desborough had received the terrible news. The British constantly are ridiculed for their phlegmatic, stiff-upper-lip attitude, but never by me. Not since the morning I saw that look in Lord Desborough's eyes. It dispelled all thoughts of returning to America. I went back to the flat and I wrote "The British Volunteer," England's first war song, in a burst of determination I never have been able to recapture.

I'm proud of the roaring reception "The British Volunteer" received at the London Hippodrome when Violet Lorraine stepped to the footlights and sang:

> He comes from his desk in the City,
> He comes from his place in the bank.
> He's never been a soldier,
> He's never been a sailor,
> He's never held an office or a rank.
> He's never been promoted
> And his name you never hear.
> But when he's marching down the street,
> You feel you want to cheer
> The British Volunteer!

During my spasmodic song-writing career, I've turned out some forty numbers, but "The British Volunteer" is my favorite for a very special reason. I don't want to sound like one of those broken-down "and-then-I-wrote" hacks who helped to kill vaudeville, but I did have moderate success with my compositions. "The Singer" was used for years by Nellie Melba and Frances Alda as an encore in recitals. Eleanor Steber, Lauritz Melchior and Lawrence Tibbett have given my selections public auditions. I wrote special material for Ina Claire, Marie Dressler, Grace LaRue and Alice Delysia, all big stars. "The British Volunteer" didn't bring a fraction of the money I earned on "the Tango Dream"; in fact, I gave it away, glad to have Violet Lorraine sing it as my modest contribution to the war effort. It wasn't as good a song as "Tipperary," "Over There" and "Madelon," yet it had one distinction that is a source of pride to me. It's a matter of record that I, an American, wrote England's first war song.

I promptly followed up with two other patriotic songs. "Carry On" was fairly popular with the British Navy, but "Shine Little Searchlight" died suddenly due to natural causes. Soon after hostilities started, the Germans boasted that they would bomb London from their Zeppelins. The government set up batteries of huge searchlights in anticipation of air attacks, but to most civilians the whole thing was an awful nuisance. The idea of gas bags flying hundreds of miles across the North Sea at night was dismissed as fantastic nonsense and people complained bitterly that the garish searchlights accomplished no other purpose than disrupting their sleep. A generation later the people of London were to endure too many sleepless nights without a whimper, but in that primitive era of the air age they were more annoyed by, than apprehensive of, the threat of bombing from the sky.

One trick of popular-song writing is to reflect current moods, and the last five lines of my ditty were written strictly for laughs:

> Fade little searchlight, fade forever.
> Please go without a fuss,
> For you don't interfere
> With the zeppelins, dear,
> But you do interfere with us.

One night Alice Delysia, who performed the number at the Empire Music Hall, waited for the audience's usual roar after the last line. The orchestra still was holding the final note when the angry, deep-throated barking of antiaircraft guns overrode all other sounds. After an agony of suspense, three heavy thuds were felt and heard in the theater. History had turned a dark corner with the first volley of air warfare and "Shine Little Searchlight" no longer was a laughing matter.

Many more important things than a topical song were discarded during the grim winter of 1914–1915. The casualty lists mounted with discouraging news from France. Austerity replaced gaiety as the home front dug in for a long, bitter struggle. The government asked all civilians who were not actively engaged in the war effort to leave London and move to the country, if possible, to reduce the transportation strain on food and fuel. Dickie and I found accommodations in a little inn at Marlow-on-Thames and tried, without much success, to relieve the boredom and frustration that filled our days.

We needed a shock to bring us out of the torpor and we got it early in May, 1915. Haddon Chambers, a playwright who was a neighbor, came to us, pale and shaking, with the news that the Lusitania had been sunk with frightful loss of life. Among the victims was Charles Frohman, who had produced many of Chambers's plays.

"According to the survivors," Chambers said brokenly, "they heard Frohman say, 'Why fear death? Death is life's greatest adventure.'"

Chambers glared at me. "Your President says his country is too proud to fight. What do you think of that now?"

I had no heart to argue with Chambers in his emotional state. I was sure that Woodrow Wilson had been misquoted or his statement had been taken out of context and misinterpreted. I didn't know what to think. The death of Frohman, whom I had known through my association with Marie Doro, and Chambers's bitter indictment of America were numbing blows that could not be thrown off immediately.

When Chambers left, I tried to marshal my thoughts. I had been away from America for seven years. I loved England and admired her people, but my roots were imbedded in my own country. I had seen too many American women who had become more British than the Union Jack and still were aliens in a foreign country. Besides, I was serving no worthwhile purpose, while a struggle for survival was raging. Maybe, in some small way, I could help alert America to the menace of Prussian militarism.

Dickie knew me well enough to read my mind. "How would you like to be on board a ship sailing for New York?" she asked suddenly.

That night Dickie and I went to London and bought passage to America.

Chapter 6

HOME had been purely a figure of speech to me for nearly ten years, but I didn't realize it until I landed in New York. I was as much a stranger in the city as Dickie, who was making her first visit to America. The New York I remembered was a raucous, provincial town trying too eagerly and self-consciously to assume the air and attitude of a metropolis. The metamorphosis was almost complete in the summer of 1915. In seven short years New York had graduated from shirtsleeves to white piping on the vest.

With England concentrating its energies on the war, London no longer was the world's financial and business center. New York's Wall Street had supplanted London's City as the master switchboard of international banking, and the new prosperity was in evidence everywhere. I gave up trying to identify familiar landmarks after a sentimental pilgrimage to my old boardinghouse and nickelodeon. Both were gone. A new hotel had displaced the boardinghouse and a skyscraper was rising on the site of the firetrap where I had pounded the piano.

New York's appearance was not the only thing that made me feel out of place. Its bustle and gaiety seemed indecent after London's somber atmosphere. Of course, I was wrong in resenting my country's apparent indifference to the war.

America still was neutral, and none of the other powers was motivated by idealism in entering the conflict. Another war was to teach me that Americans could respond as quickly and as vigorously as any people on the face of the earth when their freedom and security were threatened. But I was so violently pro-British in 1915 that, like all rabid propagandists I had no patience with objectivity or another viewpoint.

I had to adjust myself to a series of shocks in New York, the first one less than half an hour after we cleared customs. The hotel where we had reservations was flying a huge German flag. The reason for the display was Count von Bernstorff, the German Ambassador to the United States, who was standing in the lobby as large as life and twice as sinister. It was all I could do to restrain Dickie from crowning His Excellency with the nearest chair.

The British were playing football to tremendous crowds and betting heavily on horse races when we sailed, but I was outraged to find newspapers in New York featuring baseball scores. I asked the same question — although a good deal more caustically — that bewildered Marshal Joffre when he came to the United States the following year.

"Which side are the Giants on?" Joffre inquired when he saw the headlines.

Perhaps the most difficult adjustment was learning to ignore the anti-British statements I overheard constantly in the street and read in the papers. New York had large groups of people with emotional ties to countries fighting the British. It took a lot of doing, but I finally managed to understand how their sentiments influenced American public opinion.

I never was reconciled, though, to the complete lack of responsibility shown by New York's social leaders. To them, the war was a beastly inconvenience that interfered with annual pleasure trips abroad. New York's elite was a collection of pompous mediocrities occupied only with petty feuds and suffocatingly dull receptions.

The "young" Mrs. Vanderbilt — then a woman of fifty — was trying to prove to her jealous mother-in-law, the "old" Mrs. Cornelius Vanderbilt, that she could pack more deadly bores into her drawing room than any other hostess on the North American continent. Charity work was measured by the space allotted to it in Cholly Knickerbocker's column. If dear Cholly neglected to give prominent mention to a committee, the members resigned in a body and scurried around to find another activity that would get their names and pictures in the paper.

There were exceptions, of course, most conspicuously Mrs. O. H. P. Belmont, probably the most misunderstood woman in America. Sycophants feared her social power, but no one cared less about exercising it than Mrs. Belmont. The former Alva Smith, of an old Southern family, she made an unprecedented splash in society with her marriages to W. K. Vanderbilt and Oliver Belmont, then married her daughter, Consuelo, to the Duke of Marlborough. Having proved that she could call her shots as she pleased, Miss Alva, as she was known to intimates, proceeded to give High Society the back of her neck.

"It's all a pack of nonsense," she used to say. "The Smiths of Alabama cut me dead for marrying W. K. Vanderbilt because his grandfather peddled vegetables. Then they cut me dead all over again for divorcing him. I can't be bothered with stupid prejudices."

Anything smacking of hypocrisy was a target for Mrs. Belmont. She did not hesitate to cross swords even with Bishop William T. Manning, the most powerful Protestant clergyman in New York. While she was married to Vanderbilt, she spearheaded fund-raising drives for Bishop Manning's charity organizations and was instrumental in collecting millions of dollars for him. After her divorce from Vanderbilt, she received a form letter from the bishop asking for her usual donation. Noticing that the letterhead looked strange, Mrs. Belmont examined it and found that she no longer was listed as the chairwoman of the board of directors. She went to Bishop Manning and asked why her name had been dropped. He hemmed and hawed and finally told her he did not deem it proper to have the board headed by a divorced woman.

"I suppose it's perfectly proper, though, for you to accept my tainted money," Mrs. Belmont retorted. "To spare your future qualms of conscience, I'll give it to organizations more concerned with charity than appearances." Antagonizing Bishop Manning was tantamount to committing social suicide, but Mrs. Belmont successfully waged a running feud with him until her death in 1933. Although she rarely bothered to assume the role, she still was the undisputed Queen of New York society at the end. There was no heiress presumptive to take her place and no one since has had the qualifications to claim the title.

It has been said that an era passed with Mrs. Belmont, but it is more accurate to report that she was twenty years ahead of her generation. She clearly foresaw that high society was moribund and she took a perverse delight in bucking stuffy convention wherever she found it — even in her own home.

She loved to needle her son, Harold Vanderbilt, the internationally famous yachtsman and bridge player who devised a system of bidding that addicts accepted as the Ten Commandments of the game. Mrs. Belmont pointedly flouted the system whenever they played.

"The Professor" — her nickname for Harold — "goes crazy when I'm his partner," she admitted cheerfully, "but he cannot make me obey his hidebound rules. As long as I pay my losses, I'll bid any way I please."

Pretenders to Mrs. Belmont's position accused her of making remarks deliberately designed to shock people, but she was utterly sincere in her convictions.

"Every woman should marry twice," she told me early in our acquaintance. "The first time for money, the second time for love."

It did sound like one of those sardonic cracks iconoclasts are fond of tossing off, but Mrs. Belmont never did sound off just to hear her own voice. One day in 1920, she sent for me, as soon as she arrived in Paris. I seldom had seen her so animated.

"I met a girl on the boat who has all the earmarks of talent and success," she said enthusiastically. "She's only seventeen and she's poor, but she has the beauty and brains to go as far as ambition will take her. Remember her name — Clare Boothe. If she gets half the advantages she deserves, you'll be proud to know her twenty-five years from now. I'm going to give her a push in the right direction."

Mrs. Belmont's word was as good as her prediction. She introduced Clare to her first husband, George Brokaw, a wealthy New Yorker, and, although I'm getting ahead of the story, I had a little something to do with Clare's second marriage, to Henry Luce. I'm sure Clare's old sponsor, and mine, would have thoroughly approved the match. "The thing that scared me," said Clare to me not long ago, "was Mrs. Belmont's wild desire that I should marry her son Willie K. — who though charming appeared rather an elderly gentleman to me at the time."

I, too, became one of Mrs. Belmont's protégées soon after arriving in New York in 1915. She took under her wing any young woman with get-up-and-go and interest in her pet projects. The scope of Mrs. Belmont's activities ranged from music and French literature to campaigns for eliminating the ugly brownstone-front houses that disfigured New York's best residential sections. In 1915, she was a leading figure in the Women's Party that was crusading to give women the right to vote, and she drew me into the thick of the suffragette movement. She put me to work composing the music for an operetta, *Melinda and Her Sisters*, which she had written.

The *première* of *Melinda* was unveiled at the old Waldorf-Astoria on February 18, 1916, to an audience that had paid as high as $125 for box seats. The newspapers properly described the players as "a ten-million-dollar cast." The stars were Marie Dressler and Marie Doro, with Josephine Hull and Addison Mizner, the architect who built Palm Beach in the Florida wilderness, in supporting roles. Frances Alda, of the Metropolitan Opera, sang a special number. Among the chorus girls were Maud Kahn and Kitty Bache, the daughters of two Wall Street bankers.

On the strength of the publicity Melinda received, the Women's Party was deluged with applications from 10,000 members within a week. Unfortunately, one of Mrs. Belmont's idiosyncracies sent the new suffragettes fleeing in terror as fast as they were recruited. She had obtained from a German doctor the secret formula for a concoction she called Victory Laxative Tablets, which, she insisted, agitated feminists had to take once a day to keep in the bloom of health.

Mrs. Belmont was, I must admit, a martinet who ruled everyone, including her children, with an iron whim. She was much more lenient, however, with William K. Vanderbilt, Jr., than she was with Harold and Consuelo. I asked her once why she was so partial to Willie.

"He's the only Vanderbilt in captivity who ever got over his accident of birth," she snapped.

Her ferocious fits of temper invariably were followed by remorse and little gestures of consideration. One day, while I was having lunch in her home at 477 Madison Avenue she suddenly hauled off and threw a plate at Azar, the Egyptian butler she had inherited from her late husband. I stormed out of the house swearing I never would have anything to do again with such an ill-mannered tyrant. By the time I got home, a lovely bunch of roses had been delivered by Mrs. Belmont's florist and she phoned a few minutes later to apologize profusely for her conduct.

"I know there's no excuse for my behavior, but Azar drives me out of my mind," she explained. "The man is a sex maniac. He keeps my maids in a constant turmoil with his advances. You didn't see it, but during lunch today he pinched the waitress while she was serving me. There are days and days I have to keep Azar locked up in a closet. If I don't he'll turn my house into a harem."

Why didn't she fire him?

"Oh, I couldn't do that. He was so devoted to my husband. I've soothed Azar's ruffled feelings by giving him an extra week's pay. That will hold him until the next seizure."

On another occasion, Mrs. Belmont came up to see how Dickie and I were getting along in a little apartment we were furnishing on Madison Avenue. She asked me whether we had a set of silver. I laughed and told her we were eating off a wooden table in the kitchen with utensils that came from the open stocks on Mr. Woolworth's shelves.

"That will never do," she said, marching to the phone. The previous week an advertising agency had offered her a sizable sum for a personal testimonial endorsing a brand of silverware. She had rejected the offer indignantly, but our bare buffet overrode her objection to exploiting her position. She called on the advertising agency.

"I'll go along with your proposition on one condition," she told the man. "You've got to kick in with a complete set of silver. Send it to Elsa Maxwell and make out the check for my fee to the Women's Party."

I often was the recipient of Mrs. Belmont's generosity, including a lavish free junket to Egypt in 1930, but I had the good sense to refuse her handsomest gift. A few years before she died, Mrs. Belmont asked me to call at her home.

"I was thinking of you last night," she said. "I'm worried about you because you'll never marry. I've decided to leave you some money in my will. Enough to take care of your old age."

"Please don't do it," I said. "Security is not for me. If I have money, I'll settle down in a rut and never do a lick of work again. It's work and striving that keep people young."

It was the wisest decision I ever made, for more than one reason. When Mrs. Belmont's will was read, a codicil was found revoking a substantial bequest she had made to a woman who later disappointed her. The woman contested the will and maintained that I had exerted undue influence on Mrs. Belmont when she made out her codicil, which I witnessed. Had I been mentioned in the will, I would have been vulnerable to the specific accusation as well as the more damaging charge of being a sycophant who used friends for personal gain. Under the circumstances, however, my testimony was brief. As I pointed out to the judge, I could not have had any ulterior motive when the codicil was drawn since I was not a beneficiary. The case was thrown out of court.

I was with Mrs. Belmont when the end was approaching. Although she had suffered a stroke, her spirit still was indomitable and she was fuming at the nurses because they had let her hair turn gray. Mrs. Belmont, who was vain about her appearance, dyed her hair a titian red and badgered the nurses by demanding to have a hairdresser brought to her room.

"I don't want to die with white hair," she told me. "It's so depressing." She was silent for a few moments, then smiled wanly. "It makes no difference now. The important thing is knowing how to live. Learn a lesson from my mistakes. I had too much power before I knew how to use it and it defeated me in the end. It drove all sweetness out of my life except the affection of my children. My trouble was that I was born too late for the last generation and too early for this one. If you want to be happy, live in your own time."

As always, Mrs. Belmont was right.

Helping Mrs. Belmont promote women's suffrage in the

winter of 1915–1916 was a worthwhile cause, to be sure, but a more urgent purpose had brought me back to the United States. In my own vague way, I was hoping to rally support for the Allies, a tricky public-relations job that was taxing the ingenuity of high-powered press agents in New York and Washington. I had no special contacts with big wheels, yet a twenty-one-year-old boy and I joined forces and made the experts look like novices from the sticks. My young confederate was a young man named Walter Wanger, who later was to command a good deal of attention in Hollywood as a movie producer and the husband of Joan Bennett. Fortified only with grandiose ideas and the gift of gab, Walter and I cooked up stunts which seldom have been topped for bare-faced audacity.

The first scheme was relatively simple. It merely involved getting permission from New York's Mayor John Purroy Mitchell to stage a "Wake Up, America" parade on Fifth Avenue. Mitchell, whose promising political career ended during the war in the crash of a fighter plane he was piloting, had a wry sense of humor. I've always suspected he gave us the permit for the parade just to watch the expressions on the faces of his predominantly Irish police department when the cops saluted the British flag. One hundred thousand volunteers marched in the procession, which was led by Mrs. George F. Baker, Mrs. James Eustis and Mrs. Lydig Hoyt, all on white horses. There were no untoward incidents among the spectators or the police force. The impassivity of the cops when the onlookers cheered perfidious Albion's banners was a splendid testimonial to their discipline.

The second stunt was such a brilliant coup it was a wonder

it didn't cost me my citizenship. That little gem involved the "kidnapping" of Marshal Joffre, the hero of the Marne.

Papa Joffre, the idol of France, was coming to the United States with a mission seeking American aid for his desperate country. When the announcement was made, I immediately conceived of a gala benefit for the war orphans of France, with Joffre the big drawing card. I sought the advice of Mrs. Harry Payne Whitney, the famous sculptress, who was an ardent Francophile.

"It's a wonderful idea," she agreed, "but I'm afraid it won't work. I understand the French Foreign Office and our State Department have turned thumbs down on public appearances by Joffre. The war is going so badly they think it's advisable to keep the old man under wraps."

"Just let me use your name to get past the door of the Metropolitan Opera House and I'll take care of the rest," I told Mrs. Whitney.

Gatti-Casazza, the general manager of the Met, received me with all the cordiality he reserved for an amateur soprano recommended by a singing teacher in Cattle Crossing, Colorado. The room temperature took another precipitous drop when I told him I wanted the Met, rent free, for a benefit. He tried to get rid of me by telling me I would have to arrange it with Otto Kahn, the chairman of the board of directors. Before Gatti-Casazza could reach across his desk to stop me, I picked up the phone and told the operator to get Kahn. I never had met the banker, but the call was put through to him at the mention of Mrs. Whitney's name. Kahn listened patiently to my spiel for a while, then cut in.

"My dear girl," he said, "several people have had the same

idea. I even guaranteed the services of Caruso and Geraldine Farrar if Joffre would make a token appearance at a benefit, and I was turned down, politely, but firmly."

"I'll attend to that little detail if you let me have the Met," I answered, trying to communicate a confidence I certainly didn't feel.

Kahn laughed. "If you can fix that 'little detail' you can have my shirt."

Wanger, who sounded as impressive as a travel agent on the phone, called the State Department in Washington to be put in touch with Joffre. The third assistant in charge of calls from pests and crackpots told him to forget the whole thing. The marshal's public appearances were to be confined to a formal call at the White House and a reception in New York given by Mayor Mitchel at the public library on Fifth Avenue.

"It looks as though we're licked," Walter said dejectedly. "What do we do now? Tell Mrs. Whitney and Kahn it was a pipe dream?"

I had one of those brainstorms that passes for an inspiration. "Go up to Albany and see Governor Whitman. He and Mitchell have been cutting each other's throats and maybe Whitman would like to steal a march on the mayor."

Walter must have scaled hitherto unconquered heights of eloquence, for he returned from Albany with a stack of official stationery and permission to send out letters with a rubber stamp of Governor Whitman's signature. We addressed letters to about fifty prominent New Yorkers asking them, in the name of Governor Whitman, to attend a meeting of "utmost importance and urgency" at the Met. Practically everyone turned up and climbed on the bandwagon when I announced that, in addition to Joffre, Caruso, Farrar, Paderewski, Rubinstein and a score of other stars would appear at the benefit. Within five minutes we had pledges for seats amounting to $92,000. Choice boxes went for $5000 apiece.

"Just between us, how do you expect to get Joffre?" Walter asked when the meeting ended.

"I wish I knew," I answered. That was the only truthful statement I had made all day.

I went to Washington and by speaking fractured French to American attendants and flashing business cards at French bodyguards I managed to get into the hotel suite occupied by the French mission. That appeared to be the end of the line though. René Viviani, a former prime minister and a member of the mission, said Marshal Joffre positively would not be available for the benefit.

"But I shall be delighted to represent my government," Viviani added. He had a reputation as a formidable orator and he expected me to fall all over myself in accepting his offer. He blanched when I told him the sponsors of the benefit were interested only in Joffre. Viviani was so furious that he stormed out of the reception room of the suite.

A reporter who had been waiting for hours to get a five-minute interview with Joffre enjoyed seeing somebody else get the cold shoulder. "It's a cinch to see the old man," he snickered. "Just go in and talk to him."

He pointed to a closed door off the reception room. I figured my life wasn't worth two cents anyway, so I barged through the door. Joffre was dressing for dinner and, fortunately, had progressed as far as his trousers. His aide indignantly told me to get out and moved toward me as though to implement the order, but the old marshal stepped forward and asked what I wanted.

I talked fast. I repeated several times that a brief appearance by him at the Met would mean more than one hundred thousand dollars to French orphans. Joffre shook his head sadly.

"I would be most happy to accommodate your very gracious committee," he said, "but alas, my time is not my own. I am a soldier. I am subject to the orders of my government. There is only one way I can attend your gala." He chuckled and added in a stage whisper, "You will have to capture me by force and make me a prisoner of war."

How do you go about "capturing" a general, even in mock warfare, from a defensive force playing it straight? My ignorance of military tactics was staggering, but I had read enough to know that the element of surprise is a vital factor in mounting an attack. I had to forfeit that trump card by announcing that Joffre positively would appear at the benefit. It was necessary to stimulate the sale of tickets and to pacify the sponsors underwriting the show.

In the meantime, the affair had become a political football. Newspapers favorable to Governor Whitman gave the benefit a good publicity build-up. The pro-Mitchel press, assured by the State Department that the Met was not on Joffre's itinerary, branded the whole thing as a gigantic hoax. The committee's social lights, caught in the cross fire, sent Walter and me into hiding with their frantic phone calls. In the confusion, Maude Adams came out of retirement to offer her services at the gala and Paderewski sent a telegram informing us that he was interrupting a transcontinental tour for the privilege of playing for the marshal. Practically every artist under con-

tract at the Met was on the program, but the only star the
audience wanted to see and hear was Joffre, and there would
be plain and fancy hell to pay if he didn't show up.

Walter and I went into a trance and came out of it with a
scheme so insane that it had a prayerful chance of succeeding.
We asked Governor Whitman for a National Guard cavalry
escort for Joffre and took the young captain in charge of it
into our confidence. We told him we "believed" Joffre would
submit willingly to capture and asked him to take it from
there. The captain, an Irish bucko, was so intrigued with the
idea of seizing a war hero who had thrown back the German
army that he agreed enthusiastically to raid the reception at
the library.

"You can count on me," he said. "I'll bring the old boy to
the Met even if we have to shoot our way out of the joint."

According to the schedule, the audience was to be seated at
8:30 P.M. and the performance was to commence fifteen
minutes later, when Joffre took his place in J. P. Morgan's
box at the Met. The first part of the plan went off without a
hitch. The audience arrived early and the Diamond Horseshoe
never was more somber — or more impressive. All the women
wore black evening gowns unrelieved by jewelry as a mark of
sympathy for the terrible losses France was suffering during
the war.

Sharply at eight-forty-five, the orchestra began to play
"Sambre et Meuse," the marshal's favorite march. At the finale,
the jammed house turned en masse toward Morgan's box. It
was empty. The conductor rapped on the podium with his
baton and swung into the march again. The expectant hush
had icicles around the edges when the last notes faded. Still

no Joffre. I rushed from the Fortieth Street entrance of the opera house, where I was awaiting Joffre with my reception committee, and signaled the conductor to play the march once more. Nobody had to tell me that the musicians and the audience would start to throw things if we attempted to stall much longer.

At nine o'clock the house lights were dimmed and Louise Homer sang "The Star Spangled Banner." When the grim audience rose with a scraping of feet for the national anthem, I thought for a paralyzing moment that the customers who had paid unpopular prices for seats were coming after me. By nine-fifteen, Wanger and I alone were holding the fort at the entrance. My reception committee had left in a gamut of emotions ranging from Mrs. Whitney's inarticulate despair to Gatti-Casazza's raving profanity in Italian. Maurice, the ballroom dancer, joined us with the bleak observation that he thought it safer to be on the street when the ugly mood of the crowd erupted in a riot.

We were standing there, waiting for the blowoff, when we heard a sweeter sound than my million-dollar cast could produce — the clip-clop of horses' hoofs on the pavement. "Joffre is coming!" I yelled. "Where is the reception committee?"

People began to spring up out of nowhere as the grinning marshal stepped out of the carriage. Joffre, who seemed to be enjoying the tumult immensely, winked at me and tweaked my ear. I was afraid to ask my gallant, cocky National Guard captain whether I was to be held as an accessory to a criminal assault, or something, but he took me off the hook.

"It was a breeze," the captain assured me. "The old boy made it easy for us. He faked a headache and left the mayor's shindig. There was a police escort for him on Fifth Avenue, but we pushed the cops aside and one of my men hopped into the driver's seat of the carriage. Before the flatfoots knew what hit them, we hightailed it out of there."

As Joffre entered Morgan's box, the applause that welled up from adjoining stalls spread like a flash fire throughout the house. Paderewski, who was at the piano on the stage, stopped what he was playing when he heard the ovation and burst into Chopin's Military Polonaise. He never played with more brilliant exuberance, and he never had a less attentive audience. The people screamed and stamped for ten minutes as Joffre acknowledged their tribute. Me? I went home and had a quiet nervous breakdown.

The Joffre success established me as a triple-plated wonder-worker, and in the months that followed I was asked to join every committee in sight staging benefits for the Allies. Among other things, Dickie and I ran a soda fountain at the Allied Bazaar in Grand Central Palace. The moving spirit of the bazaar was Mrs. Brigit Guiness, the wife of a British banker with important interests and connections all over the world. Mrs. Guiness was the type of society woman I admired and, frankly, was trying to cultivate. She was cultured, progressive and made her beautiful home on Washington Square a salon in the European tradition. All the outstanding musicians, artists, writers and composers in New York, the sort of people with whom I had associated in London, congregated regularly at Mrs. Guiness's home. Despite her enormous wealth and blue-blood background, Mrs. Guiness was a warm, democratic woman and invited everyone who worked at the bazaar to her soirees.

So I was happy when Brigit Guiness came up to me at the bazaar saying, "I'd like you and Miss Gordon to come to a party I'm giving for Muratore of the Met and his wife, Lina Cavalieri. I have a rule that everyone who's invited to my parties must do something to contribute to the entertainment. I want you to accompany Muratore and I want Miss Gordon to sing."

We were so excited about the party that we arrived at Washington Square fifteen minutes early. To kill time, we walked around the park and talked about the people we were to meet. Dickie was particularly interested in Muratore, who was being touted as Caruso's closest rival. I hooted down the claim out of loyalty to my old luncheon date in San Francisco and said the big attraction for me was a young man who had written the music for a Broadway show, *See America First*. The show was a dismal failure, but I had heard the music and thought it was unusually promising.

Dickie, whose stubbornness can be matched only by her temper, was sore because I had criticized her man Muratore. To get even with me, she began to tear into my young song writer. We were still arguing when we entered the Guiness mansion.

"The fellow must be a false alarm," Dickie scoffed. "The show is a flop."

"Pardon me for eavesdropping, but are you paging me?" a man cut in.

That was my introduction to Cole Porter, one of the closest — and unquestionably the most talented — friends I've ever known. I wish I could say that I fell for him in the first ten seconds, but Cole would correct me sharply. On the contrary,

I felt antagonistic toward him. I thought he was trying to be excessively cute, and I've always been allergic to that approach in men and women, adults and children. Further, he was dressed too immaculately for a young composer who had been roasted by the critics. I had seen too many gigolos in Europe to be taken in by fine feathers. I pegged him for a phony, easily the worst snap judgment I made in my first seventy years.

"You must be flat broke or else you wouldn't dress so well," I said rudely in my annoyance.

Cole waved airily, "All on tick, grandpa's tick." I saw that he was tight and that, too, rubbed me the wrong way. I've never been able to tolerate people who drink too much, although I must confess that Cole made a large dent in that prejudice in later years.

I had work to do and I walked away from the irritating little man. When Muratore finished singing, Cole winked at me and said, "Now it's my turn to sing for my supper."

The buzz of conversation in the room went on when Cole sat at the piano and played a few bars from *See America First*. The music was unfamiliar and so was the first number he sang, but at the end of it everyone was straining to catch the droll nuances of his lyrics. He held a critical audience enraptured for fully a half hour while he ran through his repertory of "secret" songs, which he has been writing for years and hoarding until public taste and sophistication are ready to appreciate them. At the end of that half hour I was a wild fan of the most paradoxical man ever to invade the jungles of show business.

Cole Porter emerged in the golden age of American song writing — the period that produced George Gershwin, Irving

Berlin, Dick Rodgers, Oscar Hammerstein II, Herbert and Dorothy Fields, Jerome Kern, Howard Dietz and Arthur Schwartz. Of that distinguished company, only Gershwin — a genuine genius — was a more talented musician than Cole. And no one was, or is, a sounder craftsman or a wittier lyricist than Cole. No one has composed more songs now accepted as light classics and no one has written more Broadway hit shows. As I write this in the fall of 1953, Cole's latest production, *Can-Can*, is playing to standing room thirty-eight years after his first effort. That is a record of consistency without a parallel in the American theater.

To me, Cole Porter is more fascinating as a personality than as a theatrical phenomenon. His character and career contradict every concept of a popular composer. Most song writers who fabricate the enduring favorites that are sung and whistled by the public are products of big-city environments. Cole, the most sophisticated composer of his time, was born and raised on a farm in Peru, Indiana. Poverty and struggle are supposed to serve as stimulating challenges to inherent ability. If Cole ever worried about money, it was only the problem of getting an advance of a few hundred dollars on his allowance to tide him over a week end while he was an undergraduate at Yale. His grandfather's mining and lumber interests in Virginia made Cole a millionaire long before his first royalties came in.

Traditionally, song writers serve apprenticeships in Bowery dives, cheerless back rooms or grubby studios along Tin Pan Alley. Cole's first hit, "Bulldog Yale," was dashed off in a comfortable dormitory at New Haven and I doubt that he ever has seen the inside of a publisher's office on Tin Pan Alley. Many classical and popular composers have been recognized and rewarded quite early in their careers. Cole had to wait thirteen long years after his first flop to gain a toehold in his profession.

It was during those thirteen years that legends and half-truths surrounded Cole and caused producers to dismiss him as a dilettante with too much money for his own good. Cole and his wife Linda spent a good deal of time in Europe trying, it appeared, to squander money faster than the gilt-edged investments he inherited could pile it up in the bank. In Venice they rented the 200-room Palazzo Rezzonico, where Browning lived and died. When Cole became bored with hangouts fancied by the chi-chi crowd, he bought a huge barge, fixed it up as a night club, and had it towed around the canals of Venice to accommodate his guests, who had a wonderful time eating and drinking off his impeccably starched cuff.

Cole's chief occupation in the 1920's seemed to be devising elaborate practical jokes calculated to puncture stuffed shirts full of holes. In 1925, he invented a fabulously wealthy American couple, Mr. and Mrs. S. R. Fitch, of Muskogee, Oklahoma, just to expose the silly fawning on celebrities in the international set. Cole launched the mythical Fitches on a giddy whirl by sending a note to the Paris *Herald* to the effect that they had been guests of honor at one of my dinner parties. For the next six months he continued to feed gullible society columnists so many "exclusive" tidbits about the mysterious couple that hostesses on both sides of the Atlantic were bursting gussets to snare the social lions who had been feted by princes and maharajahs.

The fact that no one in Muskogee ever had heard of the Fitches merely made them more desirable quarry for the headhunters. There was such goggle-eyed curiosity in the Fitches that more than one glib poseur enjoyed splendid free-loading on the strength of fanciful friendships with them. The Fitches were the most famous disappearing act since Houdini until the late Maury Paul, then conducting the Cholly Knickerbocker column in the Hearst papers, was tipped off to the fraud. I've always suspected that Paul's informant was Cole, who was so busy acting as the Fitches' social secretary that he had no time for his own skylarking.

On another occasion, Cole was very happy to acknowledge publicly his authorship of a social satire. He and I knew Bricktop, an American Negress who had been eking out a living playing and singing in Parisian night clubs for years. Bricktop was a proud, hard-working woman who never asked for favors, but once she confessed to Cole that she had a secret ambition. She wanted to see the charity ball given annually at the Opera by the President of France. If only Mr. Porter could hide her somewhere, perhaps behind his box, so she could see the colorful affair and the magnificent gowns worn by the women. She was particularly interested in the beautiful Princess Marina of Greece, who was engaged to marry the Duke of Kent.

"You're going to the ball and you won't have to hide," Cole said. "You're going as my guest."

"Oh, I couldn't do that," the woman protested. "I don't belong there and I don't have the clothes for such a grand party."

"You have as much right to be there as anybody," Cole said, "and I'll take care of your clothes."

Cole went to my old friend Edward Molyneux, the leading

couturier in Paris, and said he wanted an extra-special gown for a good friend. When Molyneux asked what he had in mind, Cole artfully pretended he couldn't decide on the style or color.

"To make it easy for both of us," he said, "make an exact copy of the dress Princess Marina is wearing to the President's ball."

Molyneux recoiled and said he couldn't do it. All his gowns were originals and it simply wouldn't be cricket — Edward always has been a staunch Britisher — to copy the creation he had made for the princess, a very dear friend and a good customer. Cole was adamant, though, and Molyneux finally gave in. Linda Porter was a better customer than Princess Marina.

The identical gowns worn by the princess and Bricktop at the ball were what constitutes a *cause célèbre* in the chi-chi set. Cole hugely enjoyed the rumpus and insisted that his guest looked every inch a lady as much as the princess. And on that score he wasn't kidding.

Cole was a merry Andrew, all right, but only a few of us who were his intimate friends knew the other side of the story. While he was cutting capers all over Europe, he was working hard and steadily, six hours a day, writing songs, experimenting with lyrics, polishing his technique. A perfectionist who slaves over every chord and rhyme, Cole was building up a large inventory of songs, but he had no showcase for them. After the disastrous *See America First* he did the music for *Kitchy Koo*, in 1919, and *The Greenwich Village Follies*, in 1924. Neither show set Broadway on fire.

By 1927, Cole had such a reputation as a playboy that no producer would take a chance on him. Then Ray Goetz, who was producing *Paris*, starring Irene Bordoni, went to Cole as a last resort. Goetz needed music with a continental flavor and no song writer in America was able to deliver the sophisticated score he wanted. It was suggested that maybe Cole, who had been batting around the smart spots of Europe for nearly a decade, could solve the problem. Cole could and did, practically on the spot. Now all those years of work and careful craftsmanship paid off. Cole dipped into the trunkful of songs he had been writing since he was an undergraduate at Yale and came up with a tailor-made score. Some of the songs were more than ten years old, but Cole had been so far ahead of his time that his numbers were as fresh and crisp as a dollar bill minted that same morning.

The most paradoxical side of Cole's nature is his openhand-edness with money and his miserliness with ideas. He is a notoriously soft touch for old actors, he rarely turns down an appeal from a worthwhile charity and he has provided college and musical educations for more boys and girls than he can remember. I have seen a good many two-fisted, freestyle spend-ers, but I've never known anyone as prodigal with money as Cole. He'll give a stranger the run of his house, but he won't share an idea, a line or a catchy tune with his best friend until he is ready to use it in his work. Cole never forgets or discards a line or a tune. He even exhumed the Fitch gag in *Gay Divorcee*, seven years after he pulled it. He wrote a song about the Fitches that would have been popularized by the radio if he had been able to curb his weakness for a risqué rhyme. Mrs. Fitch was described by a five-letter word commonly heard around kennels but never over the air.

Cole's hoarding of ideas was the explanation for his incred-ible starburst of eight smash musical comedies in the first nine

years after he hit the bright lights of Broadway. *Paris* was
followed by *Fifty Million Frenchmen, Wake Up and Dream,
The New Yorkers, Gay Divorcee, Anything Goes, Jubilee*
and *Red Hot and Blue.* A mortal man could not have turned
out those eight brilliant scores from scratch. They were stored
in Cole's trunk until the public was ready to appreciate
them.

Success did not give Cole delusions of grandeur. I once was
at a party with him when one of those pompous asses who
fancied himself a deep thinker buttonholed Cole.

"Do you realize that 'Night and Day' is much more than just
a song?" the man said, enchanted by the sound of his own
voice. "It is a masterful presentation of the philosophy of the
Lost Generation. It is the lament of a generation caught in
the cruel accidents of history, a great war and a calamitous
depression."

Cole laughed in the man's face. "There's as much philosophy or significance in 'Night and Day' as there is in a hardware
catalogue," he snorted. "If I had thought of another phrase
to fit the tune I would've used it."

I love Cole for his talent and his gaiety, but most of all I
admire him as a man — for his guts. In 1916 when young and
old people in his social position were making cynical wise-
cracks about fighting a war to save democracy and Wall Street,
Cole left his ermine-lined security and joined the world's
toughest military outfit — the French Foreign Legion. Only a
fool would have gone to such extremes to pull a grandstand
play, and Cole, although given many false labels, never has
been called a fool. People misled by Cole's flippant attitude
continued to regard him as an effete, pampered playboy. That

opinion was reversed completely after the terrible accident that cut him down at the very height of his career.

In 1938, the man with the light, golden touch was thrown from a horse at the Piping Rock Club on Long Island and sustained such severe multiple fractures that the doctors thought at first they would have to amputate his right leg. A series of more than twenty excruciatingly painful operations saved the leg, but specialists doubted that he ever would walk again. The doctors failed to consider Cole's unquenchable spirit. He eventually regained the use of his legs, although he still needs braces and canes to get around and will require them as long as he lives.

The ordeal would have been bad enough for anyone, but it was doubly harrowing for a *bon vivant* with Cole's ebullience and zest for living. Most middle-aged men in his financial circumstances would have gone into retirement and watched the passing parade from a wheel chair. Cole, suffering almost unendurable pain, led the parade from a hospital bed. He turned out three of his biggest, blithest hits in three successive seasons — *DuBarry Was A Lady, Panama Hattie* and *Let's Face It.*

I could go on indefinitely about the most fascinating man I know, but Cole, who can't stand maudlin friends, will begin to whistle his ominous warning, "Get out of town, before it's too late." I'll wind up on the characteristic note Cole himself struck in the grimmest moment of his life. He had just come out of the anesthesia after his first operation and didn't know yet whether his leg had been amputated. His condition was desperate, but his spark never was higher. He turned to his nurse.

"Now I know fifty million Frenchmen can't be wrong," he said. "They eat horses instead of ride them."

Soon after America entered World War I, I made another lifelong friend with a different, and equally admirable, brand of courage. She was Mrs. William Randolph Hearst, the wife of the most controversial and shrewdest publisher in the history of American journalism. Although Mrs. Hearst was as active as I in war work, we never met until she dropped me a note asking me to help her on a project. Her office, ironically, was in the Times Building, owned by her husband's bitter opponent.

I arrived at the appointed time, and seated at her desk was the prettiest creature I had ever seen. It was difficult to believe she was the mother of five sons. I introduced myself and heard for the first time that famous chuckle that has charmed her world.

Soon after I met Millicent Hearst, a cloud appeared that cast a pall over her entire life. Her husband became involved romantically with Marion Davies, a movie star of the period. When she learned the bitter truth, Millicent refused to give her husband a divorce. For thirty years she suffered humiliation in a desperate effort to maintain a semblance of family unity for the sake of her five sons.

It was only recently, several years after the death of William Randolph Hearst, that I discovered she did succumb once to the temptation of acting like an outraged wife. Cole Porter confessed that he inadvertently had witnessed the incident and reminded Millicent of it while the three of us were dining together.

Cole was in Tiffany's shopping for a trinket for his wife

many years before when his attention was attracted by a beautiful woman at the next counter. The woman was looking at pearls and was dissatisfied with all the exquisite necklaces the salesman had in the showcase. When the salesman had exhausted the stock on hand, he excused himself, went to the inner sanctum and returned with a string of perfectly matched pearls. The woman nodded approval and asked how much they were. The salesman mentioned a sum running to six figures.

"I'll take the string with me," the woman said. "Send the bill to my husband's office."

Cole, a free and easy spender himself, never had seen anyone make such an expensive purchase so casually. He stalled until the woman left the store, then rushed over to the salesman. "Who was that woman?" he asked breathlessly.

At that point in the narrative, Millicent interrupted Cole's story. "Let me tell Elsa," she said. "I bought the pearls. Some women buy a new hat when they're angry. I bought the finest string of pearls in New York. You see," she added with a wistful smile. "I was awfully angry, but I got over it a long, long time ago."

Millicent could have found happiness with another husband. A number of men were attracted by her beauty, charm and keen mind, which had been sharpened by meeting the world's leading statesmen and intellectuals in her home. Among many other things, Millicent is a superb hostess. After World War I, she pulled the social coup of the Paris season by entertaining Generals Pershing, Joffre and French at the same dinner party. A little touch that made the dinner unusual were the exotic birds in cages she gave as souvenirs to the women guests.

If Millicent had been impressed by false glitter, she could have had her pick of several high European titles, had she been willing to divorce her husband. She always was on friendly terms with the Greek royal family; hers was the only private invitation accepted in New York by King Paul and Queen Frederika when they visited the United States late in 1953. Prince Andrew, father of the Duke of Edinburgh, was one of Millicent's strongest admirers, but she never permitted their relationship to progress beyond that stage. She always was intensely aware of the obligation she owed her family. At least one persistent escort did not associate Millicent with the power and prestige of the Hearst name. He was Lord Castlerosse, and I still chuckle at his bewilderment when he discovered Millicent's true identity.

She and I were invited by Lord Valentine Castlerosse to visit him at Kenmare Castle, his ancestral estate in Ireland on Lake Killarney, in 1926. It was at the height of the agitation against England and the Sinn Feiners had inflicted widespread damage on public utilities to balk reprisals by British military forces. Valentine, our host, came to me soon after our arrival and showed me a personal message from William Cosgrave, the president of the Free State's executive council.

"I don't understand this," Valentine said. "Cosgrave has invited Millicent to Dublin for an official reception and assures her he will repair the railroad bridge that has been blown up to guarantee her a safe journey. Why is he so anxious to receive Millicent?"

I told Valentine that the newspapers owned by Millicent's husband strongly supported Irish independence.

Valentine clapped his brow. "You mean her husband is

William Randolph Hearst, the famous publisher? Good Lord. I never dreamed she was his wife."

The outstanding facet of Millicent's character is her complete loyalty to those she loves. A typical manifestation of that loyalty was shown recently when I was on a radio program appealing for funds to build for the Overseas Press Club, to which I belong, a memorial for foreign correspondents who lost their lives in the service of the press. A number of contributions were announced, and when Jinx Falkenburg interviewed me briefly I pledged $1200 in twelve monthly payments of $100. I had barely left the microphone when a telephone call was made to me at the studio. It was from Millicent.

"I just heard you promise to contribute all that money," she said. "Can you really afford to give so much?"

I told her I couldn't, but it was a good cause and I'd manage somehow to make good on the pledge.

"Now don't do anything rash or foolish to get the money," Millicent said. "I know you. You make me so — so nervous."

During Millicent's long domestic troubles, I marveled at her strength and wondered how she could be so free from the weaknesses associated with the eternal feminine. She held her head high, never tried to enlist sympathy or complained of her lot.

During the year and a half the United States was an active participant in World War I, my fighting was confined to getting celebrities and performers for the round of benefits dumped into my lap. The bloodiest engagement was the Battle of Carnegie Hall, which wound up in the riot that had narrowly been averted at the Marshal Joffre clambake. The law of averages always catches up with those who brashly thumb their noses at it.

Soon after the czar was overthrown, a delegation of Russian scientists representing the Kerensky government came to New York on a technical mission. I was asked to devise something "different" for the official reception and finally hit upon the idea of a labor debate. The big domestic news of the moment was a bitter strike in East St. Louis, and I invited former President Theodore Roosevelt and Samuel Gompers, the president of the American Federation of Labor, to discuss the issues involved.

Everything proceeded in dignified, orderly fashion until Gompers, in concluding his speech, departed from the script which had been released in advance to the newspapers. He touched off a wild demonstration among his rooters in the gallery by reading a telegram from the strikers in East St. Louis denouncing the "tools of capitalism." Roosevelt was incensed by what he considered a low trick. He was working up to such a choleric rage that Gompers rose to pacify his adversary. Roosevelt shook his fist in Gompers's face, but in his frenzy he waved it so vigorously that he hit the small labor leader on the top of the head. Gompers sagged to the floor.

That did it. The people in the gallery hurled newspapers, hats and remnants of box lunches on the stage. A dozen fist fights broke out on the orchestra floor. Belligerents leaped on the stage and embroiled the Russian scientists in the free-for-all. The few policemen on duty were lost in the shuffle. By the time reinforcements arrived, Carnegie Hall was a shambles and the voice of sweet reason I was trying to introduce in labor-management relations by bleating, "Gentlemen, please," was as effective as a parasol in a tornado.

I felt even more out of place the day after the Armistice was signed. Everyone I knew was trying to get boat accommodations to Europe. Paris, the scene of the peace negotiations and the center of forthcoming social activity, might just as well have been on Mars for all the chance I had of getting there. As always, though, my luck held true. Mrs. Edward Stotesbury, the wife of the banker, asked me to go to Paris with her recently divorced daughter, Mrs. Louise Brooks.

Since I've been the beneficiary of so many similar windfalls, this is a good time to make one thing clear. I never have been taken on a free trip as a companion or a chaperone, two words with connotations I detest. A companion suggests a handmaiden or a stooge who truckles to the whims and vanity of the person picking up the checks. A chaperone in my book is a dried-up, professional killjoy, with little beady eyes that see sinister implications in every natural impulse.

Mrs. Stotesbury, and all the other women who cultivated my friendship, did it for one reason. I was a gay and amusing guest. I always contributed as much, at least, as I received. With Louise Brooks, I more than repaid my boat passage and my board at her mother's house in the Rue des Saints Pères. Louise went to Paris determined to marry the youngest brigadier general in the United States Army, and the parties I whipped up helped her to capture her man. A dashing fellow named Douglas MacArthur.

Chapter 7

THERE is a dwindling company who witnessed at close range two attempts to build a brave, new world in the span of a quarter century. Those of us who had ringside seats at both events were buoyed by a surge of optimism at the Paris Peace Conference in 1919 which never was recaptured at the United Nations meetings in San Francisco in 1945. I don't say this because we were younger and more idealistic in 1919. The world was younger, had not yet seen its illusions betrayed.

Anyone with a sense of history who was in Paris immediately after World War I had to be stirred by the realization that he was on the scene of the first effort to establish an international community of nations. By the time the United Nations assembled, two decades of broken treaties and naked power plays had made everyone cynical. We looked for booby traps in the blueprints of peace and progress, and they were quickly exposed. The Soviet delegation sabotaged the United Nations structure from the start by agitating for sixteen seats for its "independent" republics. The crusher was the Russians' callous rejection of the United States' magnanimous offer to share the secret of atomic energy in return for guarantees of international controls designed to eliminate it as a weapon of war.

At the Paris Peace Conference, Europe's ancient hatreds

were undermining President Woodrow Wilson's Fourteen Points, but we didn't know it. We never dreamed that the United States Senate would refuse to ratify America's participation in the League of Nations. We did not foresee the day the League would be reduced to such a meaningless instrument of collective security that Japan, Italy and Germany could flout its authority without reprisal. Statesmen were rendering lip service to Wilson's program and we believed them because we wanted to believe war could be outlawed by legislation.

It is difficult to describe the exhilarating atmosphere of Paris during the peace negotiations. Every day was like a sparkling holiday. There was an aroma in the air as though a thousand girls wearing a wonderful perfume had just passed. The city echoed to the music of bands welcoming returning soldiers. Shops, theaters and cafés were jammed with people who had lived under the drab shadows of war for four years. Everywhere, every hour of the day and night, there were parties.

No social light shined brighter than Bernard Baruch, a living legend if ever there was one. Baruch, adviser to seven Presidents and an imposing global statesman, once played another role which, I'm sometimes convinced, he relished above all others. He was an indefatigable ladies' man — and the ladies succumbed in droves to one of the handsomest men of his time.

A few years ago, when the international situation had taken another depressing turn, I sought out Barney on his favorite bench in Washington and asked for his appraisal of the situation. I never did get his opinion. I wound up answering his questions — about the women he had known. He was far more interested in recapturing the past than he was in discussing the present, and I can't say I blamed him.

Louise Brooks's house was the unofficial headquarters of the American military delegation and the younger set of foreign army officers attached to the various embassies. General John J. Pershing and his staff regularly came to Louise's Saturday-night dances, which were enlivened by the general's liquor and my piano playing.

I helped Louise plan the parties and select the guests, and in general kept the ball rolling once the festivities began. But I had not actually given a party on my own hook since that disastrous boat episode on my thirteenth birthday. At the rather advanced age of thirty-six, I didn't know what I was going to be when I grew up, but had anyone predicted I was to make an international reputation as a hostess, he would have been committed to a mental institution. No one in Paris, London, New York or points worse had less money or fewer qualifications for that nebulous distinction. Some people fall accidentally into professions and avocations. In roundabout fashion, I literally was pushed at sword's point into the spotlight as a party-giver.

I had gone to bed after one of Louise's blowouts when I was awakened by harsh, metallic sounds in the garden below my room. I went to the window and saw something that looked like a scene out of a bad operetta. A British and an Italian officer were hacking away at each other with sabers, only they weren't play-acting. They were dueling strictly on the level. I threw on a dressing gown and rushed to the garden.

"Gentlemen! Gentlemen!" I cried. "Let's — let's have a cup of coffee!"

I distracted them long enough to thrust my not inconsiderable bulk between them. They glared at each other, then seemed highly relieved indeed to accept my proposal. Louise always thought she inspired the duel, but the cause of it was Dickie Gordon, for all the good it did the adversaries. The gallants waiting on line for a kind word from Dickie stretched around the block.

The rivals swore undying friendship when they calmed down, and invited me to have cocktails with them at the Ritz the following afternoon to celebrate a bond almost sealed in blood. The ceremony went off without a hitch and as I was leaving the bar an elderly, chic woman stopped me at the door.

"Aren't you Elsa Maxwell, the woman who sings those risqué songs?" she asked sharply.

"I'm Elsa Maxwell," I snapped, "but off-color songs are not my stock-in-trade."

She waved her hand impatiently. "Never mind. I'm giving a tea at my home tomorrow for some of the diplomats of the Peace Conference and I'd like you to help with the entertainment. I'm Elsie deWolfe."

The introduction was superfluous. Everyone who stuck a tentative toe in the social swim of Paris knew Elsie deWolfe (afterward Lady Mendl), an undistinguished American actress who had made a fortune as an interior decorator after her retirement from the stage. Elsie, a shrewd businesswoman who could bargain a Yankee horse trader into the ground, had exquisite taste — and the good sense to borrow many of the ideas of Oscar Wilde, whom she had known. Practically singlehandedly, Wilde had routed the gloomy, oppressive décor and the ugly gimcracks of the Victorian era by painting rooms in light colors and using cheerful fabrics for upholstery and draperies. Elsie copied many of Wilde's innovations and numbered the wealthiest people in America and Europe among her clients, and successfully cashed in on it. She was a wonderful friend — and the Duchess of Windsor learned many of her ideas on quaint cuisine from Elsie, whom she deeply admired. Elsie's home was a combination of the aesthetic and the rug seller in a bazaar. She loved beauty more than anyone I have ever known, and to pull off a sharp bargain was her very champagne of life.

Although Elsie's rather patronizing invitation to tea annoyed me, I could not resist the temptation to meet the Conference celebrities and to see her famous "Trianon" villa in Versailles, probably the most beautifully furnished house in Europe. The chief luminary at Elsie's reception was Arthur Balfour, England's Secretary of Foreign Affairs, whom I had met at Maxine Elliott's home before the war. The tea was a trifle stifled until I played and sang some of Cole Porter's "secret" songs. Balfour's eyebrows became an extension of his hairline when he first heard the irreverent lyrics, but his reserve soon cracked and he laughed uproariously as I dipped deeper into Cole's private stock.

"That was first-rate," Balfour said when he was leaving. "I should like to see you again."

This compliment from the famous statesman induced temporary insanity in me.

"Why not dine with me?" I said.

"I should be charmed," smiled Mr. Balfour.

"How about a week from tonight at the Ritz?" I heard myself ask from a great distance.

"I shall be there," Balfour bowed.

I was numb when I came down to earth with a sickening

thud. My financial resources couldn't stand the strain of ordering an omelette at the Ritz, the most expensive restaurant in France. Then there was the important question of protocol. A man as important as Balfour could not be seen dining in public with people who did not rate the distinction. Fortunately, the one person in Paris who could bail me out of the jam had arrived that day. I went to Lady Colebrook, an old friend from the Allied Bazaar in New York, and told her my sad story.

"Don't worry, Plumpy," she said. "I'll see to it that you don't let down my country's foreign secretary. I'll stand treat for the dinner. Now, let's decide whom you'll invite. Eight always is a nice number for a dinner party."

"Eight?" I echoed bleakly.

"I told you not to worry about the expense," Alex said. She took a piece of paper and began to jot down names. "You'll ask Mrs. George Keppel, the Princess Edmond de Polignac, Lord d'Abenon, Lady Ripon, the Grand Duke Alexander of Russia, the Marquis Boni de Castellane and Sir Ronald Storrs. That will balance your table quite nicely."

"Well, that's just dandy," I said hollowly. "But the only one you've mentioned whom I know is Mrs. Keppel."

"Don't worry about that either. I'll see to it that they'll come."

"But I have nothing to wear except my old black chiffon dress," I wailed. "I can't be the hostess at a dinner looking like a charwoman."

"Someone just gave me a beautiful scarf," Alex said blandly. "I'll paint some Chinese sampans on it and the effect will be so striking that it may even start a new fashion. Now run along to the Ritz and see Olivier to order the dinner."

I didn't dare confess to Alex that conferring with Olivier was the most frightening part of the whole thing. Olivier, the world's greatest snob and headwaiter rolled into one, was a towering iceberg of etiquette who had been known to freeze grand dukes with a glance. I knew he would spot me instantly as an impostor, but it was too late to back out. Years later, Olivier wrote his memoirs and paid me a supreme compliment by stating that only three people in all his experience knew how to order a dinner properly — the Prince of Wales, afterwards King Edward VII, Prince Esterhazy of Hungary, and Elsa Maxwell. The Prince of Wales would write two weeks ahead to order a dinner for twelve. Prince Esterhazy of Hungary would bring his own gypsy band and ordered his dinner for fifty one month in advance. And Elsa Maxwell would rush in six hours before to order a dinner for two hundred.

In 1919, my knowledge of ordering dinners was confined to asking for the blue-plate special in a cafeteria.

To prepare for the great confrontation with Olivier, I went to the Paris office of the New York *Herald* and asked to see their old files. I once had heard that Boni de Castellane had given such a sumptuous dinner before the war that the menu was reprinted in the newspapers. It must have been some dinner, for the librarian remembered the date and pulled the menu out of the files for me. I spent two hours memorizing the courses and the vintages of the wines, then girded myself for the ordeal with Olivier.

Olivier, a melancholy man, began to write down my order on a desk pad, but after taking the first two courses he put aside his pencil and stared at me. When I had struggled through the menu, Olivier rose and bowed from the waist.

"This dinner, mademoiselle, lacks only one thing to make it perfect — the presence of the Marquis de Castellane," he said dryly.

The big night passed in a daze for me. The food tasted like ashes and the wine was as flat as water in my parched mouth, but Balfour went into raptures and said it was the finest dinner he had ever eaten. Mrs. Keppel, King Edward VII's favorite hostess, remarked on my flawless menu. The Grand Duke Alexander raved that the white wine was the best since 1897, which was a long time between drinks. The only guest who appeared unappreciative was Boni de Castellane. Since I was a plagiarist beyond the reach of the law, his only satisfaction was to glare at me malevolently.

"That was so good I hate the thought of going back to my depressing hotel," Balfour sighed.

I cast caution and Alex's credit to the winds. "How would you like to go to the new night club Paul Poiret has just opened?" I suggested.

"I've never been to one of those places," Balfour said, "but this seems to be a splendid evening for experimenting."

As we walked through the lobby of the Ritz, it was a moot question whether Balfour or the armada of sampans Alex had painted on my scarf aroused more of a stir. I don't know how chic Alex's creation was, but it certainly was unusual. We stayed at the night club for four hours, giving Balfour ample opportunity to ponder the undressed French chorus girls' strange immunity to pneumonia. He also heard ribald jokes which probably never before had assaulted the ears of one of His Majesty's elder statesmen, but he chortled like a schoolboy. As the party broke up, Balfour took my hand.

"My dear Miss Maxwell," he said, "allow me to thank you for the most delightful and degrading evening I ever have spent."

In the jungles of high society, the capture of a lion as imposing as Balfour invariably brings on the double the herd of headhunters consistently prowling for big game. The all-star supporting cast Lady Colebrook assembled for me further excited so much attention that people began to ask questions about that fat, jolly woman who seemed to have an "in" with the bon ton. The herd came trumpeting after me as though I were someone of importance, and I did nothing to disabuse them of that foolish notion. I was having too much fun accepting the invitations showered on me and rubbing my threadbare elbows against the ermine capes and tailcoats of those in the news.

It is an ironic twist that the Balfour dinner, which launched me as a hostess, saw me in a complete reversal of my future role. The tone of the dinner was set by Lady Colebrook's guest list and Boni de Castellane's menu, not the distinctive touches that made my later reputation as an organizer and social director of gala affairs. I would have needed a good deal more foresight than I possessed to have guessed that I was to carve that niche for myself. A party-giver, by definition, gives parties. At that time, I couldn't afford to give a taffy pull in a telephone booth.

Although I began to earn some money again in 1922, I had no regular source of income during the first three years that followed World War I. I have a vague recollection of writing an occasional newspaper article and turning out a few special songs for professional entertainers, but if a gun was held to my head I couldn't explain now how I managed to get along. It was possible then to live in Paris for almost next to nothing, and I suppose Dickie Gordon paid our meager bills until I was able to hold up my own end.

A single woman has three major items of expense — rent, food and clothes. Rents, frozen by the French government in 1914, had not been de-controlled and were ridiculously cheap. After Louise Brooks went back to America to marry General MacArthur — in 1922 — I stayed with Lady Colebrook for a while, then moved in with Dickie in a little apartment in Montmartre which cost less than $100 a year. That's no typographical error. The rent was less than $100 a year. Food was the least of my worries. There were so many invitations to lavish luncheons, dinners and suppers that I was happy to stay home occasionally and make a feeble gesture at dieting on the meals prepared by Dickie, an excellent cook when the spirit moves her.

Clothes? There was a running gag that Elsa Maxwell always traveled with fourteen trunks and a hatbox — the trunks for her clippings and the hatbox for her other dress. A base canard. I didn't own another dress. My wardrobe consisted of one suit and one twenty-dollar evening dress I picked off the rack of a department store. It was just as well that my vanity was as negative as my bank account. I didn't have the figure or the flair for wearing clothes, and I would have looked ridiculous had I tried to compete with the wealthy women who were walking advertisements for the leading couturiers of Paris. I circulated in a set where chic clotheshorses were a dime a dozen. While they were knocking themselves out trying to look distinctive, I achieved the same effect by making my one

suit and one dress my trade-marks. Ask the veteran habitués of
Paris society who was the best-dressed woman in the early
1920's and you'll get a dozen different answers, but the nom-
ination for the worst-dressed woman stops with me.

Anyway, the women who really were worth knowing were as
casual about clothes by choice as I was through necessity.
There was the Princess Edmond de Polignac, the former Winnie Singer, a daughter of the fabulously rich and prolific sew-
ing-machine magnate. Winnie had more money than she possibly could count, as she informed the Duchess Mattie de la
Rochefoucauld, another American heiress, during an argument.

"My name is just as good as yours," the duchess said haughtily.

"Not at the bottom of a check," the princess snapped.

The de Polignac salon ranked with the most lavish in Paris,
but Winnie deliberately dressed badly, to the point of shabbi-
ness, to show her contempt for women who were enslaved by
dressmakers. The Paris police once ran a big outdoor benefit
at which donations were solicited for their welfare fund. Winnie stood in a long line waiting to make her contribution. Just
as she reached the desk an officious young squirt, thinking she
was a poor woman of the neighborhood, said he was closing up
and brusquely told her to come back the next day. Winnie
gave him a check for ten million francs and walked off without
a word.

Princess Jane di San Faustino was another American heiress
who might have been mistaken for the poor relation of women
she was able to buy and sell ten times over. Jane, a redhead
from New Jersey who became the arbiter of society in Rome,
affected an unvarying costume after the death of her husband.

She wore a peaked widow's cap, a loose gray or white gown that reached to the floor and a veil. She looked as ethereal as a figure out of a medieval painting and had a tongue like a fishwife when she turned it on arrogant poseurs. She ruled social Rome with an iron hand — as she did the Lido Beach in Venice.

Jane's contempt for the mediocre wives of some of our great statesmen was evidenced when Mrs. Stimson, wife of our fine Secretary of State, came on a visit to Rome. Of course she was brought to Jane's for tea, and I trembled at the encounter.

"Oh, Princess," drawled the estimable Mrs. Stimson. "How lovely to live in the shadow of the Coliseum where Nero fiddled while Rome burned."

"It's difficult," snapped Jane. "Now the men fiddle while the women burn." Mrs. Stimson almost had a syncope.

Jane's grandson is Gianni Agnelli, the young Italian industrialist who is the head of the Fiat automotive empire, and I think that Gianni inherited his drive and quick, agile mind from Princess Jane. Although I never have seen a demonstration of it, I rather suspect that Gianni inherited his grandmother's temper, too. Gianni, who has a classic profile like the etching on an old Roman coin, was engaged to Winston Churchill's former daughter-in-law, Pamela, but they broke up in a violent quarrel in 1952. Gianni left Pamela in a blind rage, roared off in his car and wrecked it against a stone wall, smashing himself so terribly that he may never walk again without the aid of canes. Happily he has found a lovely wife in Marella Carraciolo.

Several paragraphs ago, before Gianni Agnelli was born, a question was posed: How do you become a party-giver without giving parties? I simply did what came naturally to my

gregarious disposition. It might be described as another example of nature rushing in to fill a vacuum. I always have been
a complete hedonist whose cult is happiness. There is nothing
I adore more than laughter and gaiety, and my enthusiasm
must have been infectious or else people would not have been
attracted to me.

The process began with my piano playing. Music always
stimulates a social gathering and, if I say so myself, I was a
darned good pianist. Europe was swept by a dance craze after
World War I and in those days it was not possible to hear the
latest recordings by flicking a radio or a phonograph switch.
People went wild over the new school of jazz that had been
developed in America during the war and I was among the
first to import it to Paris and London. I was in constant demand to play for dancing and to sing numbers from new
Broadway shows. With my vaudeville training, I had the poise
and the polish to put on a pretty good one-woman show, and
acquaintances began to build parties around my performance.

For the sake of the record, I want to repeat that I was not
a paid entertainer, nor did I serve as a mistress of ceremonies
to curry favor with the rich. I played, sang and invented games
simply because I enjoyed every minute of it. If someone in the
crowd could cut a better caper, I was more than happy to yield
the spotlight and become part of the audience. When I began
to run my own parties, I always tried to invite guests more
talented and amusing than I was. They weren't difficult to find,
but most hosts and hostesses seldom looked beyond their check-
books in planning a social function.

On one of the very few occasions I paid an entertainer to
perform at a party, I "discovered" an unusual talent. Noel

Coward and Gertrude Lawrence had just opened on Broadway in *Tonight at* 8:30, and to celebrate the smash hit I threw a party for them at the Waldorf on December 11, 1936 — a date memorable for the abdication of Edward VIII. Noel and Gertie were depressed, as loyal Britishers, by the crisis at home that had forced Edward off the throne, and they tried to beg off the party, but I promised them a treat and, at my urging, they finally came.

A few days before a thin, balding young man called on me at the Waldorf and asked whether he could appear at the party. He was bearing a black case and looked like a door-to-door salesman peddling the life of William Jennings Bryan in six volumes.

"What do you do?" I asked him.

"I'm a ventriloquist," he answered.

"Isn't that a rather hackneyed act?" I replied haughtily.

"Not the way I do it," he said, opening the case and bringing out a little figure that was to be known presently all over the world.

That was my introduction to Edgar Bergen and his *alter ego*, Charlie McCarthy. He went through a bit of his routine and after I stopped laughing I engaged him for the party. He seemed to have such a refreshing sense of humor that I told him little details about the personalities who were to be at the party and asked him to have Charlie make some amusing comments about my guests. Charlie was such an uproarious success at the party that I gave Bergen $150 for the night. It probably was the biggest fee he ever had received and I'm sure he didn't expect it. He would have worked for nothing just for the recognition.

I became such an immediate Bergen fan that I pestered Rudy Vallee to put him on his radio show in the spot preceding mine. Bergen proved that it often is more difficult to get a chance than it is to make good. Within two years he was earning a half-million dollars. The thing that pleases me most about Bergen is that he never has lost his diffidence, his charm or his gratitude to me for having given him the one big break he needed.

The best parties are given by people who can't afford them. They must use imagination and ingenuity as substitutes for money. The glimmer of an original idea can make an evening more successful than a lavish dinner and a well-stocked bar, and the conclusive proof of it is my career. My parties were memorable for the entertainment, not the food and liquor I provided. Guests who heard Rubinstein, Milstein, Melchior and Coward perform for me, didn't know, or care, what they had to eat. Anyone who participated in one of my scavenger hunts or murder parties didn't need the artificial stimulus of liquor.

It was only when hotels eager for publicity later gave me carte blanche to serve elaborate dinners that I devoted attention to that phase of parties. The time I spent studying food and wine could have been put to a more useful purpose, certainly a more interesting one as far as I was concerned. If the truth must be known, though, I was embarrassed exposing my ignorance of such refinements to the austere headwaiters whom I had to consult in making the arrangements. Having been raised in a middle-class American home, I was not accustomed to fancy cooking. And when I was scrambling around and doing the best I could, my chief preoccupation with food was quantity, not quality. As for fine wines and liqueurs, I've been a teetotaler all my life. To avoid making tiresome explanations, I take a glass of champagne or a cocktail when I'm in a group of drinkers, but I nurse it all night. It's not that I have any scruples against drinking. I simply have never felt the need for it.

To take full advantage of the superb cuisines and cellars at my disposal, I studied menus of dinners given by gourmets and the authoritative essays of Brillat-Savarin, the famous epicure. I asked men acquaintances who were connoisseurs of fine wines and liqueurs for guidance in the mysteries of their hobby. I subscribed to bulletins and handbooks published by gastronomical societies and waded through stupefying lists of recipes and vintages. If a guest of honor had finicky tastes, I scurried around until I found out what his preferences were.

A dinner I gave for Queen Marie of Romania in Venice in 1921 is an example of the careful planning that went into some of my more elaborate parties. It was an alfresco affair on the beach at Lido, and I had a grand piano moved outdoors so that George Copeland could play Clair de Lune as the moon rose over the Adriatic. The marvelous sea food in Venice's back yard recalled San Francisco and the old-fashioned clambakes I attended when I was a girl. The Venetians never had heard of a clambake and they thought I was crazy when I had them dig pits and cover the fish with seaweed. It was the Venetians' turn to go crazy when the food was served.

"This is utterly delightful," Queen Marie said. "Exotic food and Debussy in the moonlight. It must be wonderful to be able to plan such a perfect evening."

I told the queen that was a rather strange comment coming from a woman who managed her country's economic program, wrote books and was a symbol of glamour throughout the world.

Marie glanced at the table where the fat, repulsive King Ferdinand was ogling the young, pretty girls he had brought in his entourage. She laughed sardonically. "Yes, I am glamorous. There is nothing more I can achieve socially. I control Romania's economic policy and I write books and diplomats court me. And sometimes," she added bitterly, "I am even an occasional wife."

Like everyone who ever has been to Venice, I fell in love with the most romantic city in the world. The following year Dickie Gordon, who was paying most of our expenses, and I returned to Venice with an obscure young man whom I spontaneously invited to go with us as a guest. Had anyone suspected he was to become the most versatile figure in the English-speaking theater, he wouldn't have had to wait for us for his first break.

In those days Dickie and I practically commuted between Paris and London. On one trip we were invited to a party Lady Colefax gave at Oxford for her son Peter, who had just been graduated from the university. I was installed at my customary place at the piano and I could not help but notice a young man with an unusual, almost Mongolian, countenance watching me intently. After playing popular songs for a while, I drifted into my old meal ticket, "The Tango Dream."

"That's a beautiful song, Miss Maxwell," the young man said. "I wish I could compose a number like that."

His effort to make a good impression on me was both flattering and touching. "The Tango Dream" was ten years old and the youngster obviously had gone to the trouble of learning something about me.

"There are so many things I want to do," he went on. "I want to be like your compatriot, George M. Cohan. I want to write songs, produce, and act in my own plays."

"That's a large order, but you may get there someday if you work hard enough," I answered. What else can you say to young people with grandiose ambitions?

He shook his head. "I've been on the stage ever since I was a child and I don't seem to be getting anywhere. I'd chuck the whole thing if there was some other way I could make a living."

He seemed so dejected and so terribly earnest that I wanted to do something to buck up his spirits. "What's your name?" I asked.

"Noel Coward. I know this is a frightful imposition, Miss Maxwell, but I'd be most grateful if you can have lunch with me tomorrow. I'd like to get the benefit of your advice."

"I'm leaving for Venice tomorrow," I said. I've always been an easy mark for struggling actors and musicians. On an impulse I added, "Why don't you come along? I'm giving a party for His Royal Highness the Duke of Spoletta. It will be great fun."

"I have no money and my mother runs a boardinghouse in Ebury Street in London," Coward blurted in embarrassment. "I'm much too poor to afford such a trip."

"That's why I'm inviting you to come as a guest," I said.

Dickie was so openhanded with money that I knew she would not object to an added starter on the excursion.

In Venice, we took two modest rooms at the Hotel Victoria. The manager of the stylish Hotel Excelsior, remembering the stir created by my party for Queen Marie the previous year, sent word that he would consider it a great privilege to provide the facilities and the necessary refreshments if I gave the party for Spoletta at his establishment.

A hostess to royalty is required by protocol to submit a list of prospective invitations for approval so that no one unacceptable to the guest of honor for social or political reasons is among those present. I sent my list to Spoletta's equerry and it came back intact save for one change. Noel Coward's name was crossed off. Spoletta's objection to Coward could have stemmed only from one source. Dorothy di Frasso had made the mistake of trying to match Coward's sharp wit at a party in London and had been routed in the exchange of repartee. I suspected that Dorothy, who knew Spoletta well, was behind the blackball to get even with Coward, and inquiries through the grapevine confirmed my hunch.

I was so furious about the shabby trick that I sent for the Duke's equerry and told him there would be no party without Mr. Coward. Within the hour, my original list was returned without an omission. I still was seething on the night of the dinner when I ran into Dorothy in the lobby of the Excelsior. I told her to take a flying jump in the Grand Canal and tried to implement the suggestion by grabbing her hair. We were separated before we set a new style in coiffures.

My ultimatum to Spoletta was not the last time I fractured protocol. At a dinner for Prince Andrew of Greece, I caused a terrific sensation by seating His Royal Highness on my left at the table with Cole Porter on my right, in the favored position. Guests who didn't know Cole assumed he was royalty and bowed and curtsied to him all night. That's the way it should have been. Cole was ranking royalty by virtue of his talent.

Chapter 8

EVER since the newspapers began identifying me as the Number One party-giver back in the 1930's, I have been receiving on the average of 300 letters a month asking how I do it. Most of the letters are tinged with overtones of despair. Parents want to know how they can create a social atmosphere at home that will keep their children out of night clubs. Wives beg for suggestions that will rouse lethargic husbands out of the doldrums or, more urgently, curb their explorations in more inviting pastures. The most pathetic letters come from girls who have no social life and wonder wistfully how they can meet young men.

The letters are depressing because they imply that I have a mysterious formula which, if divulged, will guarantee automatically the success of a party. That's utter nonsense, of course. The principal element of a party is perfectly obvious. Congenial, stimulating people make good parties. If guests are provocative or amusing conversationalists, a hostess merely has to bring them together for an enjoyable evening. Since conversation is a dying art, though, it usually is necessary to have in reserve a novel idea that will prop up a sagging party. If I have any formula it is nothing more than a little originality.

Virtually every woman who asks for advice makes the

superfluous point of reminding me that her limited budget does not permit elaborate entertainment. As though I didn't know. I wasn't trying to contrive an epigram in the last chapter when I wrote that the best parties are given by people who can't afford them. Sure, my most publicized affairs are fancy galas and costume balls. But in the last thirty years I've given a thousand small, intimate parties that were just as much fun, and within the reach of anyone's pocketbook.

Only once in a blue moon did a wealthy friend like the Baron Nicky deGunzberg tell me to shoot the works in staging something extra special in the way of parties. It happened so rarely that I remember the exact date, June 13, 1931, of the *fête champêtre,* or rural gala, I put on in Nicky's house in the Bois de Bologne. The house was transformed into a glorified farmhouse by the late brilliant artist and scene designer Christian Bérard, who painted a fantastic farmyard on wood frames, and covered the entire house with blue satin. Cole Porter had composed a special score for the orchestra, and Lauritz Melchior and Frieda Leider sang the love duet from Tristan und Isolde. Serge Lifar made a grand entrance on a white horse, his body painted entirely in gold. There would be far less unrest abroad in the world if all farmers were as gay as our 400 "peasants." The Cole Porters arrived in a Sicilian donkey cart loaded with orchids and gardenias. Daisy Fellowes came as Circe, with the Baroness Lillian LoMonoco as her bewitched swine. Bérard's backdrop and the costumes were so beautiful that an entire issue of *L'Illustration,* France's famous art magazine, was devoted to the event, as though it had been an exhibition.

Now no one has to tell me that few people have the facilities, much less the money, to entertain so lavishly. Lord knows I wasn't able to do it. In the decade following the First World War, I lived in tiny, two-room apartments, and the only servant I had was a cleaning woman who came in twice a week. I barely had enough money to meet normal expenses. Yet it was during that period that I made my reputation as a hostess. How? I threw convention out of the window.

You say you haven't adequate space or servants for a proper sit-down dinner? So what? A buffet dinner is much more fun anyway. Guests are free to circulate and mingle with everyone instead of being anchored at a table with the partners on either side of them. Any informal touch tends to break down reserve and make for conviviality in a group. A buffet is cheaper, too. A hostess can get by nicely with one main course, salad and dessert. The food must be simple, of necessity, since guests serve themselves and eat under makeshift conditions. There is another advantage in a buffet that solves a ticklish problem for the hostess who does not have complete sets of china, glasses and silverware. In the pleasant milling around, critical guests are less apt to notice that the table appointments do not match perfectly. It's a triviality, perhaps, but it disturbs the overly sensitive hostess.

What about the preparation of the dinner? That headache can be turned into the highlight of the evening by adopting a suggestion which, at first shock, appears to be a brainstorm. Have the men cook the dinner. Men always brag that cooking is a cinch they can master any time they put their hands to it. Call their bluff by turning them loose on an easy recipe that can be salvaged no matter how badly it is manhandled —

something like spaghetti and meat sauce, shrimps creole or Welsh rarebit. I won't vouch for results, but I can promise a hilarious hour while the men are making messes of themselves and the kitchen.

No one will mind that dinner is late. Half the guests will declare, to a man, that they never had a better dinner. If wives are as smart as I know they are, they will play along with the gag on the off chance that their husbands will get delusions of grandeur and relieve them occasionally of kitchen duty. That's beside the point. Even if the dinner is a culinary catastrophe, it will be fun at the moment, and that's the main purpose in giving a party.

Food doesn't make or break a party. A chef with the Cordon Bleu can prepare dinner and the evening still can fall as flat as a cold soufflé. The critical turning point of a party comes after dinner. That's when the ordinary hostess sees her party slough off into one of two ruts. Guests sit around and make desultory conversation, or they play cards. In either case, it is a dull, static routine and the hostess pays heavily for it in the liquor lapped up. Most people drink to escape boredom. They don't need bottled stimulation if they are shown how to draw upon their own resources for amusement.

The consumption of liquor at my parties always was astonishingly low — and I had more than my share of cutups who were waging crusades to keep the distilleries of France and England working overtime. Excessive drinking turned only one of my parties into a rowdy affair. That was the "Come As You Were" party I gave in Paris in 1927. The big idea was that the sixty guests were pledged to appear dressed exactly as they were when the invitations were received. To make sure of a wide variety of getups, I had the invitations delivered by messengers at odd hours of the day and night.

Knowing my customers as well as I did, I chartered two busses and personally picked them up at their homes. Parisians are accustomed to strange sights but, after all, there are limits to their tolerance. Hiring the private busses proved to be a necessary precaution. The Marquis de Polignac was attired in full evening dress save for one conspicuous omission. He wasn't wearing his trousers. Daisy Fellowes carried her lace panties in her hand. A half-dozen women who are respectable grandmothers today came in slips that definitely were not shadowproof. Bébé Bérard wore a dressing gown, had a telephone attached to his ear and had white make-up on his face to simulate shaving cream. Several men who rated honor above vanity came in hairnets. Jay O'Brien was a fashion plate in tails, except for one minor detail. He wasn't wearing a white tie and somehow he looked more disreputable than anyone else.

I made two mistakes in my otherwise careful planning. I installed a bar in each bus and I neglected to account for Paris's monumental traffic jams in my timetable. The busses began to pick up people at seven o'clock in the evening, but it was nine o'clock before they arrived at Meraud Guevara's apartment in Montparnasse, which I had borrowed for the occasion. By that time everyone was flying so high that there were drastic changes in some of the costumes. Countess Gabriella Robilant, an Italian, lost her skirt during maneuvers in one of the land-going hangers. Gabriella was unconcerned, but Countess Elisabeth de Breteuil, a Frenchwoman, was outraged.

"I refuse to be seen in my country with anyone in that scandalous condition," she said indignantly.

"To the Bastille!" Gabriella cried, yanking off Elisabeth's skirt. "Now a French and an Italian countess are equals."

I gave up trying to bring the situation under control after a plea for a little restraint was answered by a volley of hard rolls fired at me by my guests. The neighbors cheered my hasty retreat. They didn't want spoilsports, including the police, throwing a wet blanket over the free floor show in the garden. It looked like the rehearsal of a French bedroom farce.

There are safer gambits for getting guests to throw off their inhibitions at a party. My favorite device for giving a dull gathering a shot in the arm is a game, the sillier the better. I know it sounds corny, but it never has failed to work for me with people who make a fetish of sophistication or fancy themselves too dignified to lend themselves to that sort of thing. Personally, I prefer guessing games that test wit and knowledge — Twenty Questions, Categories, Charades and the like — but they backfire if all the participants are not on the same general intellectual level. In a large group, a few players usually wind up dominating the game and those who are not as quick on the uptake retire to the sidelines with a feeling of inferiority. The best games are those in which failure is comical rather than embarrassing.

The list of possibilities is almost endless. For example, to demonstrate how the sense of smell is governed by visual association, have blindfolded players identify a series of familiar articles without touching them. The ludicrous answers will give everyone a laugh. Bananas will be tagged as violets and a sprig of parsley as expensive perfume. A hostess can save enough on liquor bills to buy herself a new hat by putting up an eighty-nine-cent bottle of domestic wine as the prize in an absurd contest such as button-sewing or draping a live model with a few yards of cheap material for the most stylish effect. The Mayfair set once rooted more frantically for their entries in a race I put on than it ever did at Epsom Downs. The entries were mechanical windup toys I borrowed from friends with children.

What if you're stuck with stuffed shirts who refuse to play along with your amiable stunts? I'm tempted to suggest that you cross them off your list, but I realize it may be necessary to entertain them for business or social reasons. Every hostess I know tries to make the best of a sticky situation by balancing bores with bright, amusing people at the same party. It never works. One group cramps the style of the other and, as always, mediocrity pulls talent down to its level. Attack the problem boldly. Fight fire with fire. If you must have bores, always put them together or at the same table, and be prepared for a surprise that must be seen to be believed.

For some reason I've never been able to understand, bores have an effervescent chemical reaction on one another at a party. They invariably have a marvelous time trading banalities in the absence of competition. Clichés roll trippingly off the tongue like sparkling epigrams and trite observations acquire depth sinking into receptive minds. Don't ask me why. I only know it is an unfailing phenomenon. It's worth a try, accept my word for it. Anything is better, as far as I'm concerned, than the alternative catchall for repaying second-class social debts — a cocktail party.

The cocktail party easily is the worst invention since castor

oil. I've never given a cocktail party and I'd sooner go to the
dentist than be found at one of those social abominations.
The disorganized routs always are flops because they violate
the first principle of party-giving. The host and hostess must
have a good time themselves if their guests are to spend a few
pleasant hours in their home. That is manifestly impossible
under the conditions that attend a typical mob scene.

You know what usually happens. The condemned couple
greets you at the door with a clammy hand and a despairing
eye. They know better than anyone the torture about to be
inflicted on you. They can't accommodate all the people who
have been invited and each new arrival means so many more
decibels of noise and so many more gallons of noxious cigarette
smoke. Everyone is screaming and smoking in self-defense.
The limp anchovies on soggy crackers are an offense to your
stomach and it is compounded by lukewarm, prefabricated
drinks. The hostess anxiously wonders how many diehards
will hang on to the bitter end in the delusion that dinner is
to be served. The host wonders how long his liquor and ice
will hold out and decides to make deep inroads into both in
the hope that everyone will go home when nothing is left to
drink. Eventually, and not a moment too soon, the condemned
couple is reprieved by the fatigue that drives their guests into
the night in search of a place to sit down.

Inadequate seating arrangements may seem to be a minor
detail, but that detail has ruined more parties than any other
single factor. I didn't go to Perle Mesta's ball the night of
Queen Elizabeth's coronation. The ball was held in a long,
narrow room at Londonderry House, and there wasn't a comfortable chair in the place where a guest could escape being

trampled by the aimless, milling crowd. The small fortune Mrs. Mesta spent on the ball went down the drain. The notables left early.

More than one woman since Lot's wife has betrayed herself by looking back, but I can't help shedding a nostalgic tear for the decline of my favorite entertainment — the costume party. I've given so many dress-up soirees that Janet Flanner once described my party activities under the generic title of "Come as Somebody Else." I suppose the ham in me partly accounts for my fondness for costume balls. I always had the uncanny knack, even when I was much younger, of getting tricked up to look like any elder statesman I chose to impersonate. Among my roles were Herbert Hoover, Ben Franklin, Edouard Herriot and Aristide Briand. On one occasion my make-up fooled entirely too many people.

During the Peace Conference in 1919, Prince Murat picked me up in his car on the way to a costume ball in Paris. The prince was masquerading as Clemenceau and I as Lloyd George, the respective leaders of the French and English delegations to the Conference. Passersby caught a glimpse of us as we rode down the Champs-Élysées and thought we were the diplomats in the flesh. In three minutes traffic was blocked by the dense, cheering crowd that surrounded the car. I explained to the frantic gendarme trying to clear the jam that we were impersonating the heroes.

"You *are* Lloyd George and Clemenceau," he whispered furiously. "Bow to the crowd and tip your hats. There will be a riot if it is discovered that you are impostors. I will do nothing to protect you from the physical violence you deserve."

Every costume party in my experience has been a rousing

success. There is a sound psychological basis for it. By identifying themselves with another character or historical period, people assume new personalities — and the change usually is a distinct improvement. There is a touch of Walter Mitty in all of us. We love to romanticize ourselves, imagine we are fascinating and/or dashing creatures, and a costume party is an ideal springboard for fanciful flights. I'm told that costume parties, once popular on all social levels, have been supplanted by movies, television, soap operas and other synthetic escapes from drab reality. That's only half the story.

I know the course of history will not be altered one iota if no one ever gets tricked out again as Marie Antoinette or Don Juan. To me, though, the whole thing is symptomatic of an attitude with broader implications. People simply are too lazy to take the trouble of expressing their individuality even in an area as inconsequential as a party. It is said that costume affairs are expensive. Ridiculous. It is cheaper to hire a costume than it is to go out and buy a new dress — and what's the matter with a homemade outfit that shows a spark of ingenuity?

Actually, a costume affair is the easiest party to run. You merely select a theme and the guests will take it from there, making their own fun. What theme? There are dozens of motifs that can be developed without renting eighteenth-century gowns and silk knee breeches. According to the 1950 census, only .0008 per cent of the population in the United States is of full-blooded Indian stock. All the rest of us are descended from immigrants. Have guests come in costumes that denote the foreign origins of their families. For an amusing switch, guests can satirize national traits with gag props ranging from a piggy bank for the Scottish to a stolen toy horse for countries that shall be nameless here. A party pegged to outmoded fashions in clothes always is a howl. (Remember the shapeless flour sacks of the 1920's and the Princess Eugénie hats of the 1930's?) The outfits can be found in closets and attics people have been meaning to clean out for years. One of the most hilarious — and revealing — affairs I ever gave was a "Come as Your Opposite" party. Had it been cricket to do so, I could have met my expenses selling tickets to psychiatrists.

I hope I've demonstrated that the knack of giving good parties involves no special talent or training. It requires only a desire to improvise fresh ideas and the willingness to spend a little time developing them. My one regret is that I lavished too much time on parties, an effort that could have been devoted to more aesthetic pursuits. I wish I had written a sonnet that is reprinted in an obscure anthology or composed an enduring song that is whistled in the still of the night. Yet there is a certain satisfaction in being the best in any field, even if it is as superficial as painting Easter eggs, hitting a golf ball into a tin cup or giving parties. After all, not every hostess has had the distinction of being denounced twice in the House of Commons as a menace to the dignity of the British Empire.

The reprimands were aftermaths of two frolics that were projects rather than parties, considering the planning that went into them. The first one was my famous — or should it be infamous? — scavenger hunt in Paris in 1927. A gallon jar of Patou's Joy perfume was offered as a prize to the player who brought back in one hour the most items, or the most unusual specimen, on a list. The objectives were a slipper taken from Mistinguett on the stage of the Casino de Paris; a black swan from the lake in the Bois de Boulogne; a *pot de chambre*; three hairs plucked from a redheaded woman (the Duchesse of D'yen, a flaming redhead, locked herself in a room to protect herself); a pompon off the cap of a French sailor; a work animal; and a handkerchief from the Baron Maurice de Rothschild's house.

The players took off, and a series of disturbances promptly broke out all over Paris. The manager of the Casino de Paris put in a riot call for the police when two hoodlums barged on the stage and grabbed Mistinguett's slippers, then ransacked the shoes in her dressing room, forcing her to finish the performance in bare feet. The black swan in the Bois, a vile-tempered beast, put up such a fight that two bird fanciers went to the hospital for repairs. My landlady had hysterics when a donkey, borrowed from a peddler, started to kick out the walls of my apartment. The Grand Duchess Marie of Russia played a lone hand and came back with the trophy that won first prize. It was a most unaristocratic exhibit — a pot de chambre with two big, blue inquisitive eyes painted on the inside.

The following day a man from the Sûreté Nationale paid me a visit that was not entirely unexpected. He accused me of instigating heinous crimes ranging from the riot at the Casino to attempted robbery of public property in the Bois. He went away, quietly and quickly, when I informed him that the rowdies who had assaulted Mistinguett were Robert de Castellane, the mayor of Paris's son, and the nephew of the prefect of police.

A more serious contretemps was not resolved so easily. It

seemed that Lady Elsie deWolfe Mendl, who was married to Sir Charles, a staff member of the British Embassy in Paris, had created an international incident in going after a French sailor's pompon. She was charged with violating France's sovereignty by invading the Ministère de la Marine and stealing the cap of the sailor on guard duty. A stiff note of protest was dispatched to His Majesty's Government, causing a frightful tizzy in Commons. I was roundly condemned as the pernicious influence responsible for the deplorable action by the wife of one of His Majesty's civil servants in Paris.

Two months later, when the coast was clear, I went to London to stage a murder party at the opening of Lady Ribblesdale's house in St. James Park. Neysa McMein, the American artist, invented the murder game which I had introduced in Europe the previous year at a party given by Lady Mendl in Paris. I became the foremost expert at the game because nobody else was willing to make the elaborate plans necessary to fake a murder that was realistic enough to fool a large group.

Only four people were in on the plot in London — Lady Ribblesdale, her butler, the "victim" and me. The victim was Zita Youngman, a beautiful girl. The austere Duke of Marlborough was selected as the suspect because he was to be the top-ranking guest at the party, and pointing the finger at him would create the greatest excitement. Two weeks before the party, I began planting cryptic personal messages in London newspapers as clues which could be construed, at the denouement, as circumstantial evidence of murky goings-on between Zita and "M," her distraught admirer.

On the night of the party, the company assembled for

dinner, but Zita's place at the table was vacant. Lady Ribblesdale casually remarked that Zita must have been detained in
her room upstairs and told the butler to serve dinner without
her. I was seated next to the duke and during dinner I asked
him for a cigarette. He handed me a silver case we knew he
always carried and I surreptitiously slipped into it two Turkish
cigarettes of a brand none of the other guests smoked. The
stage now was set to spring the murder.

Lady Ribblesdale, feigning anxiety over Zita's continued absence, told the butler to go to her room to find out whether
anything was wrong. The butler came back and said the door
was locked and repeated knocking had brought no response.
That alarmed everyone and we went upstairs to investigate.
Lady Ribblesdale ordered the butler to break down the door.
The guests were frozen with horror at the sight in the room.

Zita was lying on the bed with a huge blob of catsup on her
breast. A revolver was on the floor.

The butler barred the doorway and ordered everyone to
leave to preserve all possible clues. I pretended to call to police
headquarters and two actors who had been hired to impersonate detectives promptly arrived. They made a quick search
of the murder scene and snorted loudly and significantly when
they saw the Turkish cigarette that had been planted in an
ashtray at the side of the bed.

The detectives told the guests to take their places at the
table and requested them to submit their cigarettes for inspection. Several exhibits were examined and cleared before the
Duke of Marlborough's turn came. The detectives opened his
silver case, then nodded solemnly at each other.

"This confirms our suspicions," a detective said, revealing

the Turkish cigarettes I put in the duke's case. "Can you explain these, Your Grace?"

Marlborough was too thunderstruck to answer.

"Come, now, we know all about it," the detective continued. "You had a liaison with the deceased. We've been watching you ever since these threatening messages first appeared." He brandished the clippings I had put in the papers. In the confusion, no one commented that it was a remarkable coincidence the detective had the clippings handy. They were passed briefly among the guests to substantiate the charge. The stunned duke was the picture of black guilt.

"Your Grace," the detective rasped, "why did you murder Zita Youngman?"

That was the cue for the butler to plunge the room into total darkness. He knocked over a chair, stamped on the floor and slammed the door to produce the sound effects of a fleeing man. Lady Ribblesdale and I screamed. The detectives yelled hoarsely, "Stop that man!" Dishes crashed to the floor. The guests thrashed about in a wild turmoil for thirty seconds, and then the lights went on suddenly. Zita was sitting at the table nibbling on an olive.

The duke maintained his reputation as a sportsman by smiling feebly at the hoax, but there was the devil to pay when the newspapers got wind of the affair. The *Daily Express* carried the story on Page 1 under an eight-column headline:

DUKE OF MARLBOROUGH MURDERS BEAUTIFUL
GIRL IN LADY RIBBLESDALE'S HOUSE

In smaller type, the subhead read:

Elsa Maxwell Stages A Party

Again, I was denounced in Commons for shocking disrespect for one of the noblest peers of the realm. But I was already on my way to Rome to play the murder game with Princess Jane di San Faustino, who was delighted by the rumpus Lady Ribblesdale's party had provoked.

Princess Jane and I selected guests who had not heard of the game, but we neglected to consider that the police of Rome were among the uninitiated. The clues I placed in the papers were so ominous that two honest-to-George detectives wanted to arrest me as a dangerous character.

As I have said, a good party takes a lot of careful planning. I had the foresight to invite Henry Fletcher, our American Ambassador to Italy, to the party. When I told Henry what I was up to, he promptly took the police off my neck. Henry didn't want a crimp put in his fun.

Chapter 9

THERE was a serious side to the parties I gave in the 1920's — the business of paying for them. Paris was my headquarters and although the artistic climate was heady and invigorating, I couldn't live on air alone. I needed money for such luxuries as food and rent, especially when Dickie Gordon was in England or batting around the continent with her own group of friends. On such occasions I lived in a series of dismal rabbit warrens that had two things in common. The rents were cheap and the rooms were on the top floors of old, walk-up pensions built in the days when a roof and four walls were regarded as the height of creature comforts. Like Lewis Carroll's Father William, who strengthened his jaws arguing law cases with his wife, the energy I developed climbing stairs in Paris has lasted the rest of my life.

To turn a fast and reasonably honest franc, I became one of Europe's pioneer press agents. Long before exporting technical aid was a feature of American foreign policy, I was running a private Point Four program for two of Europe's major industries — its fashions and tourist resorts. Today the business of separating visitors from their money is a big business. All countries in Western Europe now maintain government bureaus operating under fancy synonyms for press agent. The titles are new, but they're using the dodges I pulled when I was working the same side of the street in Paris, Venice and Monte Carlo.

Like all of my professions, trades, avocations or whatever it is I practice, press-agentry began as a serious proposition and wound up as a lark. My first scheme was so logical it's a wonder I thought of it. Since I was spending so much time providing entertainment at parties, I decided to do it on a commercial basis in a night club. Actually, Paris was wide-open for a high-class cabaret in 1922. People looking for diversion after dinner or the theater had three choices, none satisfactory. The big hotels with dance orchestras were stuffy. The upholstered sewers of Montmartre and Montparnesse lost their dubious, gamey appeal after one slumming expedition. Most of the remaining *boites* were clip joints catering to American and British transients to whom nudity was a novelty. The secondary sex characteristics of the female had not yet been exalted by brassière ads, the plunging neckline and overdeveloped actresses with no other visible talents.

I had no trouble getting a backer for a smart night club with a floor show presenting top attractions. The first prospect on my list was Captain Edward Molyneux, a British war hero who was a rising star in the fashion hierarchy. Molyneux, formerly the chief designer for Lucille Duff-Gordon, a well-known dressmaker, had opened his own salon and was doing well, but he needed a gimmick to buck the competition of established French couturiers. That gimmick was publicity, then practically unknown in Europe.

My approach to Molyneux was based on two selling points. He could promote his salon with the clientele a chic night club would attract. It also would help to divert potential customers from Paul Poiret, a rival who was operating the club to which I had taken Arthur Balfour after my successful debut as a hostess. Molyneux was so enthusiastic about the proposition that he promptly suggested we go into it as partners.

"Splendid," I said. "Now we need someone to put up the other half of the money. All I can contribute is an old tablecloth and some new ideas."

"You deserve a half interest for conceiving the idea," Molyneux insisted. I had the courtesy to protest that he was too generous. "Never mind the expense," he said. "We'll run the club for our own amusement."

Having found a kindred spirit, I cooked up a policy for the club compounded in equal parts of a whim and a shrewd publicity stunt. I purposely made it difficult for all comers to get in, a gambit that invariably whips up curiosity by appealing to the latent snobbery in those who fall for it. We rented a room at 7 Rue des Acacias large enough to accommodate a crowd of 300 people, but the audience was limited to 50. Molyneux and I sat at separate tables flanking the entrance and personally passed on everyone admitted to the Acacia. If one of us didn't like the appearance of the people in a party or we wanted to snub them, we gave a high sign to the maître d'hôtel, who told them that all the vacant tables were reserved. Soon the socially elite were clamoring to get into the place. We let down the bars, of course, when the customers were convinced that the privilege of paying fancy prices to enjoy our hospitality was a mark of social prestige.

The first stars of our floor show were Clifton Webb, a famous dancer long before he was discovered by Hollywood, and

Jenny Dolly, who could best be described as a Hungarian Hildegarde. Jenny made a grand entrance every night in an enormous cape of fresh gardenias, an aesthetic touch wildly applauded by the florist who furnished it. The Acacia became the Number One night spot in Paris, and should have been a gold mine. The trouble was that Molyneux and I were too busy having a good time to check incoming revenue against outgoing expenses. Half the bistros in Paris must have been stocked with liquor stolen from us. There was a constant turnover among our headwaiters and chefs, who quit to open their own restaurants on the kickbacks they received for approving phony bills.

Molyneux might have managed his dressmaking business efficiently, but his solution for the Acacia's exorbitant overhead was pretty unorthodox. He suggested that we close the Acacia and open a more elaborate night club on the Rue Caumartin, near the Opera. Since it would have been churlish of me to oppose a venture my partner was underwriting, I did not question the wisdom of the move. Our new club, *Le Jardin de ma Soeur* (My Sister's Garden) was a pure delight, especially to the decorators, who were commissioned to transform a building that resembled Madison Square Garden more than My Sister's Garden into a rural setting. I don't remember why we chose that motif, but we plunged wholeheartedly into carrying out the theme with flowers, landscaping, a huge windmill and more birds in cages than the Paris zoo had on display.

If Molyneux or I had believed in signs and portents, we would have thrown the key away and forgotten the whole thing. On the night of the gala opening, Molyneux came to my flat on the top floor of a six-story walk-up to escort me to the Garden. I was waiting downstairs for him, but I wasn't exactly ready. I had been locked out of my room for failure to pay back rent. Molyneux squared the debt with the landlord — I believe it was something like 6000 francs — so I could get into my trusty, rusty black dress for the *première* of our swank enterprise.

The floor show featured Josephine Baker, who went on to establish an international reputation, and Lady Cunard, who went back to London in high dudgeon after playing a one-night stand that gave us priceless publicity. Lady Cunard, my old sparring partner, decided to create a scene when she condescended to visit our establishment. Expressing more solicitude for our feathered friends, the birds, than she ever had shown for her human friends, Lady Cunard opened the cage of a "poor, tortured" pigeon. The pigeon proceeded to show its appreciation by making an indiscretion on her ladyship's bread. Her shrieks echoed in Paris and London newspapers, which reported the incident on a tip from a certain press agent who had cleared it with the management.

My Sister's Garden was a great success. It made so much money that it took the employees two years to steal us blind.

I never knew how much Molyneux lost on the two night clubs, but he never regretted the ventures. Although it is impossible to weigh the precise value of publicity, Molyneux was satisfied that the booming prosperity of his fashion salon could be attributed in good measure to the promotion it was given by the Acacia and My Sister's Garden. I hate to think of the lawyers who would be starving if all business partners were as amicable as Molyneux and I were, and still are. He made a bow to our long friendship in the spring of

1953 when he gave an exhibition of his paintings, a talent he began to develop only recently. The critics' rave reviews sky-rocketed the prices of his pictures, but Molyneux rejected bids two and three times higher than mine to let me buy the best example of his work for 200,000 francs. The painting of a bridge across the Seine literally will be worth a million (francs) in ten years.

Back in 1924, when Molyneux was taking a daily bath in red ink at My Sister's Garden, we were on such cordial terms that he recommended me for a job with Jean Patou, a rival couturier. It was something of a trade joke that Molyneux was hoping to hasten his competitor's bankruptcy with my extravagant ideas, but Patou needed no help in that direction.

Patou unquestionably was the most flamboyant figure ever to invade the world of couture. It is commonly believed that only effeminate men are ladies' dressmakers, but those who subscribe to that opinion never met or saw Jean Patou. He had more animal magnetism and sex appeal for women than any man I've ever known. There was another facet of his personality that fascinated women. Patou had survived four years in the trenches as an infantryman in World War I, a nightmare that had left an indelible imprint of recklessness on him.

He possessed the fastest cars, boats and women on the Continent. He entertained on an incredibly lavish scale. His gambling was an incurable disease that mounted in intensity with his losses. It is safe to say that Patou wagered, and lost, more money in the casinos of France and Monte Carlo than any gambler in history. I know the apocryphal stories told of the vast sums bet at the roulette and *chemin de fer* tables. I invented some of the yarns when I was Monte Carlo's press agent, but I've never seen a plunger in Patou's class.

The recklessness in Patou exploded like a time bomb after he made a fortune as a couturier. When I first met him, he was recognized as a top-notch designer and through his connections with important politicians his shop was backed by the silk manufacturers of Lyons. He was not, however, attracting the clientele he needed to get into the exclusive inner circle on the Rue de la Paix. Patou asked me what was holding him back. I told him bluntly what his most obvious handicap was.

"Your appearance is driving customers away," I said. "You can't expect society women to come to you for chic clothes when you look like a cheap racetrack tout." Like many Frenchmen of the period, Patou's idea of snappy dressing was to wear an ensemble of the same color from hat to socks — and Patou's favorite color was a bilious green.

"Get yourself a black Homburg, conservatively cut dark suits, white shirts with starched collars and cuffs and throw away those awful, garish ties," I added. "Put on a front that is in keeping with the elegance you're selling."

The undisputed arbiter of fashion then was Gabrielle Chanel, a woman with exquisite taste and a flair for exploitation. Her prestige was so towering that deviating from her styles was tantamount to professional suicide. Her creations, displayed by Gabrielle, the most famous fashion model of all time, dominated the field. Social leaders throughout the world made appointments with her months in advance. Her annual line was awaited with the breathless anticipation that attends the drawing of the lucky numbers in a lottery. Rivals who guessed Chanel's trend correctly — or got reports of it from spies who infiltrated her workrooms — were "in." Those with inventories that did not conform to the mode she was featuring faced ruin.

Since my interest in clothes always had been negligible, I began to wonder how Chanel had risen to such eminence that she could dictate to a multimillion-dollar industry. Before World War I, I remembered, the reigning fashion houses were Worth, Doucet, Martial et Armand, Callot and Drecoll. What had happened to them? Why were they overshadowed so completely by Chanel that they hardly ever were mentioned any more? A few random questions brought the same answer. Chanel was credited with emancipating women from bulky, overelaborate clothes with the classic simplicity of her designs — but her chief innovation was the short skirt. Imitators had gone to such extremes that women were wearing garments that looked more like kilts than skirts. I had a hunch they would welcome returning to a longer, more graceful hem line.

The hunch was based on the inescapable fact that most Frenchwomen had unshapely legs. If they adopted the long skirt more attractive for them, the lucrative American market which slavishly followed French trends — as it still does — would be a plum ripe for picking. Lowering the hem line was a bold gamble, but that was what intrigued Patou most when I proposed it to him in 1924. If he ran with the pack and copied Chanel, he would be just another dressmaker lost in the shuffle. By playing a long shot, he might hit the jackpot and become overnight the new pace setter of the Rue de la Paix.

Anyone but Patou would have hesitated to accept my suggestion. In the intensely competitive fashion rat race, a wrong guess too minute to be measured in inches — the thickness of a shoulder pad, a draped hip, a pleat at the waist — can spell disaster. Patou, who was to risk ten million francs on the turn of a card, took a flyer on my hunch. He waited until all other collections were shown. Skirts were shorter than ever before. Patou then came out with a hem fully eight inches below the prevailing length — and the gamble paid off beyond all reasonable expectations. Patou's floor-length evening gowns were a tremendous sensation and formed the basis of a fortune even he could not dissipate.

Incidentally, it is interesting to note that a generation later another relatively obscure dressmaker made his name a byword in the industry by following Patou's example. Christian Dior came up out of nowhere by introducing the New Look when the easing of World War II restrictions on materials enabled him to drop his hem line. The New Look was a complete misnomer, of course. It merely was a return to Patou's skirt length. Dior overreached himself in straining for a new sales pitch and came a cropper at the 1953 showings by shortening his skirts, a move that did not catch on at all. I think it will be a long time before fashion experts make a drastic revision of the hem line. They now realize that a long skirt is more flattering to a majority of women, particularly older women, who are the leading stylists' best customers.

Once Patou was at the head of the parade, he kept his position by springing merchandising ideas that now are standard procedure in *haute couture*. On my advice, he gave free samples of his most expensive gowns to attractive, titled Englishwomen who couldn't afford to buy them. Their only obligation was to wear the clothes at court functions and important social events,

thereby advertising Patou's salon. Virtually all the top couturiers today resort to the same device. Another one of my innovations Patou adopted was launching a new line at a gala night
opening. The champagne and buffet supper he served helped
cushion the shock of the prices Patou charged for his creations.

Patou was a press agent's dream, but in the final analysis he
was a better publicity man for himself than anyone he could
have hired. He promoted his personality with an intuitive dramatic flair that even turned his weakness for gambling into a
business asset. One night at Biarritz, when he was taking an
appalling beating at *chemin de fer*, I tried to tell him he was a
sucker to continue playing for high stakes while luck was running against him. Patou cut me short with a laugh.

"Each million I lose here sells two million francs' worth of
clothes," he said. "Relax, *chérie*. It is what you Americans call
spreading good will."

It was something a good deal more subtle than that. Watching
Patou gamble was a lesson in applied psychology. His strong,
handsome face was impassive except for the flicker of a sardonic
smile when the croupier swept away his bet. When he won, he
rarely looked at the pile of chips pushed toward him. He usually
was following with his eyes the figure of a woman as she walked
across the room — an interest that was more real than affected.
I know I sound like an infatuated schoolgirl, but Patou radiated
an aura of glamour that was irresistible to women. His excessive
gambling, affairs and extravagance were the magnets that drew
women to his salon on the pretext of buying clothes.

It is singularly appropriate that the name of Patou, who died
in 1936, still is the symbol of an elegant product. The product

is an ephemeral, perishable whiff of perfume, yet it has been sustained for almost two decades by Patou's reputation. I hope you'll pardon a sentimental flashback, but it was my last professional service for a good friend. I like to remember it because Patou was happiest when he was planning a luxury for women, at once his business and his pleasure. That was the purpose of our trip to Grasse, the town in the Riviera which produces the essences for France's best perfumes. Couturiers were developing perfumes as a profitable sideline, particularly in America, and Patou, a belated entry in the field, knew he had to come up with a unique article to crash the market.

We spent the better part of three days sniffing samples prepared by the top perfume blender in Grasse, and rejected all of them. None suggested the elusive, special something we wanted. The blender, rapidly running out of patience, muttered angrily to himself and thrust a vial at us.

"If you don't like this, I'll get a job herding goats," he snapped.

Patou smelled it. "Wonderful!" he exclaimed. "This is it." He gave me the vial. The fragrance was divine.

The man snorted. "Of course it's wonderful," he said. "It's made from the finest essences available. You can't use it commercially, though."

"Why not?" Patou demanded.

"It's too expensive. The price will be prohibitive."

"That's our angle," I cried. "We'll promote it as the most expensive perfume in the world, a perfect peg for us. And I've got the perfect name for it. Joy."

"*Joie?*" the man repeated, translating the word into French.

"No," I said. "*Joy*. It conveys a meaning that's understood all

over the world. Wherever perfume is sold, Joy will be the standard of excellence, just as the Rolls-Royce is in cars."

Since it would have been silly to introduce Joy with a campaign in mass-advertising media, I hit upon a new technique for
giving it a fashionable send-off in America, our prime target. I
sent samples to 250 prominent American women friends in the
hope of arousing the comment that boosts a luxury item. The
scheme paved the way for the acceptance of Joy when it was
retailed at forty dollars an ounce, the highest price ever charged
for a perfume sold across the counter. It still retains that distinction. The last time I bought a bottle — yes, I must pay
through the nose for it — it cost forty-five dollars an ounce.
Joy is a heavenly perfume, of course, but I like to think it has
continued to sell through the years on the magic of Patou's
name.

My career as a press agent was short and sporadic, but there
are two pretty imposing monuments to it any high-pressure
expert would sacrifice his expense accounts to call his very own.
I was directly responsible for attracting the middle-class summer
tourist to the most glamorous spots in Europe — Venice and
Monte Carlo. I'm the first to concede that the charm and the
natural endowments of Venice and Monte Carlo inevitably
would have drawn the hordes of visitors that now descend on
both cities. It is not gilding the lily outrageously, though, to
say that I hastened the process.

In 1925 Venice, the loveliest of all cities, was practically a
morgue during July and August. Everyone who could afford it
fled to the mainland to escape the hot, muggy spells and the
mosquito invasion. Nine years later, *Fortune* magazine devoted
an entire issue to Italy in what was described as a study of the

"Corporative State." A chapter on Venice was included, the editors pointed out, "to serve as a reminder that all that glitters is not Fascist." I'm grateful for that editorial clarification, for the article virtually credited me with inventing the Lido, now the center of Venice's social life in the summer.

"It was in the early [nineteen] twenties that something happened to the Lido that changed it from a pleasantly smart Adriatic beach to *the* Place — magnet for the celebrities of two continents, perhaps the best known beach in all the world," the article read. "Just what that something was remains an argument. Some say it was nothing more complicated than the world boom, some say Fascism. And some insist it was just plain Elsa Maxwell."

What happened to Elsa Maxwell was that she got roped into pulling Venice out of a hole, and got into one herself by working as an unpaid, one-woman Chamber of Commerce. In 1925 I went on my annual trip to Venice to enjoy the red carpet rolled out for me by the authorities and hotel keepers. Remembering my parties for Queen Marie of Romania and the Duke of Spoletta, they always were hoping that I'd throw more of the same, and I never disappointed them. On this visit, Count Brandolin, the mayor of Venice, asked me to call on him at his office.

"We think of you as such a good friend that I am taking the liberty of requesting the benefit of your advice," the count said. "What can we do to bring American tourists, especially businessmen, to Venice in the summer?"

I might have told the count that his question was related to the problem of keeping Venetians in their native city during July and August.

Arony

My father

Taber

E. M. at four years. The medal signified that I was "the most beautiful baby in San Francisco"!

Arony

And mother

Aime Dupont

uring World War I, I became right-hand l to the Queen of Society, Mrs. O. H. P. lmont, in promoting wartime benefits.

A. Delbosq   Berlin

My great friend, the singer Dorothy Toye. I was her accompanist on a tour of South Africa.

he stock company with which I toured the U.S. Stage-struck E. M. is third from right, front.

Edward Molyneux, the famous dress designer. We ran a night club together in Paris.

Mrs. Millicent Hearst, my true frie

European

The incomparable Jean Dessès, Parisian designer. Here with Maria Riva, Marlene Dietrich's daughter. He gives me 14 of his creations a year.

Wilfred Sketch — P

Dickie Gordon was a femme fatale w out even trying. Here she is as Tosc sung at the Opéra Comique.

Culver Service

Freud. He told me I would never suffer.

Albert Fenn–Pix

Einstein. I asked him to explain his theory in words of one syllable.

Edward Ozern

Mrs. Evelyn Ward McLean, publisher Henry Luce — and the Hope Diamond.

The most beautiful actress of her day, Marie Doro, as Oliver Twist.

Caruso. The San Francisco earthquak[e] broke our lunch date.

In white tie and tails young John Barrymore watched the city burn — with me.

Barbara Hutton with Cary Gran[t] third of her five husbands. At Biarri[tz] I saw the beginning of Barbara's fa[te] at the hands of the fortune hunt[er] Prince Mdivani.

Dwight D. Eisenhower. I picked this winner five years before the race. The portrait is inscribed: "For Miss Elsa Maxwell — who has remained a most charming lady while becoming a contemporary American Institution."

Horowitz, who played at one of my parties, is probably the world's greatest living pianist.

George Gershwin inscribed this picture: "To Elsa — from one who appreciates her genius for giving pleasure to others."

*Of the 17-year-old Clare Boothe (Luce),
Mrs. Belmont said, "Remember her
name. You'll be proud to know her 25
years from now."*

*When Gary Cooper took me in hi
arms, I understood the yowling outsid
his home the night I visited there.*

*A tête-à-tête with one of my dearest
friends, the inimitable Noel Coward.*

*Salvadore Dali drawing the charming
medallion which is reproduced as the
frontispiece of this book.*

Fanny Brice, E. M., and Bea Lillie.

Mollet

I gave talented Edgar Bergen and impertinent Charlie McCarthy their first big professional breaks.

Siri

On my right, the famous British actress Constance Collier, now retired; on my left, Janet Flanner, better known professionally as Gênet.

After a memorable White House lunch. From top left: Mrs. Martha Slater, Mrs. John Hay Whitney, Miss Fannie Hurst, Mrs. Ann Benkard; below: E. M., Mrs. Roosevelt and Mrs. William Randolph Hearst.

The Duke of Windsor. Perhaps I came to know him too well.

Mollet

E. M. and Gloria Vanderbilt Stokowski. Nice as she is beautiful.

George Bernard Shaw, here looking slightly monkish, called me "the eighth wonder of the world." On my extreme left, Noel Coward.

Paris Match

The Duchess of Windsor, and the Duke — looking rather tentative.

Cole Porter, one of the three men I've been strongly attracted to in my adult life.

As Briand, the French statesman, in 1928.

As Catherine de Medici at one of my
Birthday Balls.

François Rousseaux

Mme. Brulard and I, as a pair of Me
Wests, at a recent Charity Ball in Par

A. Aguilera

t Baron Cuevas's party last year. I arrived on a donkey, but I had to leave him outside.

Bear Photo Service

ere I seem more intimidated than ual — in a prank at Treasure Island, San Francisco.

A. Sponagel

Lefty O'Doul seems to be standing almost too close to the plate. And where's the crowd anyway?

With Clifton Webb at a benefit in Madison Square Garden.

I think I made a rather effective Herbert Hoover.

Several years ago, in a brief "excursio into Hollywood, I played the part Franklin.

Olivier of the Paris Ritz. He taught me all I know about foods and wines.

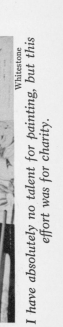

Whitestone

I have absolutely no talent for painting, but this effort was for charity.

An ill-matched but congenial trio on my farm at Auribeau in Southern Fran

Obviously a precarious seat — in a Hollywood movie based on incidents
my own life.

This record of a shoot in Hungary always gives me a laugh.

What woman wouldn't envy me in the arms of Aly Khan — even with Gene Tierney's approval?

A few dollars' worth of mustaches I passed out before a Cleveland lecture turn out to be a gag that saved the day.

At the Café de Paris, with Noel Coward, two Rothschilds, a princess a Lady Mendl.

"Women from all over the world come here to savor the romantic atmosphere of Byron, Shelley and Browning," Count Brandolin went on. "Our gondolas, museums and famous land-marks are very popular with the ladies, but men seem to prefer other places. Why?"

"You don't have anything to attract them, such as sports," I answered. This was at the height of the golf craze. "Why don't you build a golf course?"

The count looked out of the window at the Grand Canal and shrugged. "We would have nothing but splendid water hazards," he said wryly.

"You can make a good, nine-hole course on that strip of land about ten kilometers up the coast near Alberone. If you'll pay their expenses, I can get Phil May, the British professional, to bring the architect from St. Andrews and lay out a golf club. Let's see now. Why don't we do something with all this water?"

"I beg your pardon?" the count said.

"Every time I pick up a newspaper I see that Prince Carlo Ruspoli, Theo Rossi or the Duke of Spoletta has won a motor-boat race somewhere. You're letting your own drawing cards build up other resorts. Put up trophies for an annual regatta and they'll race here. That's the sort of attraction you need for men."

Count Brandolin enthusiastically endorsed my plans, but there was a complication that had to be ironed out before they could be put into effect. Venetian society was divided into rival camps that had to be reconciled to get unanimous support for the promotion campaign. One set centered around Countess Annina Morosini, who represented the old Venetian aristocracy. A livelier crowd that made its headquarters at the Lido was headed by Princess Jane di San Faustino.

In my unofficial capacity as peacemaker, I brought the two troupes together by staging formal dinners, beach parties, a fête on Cole Porter's *galleggiante*, or floating night club, and a treasure hunt. The latter affair took an unexpected turn when the police decided to get into the act and capture the prize themselves, but my guests were better sleuths than the cops. Bringing together the Morosini and San Faustino factions, more of a diplomatic than a social coup, brought me one reward. Mussolini gave me a decoration for giving Italian *turismo* a shot in the arm. I returned it three years later when I discovered the true nature of Fascism.

My promotion of Venice was so successful that the following year, 1926, Monte Carlo asked me to prescribe a tonic for its anemic pull as a tourist attraction. Before letting my enthusiasm run away with me, I had the presence of mind to get a retainer of $6000 for the job. In fact, I'm still drawing a nice little bonus from the account. During my annual two-month sojourn on the Riviera, most of my formal entertaining now is done at the Friday-night galas at Le Sporting, the open-air dining and dancing pavilion attached to the summer gambling casino. I give my "business" to Le Sporting for two reasons of equal pertinence. It is the most elegant spot on the Riviera, and I never receive a check. General Pierre Polotsoff, the managing director, extends the courtesy of the house to my party — I average twenty-five guests — in recognition of past services rendered the Principality of Monaco. If the charming general had his way — unfortunately he doesn't — he would throw in a share of the gambling loot, for Le Sporting, Monaco's meal ticket in the summer, was my brainchild.

The Riviera's development as the world's most fashionable

summer playground is such a comparatively recent boom that most of the prime movers are actively reaping the harvest. When I first went to the Riviera in 1922 to visit Mary Garden, the famous American singer, she was considered something of an eccentric for spending her summers there. Nobody who was anybody was seen in the South of France during July and August. In the words of Noel Coward's ditty, only mad dogs and Englishmen went out in the mid-day sun. Wealthy residents sought relief from the heat at Biarritz and Deauville and middle-class families vacationed in the mountains. Poor townspeople sweltered and did the best they could to make both ends meet until the winter tourist season revived business.

The startling transformation of the Riviera is a vivid memory because my visit with Mary Garden marked the end of its traditional summer stagnation — not that I had anything to do with it. Mary practically was the sole occupant of the Park Palace in Monte Carlo, and the only diversion during the day was fishing. We went out every morning, but I suspected Mary was interested mainly in catching the young, handsome pilot of the boat. In the drowsy afternoons we drove through the lovely, deserted countryside for want of something better to do. The forty-mile stretch along the Mediterranean between Monte Carlo and Cannes today is a real-estate agent's paradise where villas and cottages command season rentals not much less than the original cost of construction. In 1922, property was going begging at sacrificial prices in the area, and such renowned resorts as Eden Roc, Cap d'Antibes, Juan Les Pins and Cap Ferrat were fishing villages.

All that was changed abruptly the very next year by a fad that burgeoned into a phenomenon. Sun worship was embraced as a modern cult and the Riviera's narrow beaches became prayer rugs for the faithful. Great luxury hotels were built along strips of sand that formerly had not been able to support beach-combers. Within three years pyramided values of water-front property had turned the Côte d'Azur into the Gold Coast, but one pinpoint did not get in on the boom.

Prosperity completely bypassed Monte Carlo, once the Riviera's most glamorous attraction. The tiny Principality of Monaco, which derived all its revenue from gambling profits, was in such a bad way financially that there were rumors Prince Louis was ready to throw in the sponge and ask France to annex its eight square miles. Monte Carlo's decline started with World War I and was accelerated by the subsequent upheaval of aristocracy. Russian grand dukes, traditionally Europe's heaviest gamblers, had been liquidated by the revolution. The abolition of the German and Austro-Hungarian Empires eliminated another steady source of income. There were brief signs of a comeback right after the war when freshly minted American millionaires began to cut up *toujours gai* capers, but Nice and Cannes soon took the play away from Monte Carlo with newer casinos, operated by French syndicates.

Fancy French gambling establishments were not the sole cause of Monte Carlo's trouble. There was enough money in circulation to keep all the roulette wheels on the Riviera spinning briskly; as Mr. P. T. Barnum observed, a sucker is born every minute. The competition that was ruining Monte Carlo came from women in the upper echelons of European and American society. To be blunt, amateurs from the *Almanach de Gotha* and the Social Register had put professional cocottes out of business.

Much of Monte Carlo's old allure stemmed from notorious demimondaines like La Belle Otero and Emeline d'Lanson, who made it the favorite retreat for rich playboys on the loose. The deterioration of moral standards in the post-World War I era turned fashionable boudoirs into more accessible rendezvous. It would be a gross libel to say that infidelity was rampant in high society. Yet it was true there were enough promiscuous women in so-called exclusive circles to make a trip to Monte Carlo unnecessary for an extracurricular sexual fling. Monte Carlo had other siren songs besides gambling and sex to attract a new type of clientele, but no attempt was being made to broadcast them to the middle-class tourist, the backbone of the business.

I guessed that Monte Carlo's fading prestige was behind an invitation to lunch extended to me by Prince Pierre de Polignac, the son-in-law of the reigning Prince Louis, in 1926. My friendship with Pierre de Polignac was based on similar tastes in music and ballet, but I doubted that he wanted to see me for a cultural chat. The suspicion was confirmed when Pierre indicated a good deal more than an academic interest in the build-up job I had done for Venice the previous year.

"We need a similar effort here," Pierre said. "Monte Carlo is dying, hermetically sealed off from the tourists who are swarming to other resorts along the entire coast. Why are we missing the boat?"

"You're not rendering proper homage to the new king," I said.

Pierre was baffled. "Which king?"

"*Le Soleil,* the sun," I answered. "Life has moved outdoors. People come to the Riviera to relax, to get away from formality.

They want to play on the beach and in the water. You've got the water. Get a beach if you want tourists."

Pierre waved toward Monaco's jagged, mile-long coast line. "Where is there a beach suitable for bathing here?"

My drives with Mary Garden along the Mediterranean had not been a waste of time. "Right next door to you to the east, just before you get to Cap Martin, there is a strip of unused land that can be converted into a decent beach. If you go through the proper channels, maybe France will permit you to buy it reasonably to help Monaco out of its financial difficulty."

"Will a little beach be enough of an inducement for tourists?" Pierre asked doubtfully.

"No, you must provide other attractions. Build a new summer casino with facilities for entertainment. Build a hotel, a swimming pool. You don't need much space for tennis courts. Stage an international tournament every year after the Wimbledon matches when all the great players of the world are in Europe."

"The expense of these projects will be formidable," Pierre said.

"You've got to spend money to make money."

Pierre thought it over for a long moment, then nodded. "I like your ideas, Elsa. Will you sell them to us and supervise the plans as a sort of entrepreneuse?" That word was the closest equivalent he knew for press agent.

I was given a contract for $6000 a year, to be paid in quarterly installments. As usual, I wound up working for nothing. I promptly lost the money at roulette. I adore gambling and generally do all right at cards, but invariably I'm drawn and quartered on the roulette wheel. My gambling at Monte Carlo broke a precedent I would have been most happy to yield to somebody else. According to Monegasque law, no employee of the Société des Bains de Mer, the corporation that operates the gambling concession, is permitted in the casino as a customer. I suppose the restriction was not applied to me because the croupiers didn't know I was on the Société's payroll, or they could not resist the temptation to take a novice for a ride.

There was only one silly hitch in executing the plans for Monte Carlo's summer program. The French contractor thought I was crazy for building a huge swimming pool, fifty meters long, next to the sea, and held up work until a clause was inserted in his contract guaranteeing him full payment in the event I later was proved to be mentally incompetent. The blueprints for a hotel adjoining the pool were given to me as a present by Addison Mizner, the architect who practically created Palm Beach in the Florida wilderness. Work was rushed on Le Sporting, the handsome casino and outdoor pavilion, and it was completed in time for a gala opening in July, 1927. Grace Moore was the featured entertainer and King Gustaf V of Sweden headed the list of notables who brought back Monte Carlo's old glitter.

I got such a big kick out of engineering the revival that I continued to promote it after my contract expired. When I returned to America two years later, I told the reporters who interviewed me on the boat that Monte Carlo soon would have the finest beach in the world. I spoke simply to get a plug in the papers for an old client, but one reporter outsmarted me. He had been to the Riviera and knew there wasn't any spot along the rocky Mediterranean that could compare with America's magnificent beaches on the Atlantic Ocean. When he continued to press me for details, I boldly announced Monte Carlo was building "a rubber beach" over the rocks. That stopped the reporter, and the more I thought about the screwball scheme the more it intrigued me. Why couldn't we pour tar and rubber over the rocks, then cover it all with sand? Dickie Gordon gave me the answer.

"The tide will wash away the sand faster than you can dump it on the surface, idiot," she said scornfully. That killed the rubber beach, but the story couldn't have gotten a better play in the papers if the stunt had been practical.

Perhaps the best evidence of Monte Carlo's financial recovery was given on January 15, 1953. The gambling concession was purchased by Aristotle Socrates Onassis, a Greek whose interests hardly conform to the abstract areas suggested by his given names. A self-made colossus reputedly worth $300,000,000, Onassis ran away from home to the Argentine when he was a boy and parlayed a rowboat into control of thirty shipping companies. It was a mystery why Onassis, who is too smart to gamble himself, was so eager to get the concession that he presented Prince Rainier III with a $125,000 yacht to expedite the deal. The speculation since has been cleared up. Onassis hoped to sail his ships, the largest privately owned merchant fleet in the world, under the tax-free flag of Monaco, but found that under an arrangement with France only the French flag could be flown.

Speculation has it that Onassis and his big-business efficiency presage the passing of Monte Carlo as an institution commemorating a glamorous era that never will return. I don't believe it. I've been hearing the same complaint for thirty years, and to my mind the democratization of Monte has enhanced, rather than diminished, its glamor. There is more authentic drama in the rise of Onassis than there ever was in the vulgar spectacle of a slobbering, slack-jawed Russian grand duke betting the remains of his inheritance to buy La Belle Otero for a night. I've seen both sides of the picture, and Monte Carlo hit an all-time peak for me the night Jenny Dolly, the commoner, settled an old score with an aristocrat.

Jenny, our former entertainer at the Acacia, looked like eighteen million dollars that night when she swept into the casino. She was wearing a black gown gleaming with sequins, a wonderful picture hat with ostrich feathers and her arms were covered with jewels from elbows to fingertips. Her arm also was decorated with Gordon Selfridge, the American-born department store tycoon of England. Jenny surveyed the room and went like a homing pigeon to the *chemin de fer* table, where the Aga Khan, ex-King Manuel of Portugal and Prince Esterhazy of Hungary were playing for unlimited stakes. But Jenny rode roughshod over the big boys by playing a winning streak for all it was worth.

The Aga Khan, Manuel and the others dropped out, one by one, until only Jenny and Esterhazy were left in the game. It is protocol in the casino to gamble with dead-pan detachment, but Jenny exulted with uncontrolled vehemence as she forced Esterhazy to the wall in a personal duel. She had a stack of chips adding up to at least ten million francs when she finally cleaned out the Hungarian prince. Jenny stood up, looked at the crowd gathered around the table and laughed.

"I'm glad I whipped the great Prince Esterhazy," she announced. "My grandfather was a serf on his estate in Hungary and was lashed by his overseer."

That was democracy in action.

Chapter 10

PROMOTING the Riviera's sunshine was my job, but I preferred to bask in a headier climate — the artistic climate of Paris. The creative capital of the world ever since the vigor of the Italian Renaissance began to wane in the sixteenth century, Paris has many golden eras. No scholar will dispute the statement, however, that Paris's cultural impact reached a climax in the 1920's. In that decade, more literature and art of major stature were produced in Paris than in any other city during a correspondingly brief period.

I was running around in so many different business and social circles that I knew everyone from the geniuses to the charlatans whose only talent was for cadging free food and liquor. In the 1920's, too, an incredible torrent of preposterous pap was turned out in Paris by a prize collection of phonies and eccentrics. There were the expatriates whose loud rejection of America's materialism was rooted in an aversion for working for a living. *Avant garde* poseurs, looking for an easy substitute for the mental discipline creative effort demands, used James Joyce's stream-of-consciousness technique and the non-objective movement in art to foist their trash on the public. The dreariest bunch were the half-baked mediocrities who took sniveling refuge behind Gertrude Stein's convenient catchall phrase, "the lost generation," to excuse their inadequacies.

The lost generation's self-pity, a philosophy alien to me, further was exposed as a superficial doctrine by its chief drumbeater, F. Scott Fitzgerald. I met Fitzgerald on several occasions and he never was sober enough to carry on a coherent conversation with anyone. His wife's mental illness and his own psychological block against writing were later complications of his career. Fitzgerald then was the handsome, fabulously successful, fair-haired boy of literature, yet he already was leaning heavily on drinking to find support for his shallow attitudes. In *Crack-Up*, his autobiography, Fitzgerald later confessed that his failure to make the Princeton football team when he was an undergraduate left him with an inferiority complex he never was able to throw off.

I can't remember meeting Ernest Hemingway, although he mentioned me twice in books written during that period. The references to me were extremely flattering, of course, but I sometimes wonder whether they were more revealing of a great craftman's basic insecurity. It seems to this curbstone psychiatrist that the gentleman protests too shrilly his virility with his emphasis on violence and the physical courage of heroes — the idealized projections of his ego? — who grow older with each book.

Hemingway has few peers among contemporary novelists, but I have greater admiration for the intellectual toughness of two British writers. I hope my long friendship with Rebecca West and the late H. G. Wells has not prejudiced my judgment. Yet I feel they made significant contributions to our times by having the perception to anticipate agonizing problems and suggest the possible solutions.

I'll never forget my last conversation with Wells. He was

sailing for England soon after the outbreak of World War II, and I was giving him a farewell party at the 21 Club in New York.

"You've been a major prophet of the twentieth century," I said to H.G. "What's going to happen in the world now?"

"Man was given a most beautiful world as a workshop and a playground," he answered in his high, squeaky voice. "He will not be content until he has destroyed it and himself. Every war, every terrible new invention brings Armageddon closer. But we must fight and win each battle as it comes to give man another reprieve in the hope that he will learn eventually to appreciate the beauty of his world."

Rebecca West is the most brilliant woman I ever have known, and I never cease marveling at her simplicity and integrity. Two little anecdotes, otherwise unimportant, illustrate Rebecca's objectivity and painstaking attention to details, the qualities that have made her a top-ranking journalist. Soon after the end of the war, I took Rebecca to one of those big parties where there are so many quick introductions that no one catches names. Russia had just pulled a typically ruthless power play in the Balkans and the general conversation turned to speculation on developments in that strategic area. A number of people at the party sounded off, basing their opinions on a book about Yugoslavia, *Black Lamb and Grey Falcon*, by an author whose name they could not recall. Rebecca had written the book in 1941 and was immensely pleased that it was remembered, but she said nothing and listened intently while her work was appraised.

"The book was so thorough that the author must have lived in the Balkans for at least five years," a man said.

Rebecca had spent only a few months on her research. "I doubt it," she said quietly. "There were mistakes in the book. The author could do better now."

The people praising Rebecca's book were furious with her for disparaging the unknown author and sarcastically demanded to know what made her an authority on the subject. Rebecca could have routed the attack with one word, but rather than embarrass anyone she left the party. The people who ganged up on her never did find out who she was.

My friendship with Rebecca goes back more than a quarter of a century and I'm still discovering facets of her personality. She taught me a new refinement as a hostess, supposedly my specialty, a few years ago when she invited me to a party at her home in London. Rebecca was aware that I never had met any of the other people she invited. So the day before the party she sent me complete thumbnail histories of all the guests — their background, work, interests and hobbies — to help me feel at ease with them. As usual, Rebecca was up to her eyes in work, yet she took time out for a thoughtful gesture.

I've dabbled in a dozen varied fields, but I must be a frustrated song writer at heart, for my most poignant memories of Paris in the 1920's center around two giants of popular music — Irving Berlin and George Gershwin. It is ironic that both suffered the torments of blighted romance long after they had made it a standard ingredient of their love songs. Berlin's romance ended on a happy, sustained chord. Gershwin's romance which never has been told before, ended on a tragic note. When America's greatest musical genius died in 1937 at the age of thirty-nine, he still was carrying the torch for a girl with whom he had spent only a few short days.

The saga of America could be written around Irving Berlin, born Israel Baline in Siberia, orphaned at five, a singing waiter on the Bowery and the world's most famous song writer in 1925 when he fell in love with Ellen Mackay, a society debutante. Ellen's father, Clarence H. Mackay, president of the Postal Telegraph Company, forbade her to see Berlin, whom he contemptuously dismissed as "that little Jew from the East Side." Mackay shipped Ellen to Europe, the classic parental remedy for breaking up an undesirable affair, but it didn't work. It never does when people are deeply in love. Ellen had just turned twenty-one — Irving was sixteen years older — when she came to Paris. I met Ellen at the Cole Porters, though we were not friends at the time. I was told that she did not like me, but I had a tremendous sympathy and understanding for a girl — the daughter of a multimillionaire — to whom love was so much more important than money.

Irving was courting Ellen with a charming device that bridged the ocean separating them. He sent her private recordings of two of his loveliest songs, "Always" and "All Alone," which he wrote while she was away. The songs expressed Ellen's own feelings so wistfully that she returned to New York and married Irving in defiance of her father's violent objection. I don't know a couple who have had a richer, fuller life together. Irving's songs are an integral part of American folk music. Ellen, while raising three daughters, wrote two excellent books that reflected her happiness. *Land I Have Chosen*, published in 1944, was bought by Warner Brothers for $150,000, then the record price for a first novel. Mackay couldn't have found a better son-in-law in the Social Register — or Dun & Bradstreet. When he was in financial difficulties after the stock-market crash, Irving offered him one million dollars in cash to tide him over the crisis. I would've given a million myself — if I'd had it — to have seen Mackay's face.

The incomparable music of George Gershwin, like all true art, arouses a wide scale of emotional responses. To me, it evokes the bittersweet memory of the most electrifying night in George's life — and the bleak aftermath. It takes me back to the night in 1929 when George's symphony, *An American in Paris*, was heard for the first time in the city that inspired it. The audience's wild ovation established George as a serious composer, the ambition he had set out to achieve a few years before with *Rhapsody in Blue*, and I can still see him radiant with the satisfaction of fulfillment as he acknowledged the applause. George had invited me to share his box at the Paris Opera and I brought along Countess Nadige de Ganny, a ravishing French beauty.

George was captivated by Nadige. He took her home after the concert, made a date with her, and for days they never left each other. George was in a dream, and confessed to me that this was the only woman he would ever marry. "Do you think I have a chance?" he would ask. I tried to warn him by explaining the difference between his life and that of an exotic Frenchwoman of a society life which he could not even imagine. Then Gershwin's dream was rudely interrupted. He had gone to her house in Neuilly to take her to dinner. The maid told him that the countess had left Paris and there was no word as to when she would return. George was so haggard and distraught that I hardly recognized him when he came to my apartment late one night just a short week after his great triumph at the Opera.

"Am I getting a runaround?" he pleaded.

I didn't have the heart to tell George there were prior claims on Nadige's affections. Whether he ever learned of her attachment with Joseph Widener, the prominent American art collector and sportsman, I can't answer positively. I think he did. Many beautiful, desirable women pursued George, but he died a bachelor. Some men never can repair a shattered illusion.

It may seem strange drawing a parallel between George Gershwin, who was so rich in talent, and Barbara Hutton, who is so poor despite her wealth, but there is a common, salient point of comparison. Both were burned in their first infatuations, although the contrast in their reactions could not have been sharper. George never married. Barbara has married too often — five times, with probably a few more divorces to come. I know Barbara as well as anyone and it is futile now to speculate on what might have been. Yet I can't help wondering whether Barbara's first marriage set the pattern for subsequent failures by accentuating as it did her deep-seated inferiority complex.

I suppose it is incomprehensible to the average person that a girl who was as beautiful as Barbara could have inherited a sense of inadequacy along with forty-five million dollars. A brief flashback into her childhood may be enlightening. When Barbara was four years old her mother committed suicide, a profound shock that left a lasting impression on her. Frank Hutton was too busy administering Barbara's trust fund from the Woolworth stores and his own business to give his daughter the affection she needed. Hutton remarried when she was approaching adolescence and Barbara, believing she had been rejected by her father, resented her stepmother as a rival for his attention.

That feeling of rejection was intensified when Hutton sent Barbara away to boarding school to relieve the tension between his daughter and wife.

"I never had a home life," Barbara once told me. "I was brought up in tearooms by governesses." A slum child was reared in a healthier environment than Barbara. The fortune she was to inherit when she was twenty-one isolated her from normal social contacts with kids her age, and, at the same time, exposed her to the pitiless glare of publicity.

Like most people living in Europe in the 1920's, I knew nothing about "the richest girl in the world," the label pinned on Barbara by American newspapers. The European press had more than enough authentic princesses to satisfy the public's hunger for glamour and ignored the Woolworth heiress. Although Mrs. Jessie Donahue, Barbara's aunt, was one of my closest friends at the time, I had heard so little of Barbara that her name didn't register at first when I met her at Biarritz in the summer of 1928. I was invited to lunch by William and Beulah Fiske, and when I arrived the only other person on the terrace was a small, fat girl who was wearing a dress too tight for her. It was too hot to make conversation with a strange child, who I guessed was about fifteen years old. I merely nodded to her and waited for my host.

With perfect poise, the girl came across the terrace and introduced herself as Barbara Hutton, explaining that she was staying with the Fiskes while her parents were away on an unexpected trip to Paris. It was not until she made a passing reference to her aunt, Jessie Donahue, that I placed the girl, whose rather clumsy body was exaggerated by her tiny hands and feet. I was also struck by her large, lustrous eyes, which remained curiously expressionless while she prattled in an obvious effort to talk like a sophisticated grownup. I had the feeling that she spent too much time alone and was pathetically grateful for any sort of attention, even if she had to call it to herself. Then the Fiskes came down and I didn't think of Barbara again until that evening.

I was staying with Jean Patou, who was giving a party the following day. Since it was going to be a sedate affair, I suggested that Jean invite Jessie Donahue's young niece, which he did. Jean then asked me to look over his guest list to see whether I had any ideas for the party. I ran down the list and stopped at a pair of names strange to me — Prince and Princess Alexis Mdivani.

"I thought I knew all the refugee Russian princes, but this Mdivani is a new one on me," I said. "Is the title on the level?"

"Such cynicism!" Jean laughed. "The Mdivanis come from Georgia, and anyone who owned three sheep in that part of Russia before the war automatically was a nobleman. You should pay closer attention to the society columns. Alexis and his two brothers are called the marrying Mdivanis. At the moment, Serge is married to Pola Negri, the actress, David to Mary McCormick, who comes from a prominent American family, and Alexis's current wife is Louise Van Allen, an heiress from Newport. In fact, he's here with her on the honeymoon."

"Is their sister the Roussadana Mdivani who has just taken José Maria Sert, the Spanish artist, away from his wife?" I asked.

Jean nodded. "The strain runs pure in the family," he murmured. Sometimes you had to be a combined genealogist and hotel house detective to keep track of the romantic alliances lower-case royalty and upper-case Society made as casually as alley cats.

Barbara was among the first to arrive at Jean's party. I tried to put her at ease, but it was an awkward situation for a young girl and she retired to a corner to watch the other guests, with her face set in a mask of studied indifference. Then something very strange happened — so strange that I cannot give a rational explanation for it.

I was standing near Barbara and I saw her plump, ungainly body stiffen with anticipation as an enormous Rolls-Royce drove up emblazoned with a coronet that couldn't have been more conspicuous had it been outlined in neon lights. Prince Mdivani, scion of a distinguished line of sheepherders, bounded out of the car followed at a discreet distance by his wife. He glanced around the large drawing room crowded with sixty people — and headed for Barbara in the corner as though he had an appointment with her.

Mdivani couldn't possibly have known Barbara was to be at the party. Neither Patou nor I had told anyone she was invited. Barbara since has told me she never had met Mdivani. Maybe he had seen pictures of her in American newspapers, although it is improbable that he recognized her instantly in a room darkened to keep out the scorching heat. It sounds insane, but I'm ready to believe that Mdivani was born with a built-in Geiger counter that led him unerringly to untapped heiresses.

Barbara and Mdivani were alone in that corner all afternoon, completely engrossed with each other. Mdivani ignored his bride, who sat dejectedly on the far side of the room and made a bad job of trying to be unconcerned by her prince's rapt inter-

est in a fifteen-year-old girl. I attempted to break up the tête
à tête by asking Barbara if she wanted to join the young crowd
in the swimming pool. She shook her head impatiently without
turning away from Mdivani. Suddenly, Mdivani looked at his
watch, got up abruptly and walked out of the house, trailed
obediently by his silent wife. He had not spoken a word to his
host or the other guests. When I went to get Barbara out of
the corner, her eyes were brimming with tears.

"What's the matter? Did Mdivani say something that offended you?" I demanded.

"No, no. He was very nice," she said quickly. "I — I just have
something in my eye."

I had seen slick, continental charm boys operate on naïve
American girls before, but I hardly believed Mdivani had made
a deliberate play for a mere child while he was honeymooning
with a gilt-edged heiress. Especially a child who had to wait
more than five years for her inheritance. His Highness from
Tiflis appeared to be the impetuous type of opportunist who
would prospect the field for a faster payoff. I grossly underesti-
mated Mdivani's patience, foresight and resourcefulness.

Barbara left Biarritz without seeing more of Mdivani. That
seemed to squelch any remote possibility that her puppy love
would turn out to be a full-grown Russian wolfhound. I didn't
see Barbara for several years, but it was easy to follow the sharp-
shooters who were taking dead aim at her fortune and scoring
near-misses. Newspapers throughout the world ran play-by-play
accounts of Barbara's entanglements as she approached her
twenty-first birthday present of forty-five million dollars.

Her engagement to Phil Plant, a Broadway character, was
announced, and immediately denied by her father. She went to

Italy and was hauled back to America by her stepmother when Prince Geromolo Rospigliosi told every reporter in Rome, in strictest confidence, that he was secretly engaged to the beauteous Barbara and all her beautiful money. She went to Hawaii and had to barricade her stateroom against the advances of Prince Boromeo, another Italian.

Mdivani, the dark horse in the five-and-ten sweepstakes, let the other contenders burn themselves out in the early running. He withheld his bid until he got a million-dollar settlement from Louise Van Allen, a windfall he proceeded to blow with the greatest of ease and éclat. He tried to see Barbara and was turned away at the door by Frank Hutton as tempers and photographers' flash bulbs popped all over the place. The disconsolate prince returned to Paris and Barbara was packed off to the Orient with a companion. Geographically, they were as far apart as the poles, and I thought Barbara was safe temporarily. Two months later I ran into Jay O'Brien in the lobby of the Waldorf Astoria in New York.

"Have you heard the news?" he asked breathlessly. "Frank Hutton just got a call from the American consul in Siam. Barbara is getting married tomorrow to Alexis Mdivani."

Although I shuddered for Barbara, I had to laugh at the bold strategy of the intrepid fortune hunter. It later developed that the marrying Mdivanis had pooled the remains of their several cushy divorce settlements to finance Alexis's trip, in the hope of rehabilitating the family's solvency. Their sacrifice was well rewarded. Mdivani agreed to postpone the wedding until Barbara returned to Paris only on condition that the formal announcement of their engagement was made immediately. The nuptials were celebrated on June 20, 1933, with a $25,000 wedding breakfast at the Ritz in the presence of a large and motley assemblage. Mdivani's wedding present to Barbara was a priceless jade necklace, for which she subsequently paid. She gave him a string of polo ponies. The prince dearly loved polo. Riding brought out the dashing cossack in him.

The couple went to India on their honeymoon, a period of emotional strain for any young bride. Barbara was in love with Mdivani, or thought she was, which amounts to the same thing. It would have been much better for her had she been less enamored, for the first month of marriage aroused her feeling of rejection stronger than ever. Mdivani was one of those men with a constitutional inability to remain faithful to one woman, but his flagrant chasing did not hurt Barbara's pride as deeply as a sneering remark he flung at her in private.

"You're fat as a pig," he told her brusquely. "Why aren't you as svelte as other women?" Barbara was overweight, but not so much that she should have been unduly sensitive about it. As she later confessed to me, however, she envisioned herself as a gross monstrosity after Mdivani's insult. That was when she began the fanatical dieting that has ruined her health permanently.

The Mdivanis returned to New York to celebrate Princess Barbara's twenty-first birthday on November 14, 1933, with a Coming-Of-Age party at her home at 1020 Fifth Avenue. Barbara, who loved Oriental effects, engaged a troupe of Chinese dancers and acrobats for the entertainment. Mdivani, whose fondness for Russia increased in direct ratio with the distance he put between himself and his native country, hired a balalaika band and a company of Cossack sword dancers.

"It was touch and go all evening whether a sword dancer

would spear an acrobat and serve Chinese shish kebab for supper," someone commented.

The flamboyant party in the depths of the depression brought Barbara a blast of the unfavorable publicity that had been mounting since her lavish wedding and honeymoon. Columnists bitterly assailed her extravagance while girls employed in her grandfather's dime stores were paid starvation wages. The fortune passed on to her became an editorial target for attacking the abuses of capitalism, and the criticism was justified. Barbara liked to dramatize herself — a holdover from her lonely childhood — and she did go off the deep end flaunting her wealth. She was shoved more often than not, though, by Mdivani, a prime cut of ham. Veteran press photographers remember him as a notorious "lens louse," an exhibitionist who would go to any extreme to get his picture in the papers.

Barbara had absolutely no concept of poverty and she was too young to understand that ostentatious princesses were offensive to the grim temper of the times. When she realized that Mdivani was using her money and position to pump up his vanity, it was too late to correct the damage done to her own public relations.

I'm not an apologist for Barbara, but I think she deserved a more sympathetic break from public opinion, which she since has forfeited. Her social consciousness is not as highly developed as it could be, yet she is not devoid of it. She gave approximately five million dollars to charity the first year she inherited her money. I can document at least two typical examples of her generosity. A few years ago, when floods devastated the Po Valley in Italy, a casual acquaintance asked her to make a donation to the relief organization aiding the victims. She hardly knew the man, an Italian, but she sent a check for $100,000 to the organization.

Recently, Gerald van der Kamp, curator of the Château de Versailles Museum, told me how Barbara saved the French government from a contretemps that could have been a pretty sticky political issue. In 1939, van der Kamp was ordered to sell as quietly as possible some of the museum's possessions to help finance France's rearmament program. He put a price tag of $300,000 on a magnificent carpet made for Marie Antoinette, and offered it to Barbara. She bought it for her home in London. After the war, an inventory check of France's art works revealed that a terrible mistake had been made. The carpet was a national treasure no one had the authority to sell. Van der Kamp frantically called Barbara and asked if it could be bought back for the price he had paid.

"Certainly not," Barbara said. "I consider it a privilege to return the carpet as a gift."

Only the watchdogs of Barbara's trust fund know how many millions she has given to foundations and charities in America. Even if the figure were divulged, it is doubtful that it would temper the hostility that comes through between the lines whenever her name appears in print. I suspect Barbara always will be resented in her own country as a spoiled snob who buys foreign gigolos. Like every four-time loser, Barbara is condemned by her past record.

Her marriage to Mdivani lasted less than two years. The day after the divorce was granted in 1935, she was caught on the rebound by Count Court Haugwitz-Reventlow, an arrogant Dane with none of Mdivani's superficial appeal. Mdivani, who was killed in a motor accident in Spain three months after the

divorce, could lay on the charm with a trowel, and he was generous to friends with his own or his wife's money. Reventlow
was a calculating cold fish unsuited temperamentally to Barbara,
but the birth of Lance in 1936 was a temporary spark in their
relationship.

For a year or so, it appeared that Barbara had made a mature
adjustment to marriage. She was devoted to her baby and she
gave expression to her definite affinity for Chinese culture by
writing three love lyrics which I set to music. Then she began
to run away again from reality — and herself. She divorced
Reventlow in 1941 after three years of separation. Her marriage
to Cary Grant went on the rocks in less than three years. Her
fourth matrimonial venture was with Prince Igor Troubezkoy,
a Lithuanian, in 1947. Barbara seemed to be on the defensive in
explaining to reporters that Troubezkoy traced his ancestry back
farther than the Romanovs of Russia and that he was a natural-
ized American interested in psychology. She also said she was
determined to make the marriage a success. Despite Barbara's
resolution and her groom's hobby, they were divorced in 1951.

I once asked Barbara why she never married an American.

"My money drove American men away," she answered. "They
were afraid people would think they were interested in me only
for my money."

Barbara's explanation may be substantially true. Yet I am
inclined to believe she would have chosen, under any circumstances, men who conformed to the type she did marry, with one
notable exception. Subconsciously, Barbara wants a husband who
is entirely dependent on her. She needs such a man to bolster
her inferiority complex.

The one exception was Cary Grant, the British-born movie

star. Cary never pursued Barbara. Their marriage in 1942 was
staged-managed by Dorothy di Frasso, who sincerely hoped that
it would be a stabilizing influence on Barbara. There were two
strikes on the marriage from the start. Cary didn't need Barbara's
money. He was earning more than enough to carry his own
weight with an heiress. And Barbara, who knew Cary was her
intellectual superior, surrounded herself with a retinue of fawning parasites, the only people she could dominate mentally.
Cary couldn't stomach Barbara's friends, who cluttered up the
house. He was working extremely hard and there always was a
stupid, noisy party going on in his home when he returned dog-
tired from the studio. It was strictly Barbara's fault that they
drifted apart.

There were no recriminations when the marriage ended in
1945. Cary, an awfully nice guy, had a sympathetic understanding of Barbara and tried hard to make allowances for her. He
continued to show his affection for Barbara for several years
with the companionship he gave Lance Reventlow, her son by
her second marriage. Lance, who went to school in Arizona to
relieve his chronic sinus condition, spent his vacations with
Cary, the emotional anchor he needed so badly.

Barbara would have repeated the dreary pattern of marrying
another obsolete European title in the summer of 1953 if not
for her son's objections. Lance disapproved, vehemently and
validly, of Baron Gottfried Von Cramm, the superannuated
German tennis player, one of his mother's old flames. She
promptly dropped Von Cramm when she and Lance went to
Deauville for the polo matches and she saw Porfirio Rubirosa,
who had recently received a cash settlement of one million
dollars in his divorce from Doris Duke. His friend Leland

Rosenberg met Lance, became friendly with the boy, and suggested that he and his mother dine with Rubi and himself. Barbara was attracted by the Dominican playboy's gamy charm and the inevitable happened. Although Rubi was involved romantically with Zsa Zsa Gabor, Barbara's "love" for him proved stronger — temporarily. Barbara's abrupt termination of the honeymoon after seventy-two days of so-called marriage was inevitable.

What is the prognosis for the poor little rich girl who, as she approaches middle age, is poorer in spiritual resources and no richer for her experience? There will be other men willing to surrender their pride and submit to Barbara's domination. She will always find husbands, but she never will find happiness. The tragedy of her life is that she has been able to buy everything except love and peace of mind.

Chapter 11

THE first time Keokuk, my old home town, or any other provincial American city heard of me, I was the butt of a joke. A radio comedian remarked that the stock market crash of 1929 was such a jolt that it even shook Elsa Maxwell out of Europe. The gag was as feeble as the implication was untrue that I had come running home like a scared rabbit because rich friends who were my meal tickets were punched full of holes by the crash. I didn't mind the rib, though. There were so few jokes, good or bad, circulating in November, 1929, that it was almost a public service to be the stooge for a wry laugh.

Just to keep the record straight, I came back to America two weeks before the bottom fell out of Wall Street and twenty-five million illusions on October 29, 1929. Black Friday had no immediate or eventual effect on me financially. Since I owned nothing, I wasn't one of the twenty-five million people who, according to a Senate investigating committee, lost fifty billion dollars' worth of paper profits in the crash. I was a model of consistency. Come boom or depression, I always was broke.

I returned to America simply because I was homesick after living abroad for ten years. I was tired of being a foreigner everywhere I went, fed up hearing myself speak French, Italian and German with abominable accents. I felt the need to re-cultivate roots in my own country. I never was an expatriate again after I realized how deeply imbedded in my childhood these roots were.

Before leaving Europe, I made a deal to stay at the Ritz-Carlton Hotel in New York, which gave me special rates, convey-ing to me the first inkling that I had become a kind of celebrity — though a minor one — during the years I had been abroad. The first thing I did was to throw a "Come As Your Oppo-site" party. George Gershwin came as Groucho Marx, Cole Porter as a football player, Fanny Brice as Tosca, Mrs. Vincent Astor as a Bad Woman, Frances Alda as Al Smith, Mrs. Harold E. Talbott as a "Madam" and I impersonated President Herbert Hoover in a dress suit borrowed from Alexander Woollcott.

There were two hundred celebrities in amusing getups, but someone who wasn't there made it the most satisfying party I ever gave.

I was checking the final arrangements when a secretary brought a message from Mrs. Cornelius Vanderbilt, who was on the phone waiting for an answer. Mrs. Vanderbilt said she had heard so much about my parties that she wondered whether she might drop in with a few friends during the evening to watch the festivities. The message touched off a chain reaction that rang a bell deep within the recesses of my subconscious.

I was a twelve-year-old girl again, choked with resentment as I sat at the window of a flat in San Francisco watching the guests arrive at Senator Fair's party for his daughter Teresa. The elegant party to which the Maxwells didn't rate an invitation. All of a sudden, everything I had done in the intervening thirty-four years seemed to be a climactic build-up for this

one delicious moment. Mrs. Vanderbilt, the self-anointed
queen of New York society, was trying to wangle an invitation
to my party. I began to laugh so hard that the poor secretary
must have thought I was mad.

"Mrs. Vanderbilt is holding the line," the girl said. "What
shall I tell her?"

"Tell Mrs. Vanderbilt the party is restricted to my friends.
You may add that I do not include her among them."

Most people remember the depression for the widespread
despair and privation that gripped the country. I would be a
hypocrite if I claimed that the depression brought any material
hardship to me. I suppose this admission violates customary
I-was-there-and-suffered-too autobiographical practice, but I
managed to get along by writing occasional magazine articles
and lecturing to women's clubs. And when the harsh facts of
life threatened to catch up with me, my old friend Mrs. O. H.
P. Belmont whisked me off on a wonderful free trip to Europe
in December, 1930.

Mrs. Belmont was approaching eighty and wanted, as she
said, "to take a last look around." She invited me to go to Egypt
with her son Willie, her daughter Consuelo, her son-in-law
Jacques Balsan and the Marquis Sommi Piccardi. Mrs. Millicent Hearst was so intrigued with the idea that she organized
a junket of her own and joined us with seven guests. The two
parties went up the Nile in *dahabeahs*, large houseboats each
manned by a crew of twenty, as far as Luxor. En route,
we were taken on a special tour of the Valley of Kings by
Howard Carter, discoverer of Tutankhamen's tomb. At Luxor,
I pulled a switch on the Egyptians and showed them a refinement of modern civilization by giving a surprise party in the

Egyptian desert. Prince Duad, the son of the former khedive, assured me it was the first time since the dawn of history that anyone had succeeded in making the desert attractive. I wouldn't know about that, but I do know the party was the most exotic affair I ever dreamed up.

With my dragoman acting as interpreter and guide, I arranged for a native dinner outside a tiny village ten miles from Luxor. I hired a caravan of camels and donkeys to transport sixty guests to the feast. When my dragoman explained there was no wood to build the large bonfires I had ordered, I told him to have camels transport dead palm trees for fuel. Oddly enough, the burning palms were the most exciting feature of the party for the Egyptian guests and the thirty Arabs who lived in the village. Wood was unobtainable in the desert and the natives were vastly impressed that I had the trees hauled from Luxor to light up the scene. It was an expensive proposition but well worth the dramatic effect. At midnight, a huge, red moon came up as though ordered by Cecil B. DeMille and outlined what appeared to be the silhouettes of enormous, fantastic birds floating slowly toward us. The bizarre illusion was created by camels carrying more palm trees across the desert. The party was topped off with breakfast at sunrise on the site of the ancient temples at Karnak.

Mrs. Belmont and Mrs. Hearst left Egypt with their guests after seven weeks of sightseeing, but I remained another fortnight to take advantage of a rare opportunity. Dr. George A. Reisner, the head of an archaeological expedition from Harvard, had recently found the tomb of Cheops's granddaughter and invited Queen Elisabeth of Belgium and me to witness the opening of the burial chamber.

It was an eerie feeling watching history roll back to a scene that had been hidden for almost four thousand years. The most poignant reminder of the past, though, was not the sarcophagus or the priceless treasures buried with the princess. The sand floor of the chamber held the perfectly preserved footprints of the last slave who left the tomb before it was sealed. The slave's mark, enduring through the ages, became a haunting symbol when I went to Italy and Germany immediately afterwards.

Although I had been away from Italy only a year and a half, I was appalled by the Fascists' suppression of civil liberties during that brief period. I had registered my protest a few years before by returning the medal Mussolini had given me for promoting Venice as a tourist resort. Mussolini then was strutting behind a false façade of social reform. A token gesture by me was meaningless, of course. Yet I felt so strongly about it as a matter of principle that I sent it back.

Millicent Hearst had been invited to an audience with Mussolini and she asked me if I would like to go along. I refused the invitation. Mussolini took her into the country on an inspection tour of public works and drove his Fiat eighty miles an hour. Millicent, who is terrified by reckless driving, suggested to Mussolini that he slow down.

"Why?" he demanded belligerently.

"You — you're breaking the speed law," Millicent said lamely.

Mussolini laughed uproariously. "I *am* the law," he blustered. But despite depressing relapses, the world does progress, slowly but inexorably. Louis XIV, who said, "L'état c'est moi," died peacefully in bed after reigning for seventy-three years. Mussolini died at the end of a rope in Milan after twenty-three years of ruthless oppression.

The week after refusing to meet Mussolini, I inadvertently spent an evening in the company of a fouler megalomaniac — Adolf Hitler. The only sop to my self-respect is that Hitler's personality was so obnoxious that I didn't bother to look at him closely enough to recognize him. Winifred Wagner, daughter-in-law of the famous composer, invited me to a dinner she was giving for Mrs. Vincent Astor at Bayreuth before a performance of the opera. I tried to make casual conversation with the man on my left at the table, but he was so rude and surly that I gave it up. Frau Wagner took us to the opera after dinner and again I found myself next to my sullen dinner partner. I asked him in German whether I could look at his program for a moment. He shrugged and deliberately turned his back on me. I was so furious that I grabbed the program from him and threw it back at him contemptuously after I had read it. Had I known of the horrors he was to inflict on the world, there would be a more forceful — and lethal — end to this anecdote.

I've always loved — and admired — Anne O'Hare Mc-Cormick, the New York Times's brilliant foreign correspondent, for the needling she once gave Hitler. Anne went to Berchtesgaden to interview the chancellor, but he was morose and uncommunicative until she asked him how far the Nazis intended to go in their anti-Semitic campaign. Hitler began to froth at the mouth and eat the carpet.

"The Jews! The Jews!" he screamed. "What are you doing about the Jews in America?"

Anne looked him squarely in the eye. "Why, nothing," she said calmly. "We think we're just as good as they are."

Dictators are notoriously poor students of history. While

Hitler was boasting he was building a New Order that was to last a thousand years, the oldest ruling house in Europe was overthrown. King Alphonso XIII of Spain, the last of the Bourbons, was deposed by the most backward country in Western Europe.

I saw Alphonso the day he began his exile in Rome. I must confess he inspired great respect for the dignity he maintained in the face of humiliation. The superstitious Italians believed there was a curse on Alphonso and muttered "malocchio" (evil eye) behind his back, then brushed their clothes with their little and index fingers to ward off the malign spirits that followed him. It was the worst hex the Italians could have put on him, but Alphonso gave no indication that he noticed it. I invited twenty titled Italians to a dinner party for Alphonso in Venice, but all refused to come because of the *malocchio* superstition. Although he knew why we dined alone, Alphonso never was more charming.

The Fascist guttersnipes went out of their way to insult him. All his life Alphonso had exercised his royal prerogative of keeping people waiting for him, but he arrived promptly at a dinner given by Mrs. Hearst in Rome. Count Ciano, a half-baked imitation of his father-in-law, deliberately was an hour late for dinner. Protocol required Millicent to serve dinner as soon as Alphonso arrived, but he asked her to wait. "Mrs. Hearst," he said, "Rome is the only city where I can live with some semblance of my former life. We will wait for Count Ciano." And when Ciano finally arrived he never uttered a word of apology or regret.

Alphonso was inherently a gentleman, a word that never will be applied to ex-King Farouk I of Egypt. Although generations of inbreeding among the ruling houses of Europe and the Near East have produced scores of strong contenders for the stigma, Farouk is by all odds the most horrid specimen of so-called royalty of the last century, at least.

I'm proud to say that I incurred his enmity soon after I first saw him in Deauville in 1950. My R.S.V.P. to an invitation to dine with Farouk was a telegram to his equerry which read, "I do not associate with clowns, monkeys or corrupt gangsters." I learned that Farouk screamed like a pig — what else? — when he saw the telegram. I also like to take a bow for attacking Farouk in my column while he still was on his tottering throne and predicting on a television show that he soon would be given the boot by the Egyptians.

On June 27, 1953, the *New York Daily News* carried a story by Issa El Korashi, its Cairo correspondent, which began: "On the ancient Moslem maxim that anybody, but anybody, who hates your enemies is your good old friend, some Egyptians today started booming Elsa Maxwell for United States ambassador to this party-loving land of the Nile. She hates ex-king Farouk like an ex-subject." The State Department did not act on the suggestion. Perle Mesta held the exclusive franchise for quaint diplomatic appointments.

In the last thirty-five years I have entertained more royalty than any untitled hostess, and I wouldn't go through the ordeal again for one million dollars. That's just about what the publicity has been worth to me, but I paid an exorbitant price for it. Once I had proved to my own satisfaction that I could dress up my dinner tables with kings and queens, it was a real job fighting the deadly pall protocol invariably casts over parties attended by royalty.

Protocol may be defined as the code of etiquette which protects royalty from the competition of intellectual and social superiors. The stuffy, outmoded tribal rites that require deference to rank kill a party before it has a chance to get off the ground. To begin with, His Royal Highness is a cinch to ruin the digestions and dispositions of the other guests by showing up late. It is a special mark of esteem to a hostess if H.R.H. keeps her guests waiting only an hour for the first drink.

When H.R.H. finally does arrive, another blight is put on the party by the formal presentation of guests. The women, usually girdled within an inch of their lives, hope they don't fall flat on their faces curtsying to H.R.H. The men know they look as foolish as they feel bowing low from the waist. Once, and just once, a Scandinavian king, lubricated with the painkiller that comes in brown bottles, curtsied back to the women. But that was in the penthouse of a sixteen-story Fifth Avenue apartment building and the height probably made His Majesty giddy.

The presentations having dragged to an end, everyone waits for H.R.H. to speak. There is a crashing silence. H.R.H. has nothing to say. The floorboards creak loudly as one and all squirm with excruciating boredom. No one can sit down or have a drink before the guest of honor indicates that is his royal pleasure. It may be another hour, but the hostess is too numb to care that dinner is ruined. In fact, a late dinner can be her one good break of the evening. She may not have to play bridge with H.R.H., who uses a bidding system that antedates the airplane and insists on playing every hand. Protocol demands that everyone hold still for H.R.H.'s mediocrity, eccentricities and inanities until he decides to leave, thereby bestowing his most gracious favor on the hostess and her stupefied guests.

It alternately amuses and annoys me that the worst sticklers for protocol come from European countries that are ostensibly republics. France abolished nobility for the third time in 1871, but a Frenchman with an extinct title sulks like a spoiled child if he is not given the red-carpet treatment. Three members of the de la Rouchefecauld family once walked out on me because each was highly offended by my seating arrangements for dinner. They never were missed. Unfrocked Spanish and Italian aristocrats run a stiff neck behind the French in demanding privileges they no longer deserve. Even the descendants of Balkan brigands get on their high horses — probably stolen — if they think they can get away with it, but they quickly swallow their pride along with a free meal.

The more authentic the title, the less fuss the holder is apt to make of it. An Englishman who can trace his lineage back to the Conqueror rarely uses his rank on the social level. The Scandinavians similarly dispense with the nonsensical mumbo-jumbo of pomp and protocol. Sweden, Norway and Denmark, the most progressive countries in adopting social reforms, still are monarchies technically because their kings realized a long time ago that they rule by consent of the governed. The divine-right boys discovered they were expendable.

Gustaf V of Sweden would have been inconspicuous in a crowd if not for his extreme height. Only two concessions had to be made to Gustaf's rank. You had to pretend he didn't peek at your cards at the bridge table and you had to brave his lisp that sprayed you when he spoke. "Bring your raincoats," I always warned guests who were dining with Gustaf V. A lot of good-natured fun was poked at Gustaf's passion for tennis, which he played until he was past eighty, but kings have been known to pursue, and sometimes embrace, gamier hobbies. I really believe Gustaf would have traded his royal prerogatives for one Wimbledon championship. Back in the 1920's, while I was promoting Monte Carlo, Gustaf was as starry-eyed as a girl on her first date when I invited him to lunch with Suzanne Lenglen and Henri Cochet, the French tennis stars. They were delayed for an hour by a flat tire on the drive from Nice and I wanted to go ahead with lunch, but Gustaf wouldn't hear of it.

"There are fifty kings and emperors," he said, "but there is only one Lenglen and one Cochet. I can wait. They are the aristocrats and I am the commoner today."

The most impressive figure of royalty of her generation was, unquestionably, the late Queen Mary of England. Nothing, not even a 200-pound weight falling on her, could make a dent in Queen Mary's monumental composure. I should know; I was that weight. In 1922, Queen Mary and Queen Victoria of Spain attended a musicale for charity in Mrs. Benjamin Guiness's home in London. I was asked to accompany Lauritz Melchior and was told to curtsy deeply to the queens before and after the selection.

I was much heavier then than I am now and I got by on the first obeisance with only a few tremors. But in making the second curtsy I lost my balance and fell with a frightful crash on, not at, Queen Mary's feet. I wanted to crawl into the woodwork and die of embarrassment, but Queen Mary saved me from utter mortification by helping me rise as though the accident was an everyday occurrence. Then she broke the ghastly silence and covered up my retreat by complimenting Melchior on his singing until I fled from the room.

There have been queens who generated more personal warmth, but none surpassed Mary in the quality that is the only justification for the existence of royalty. She had a tremendous sense of *noblesse oblige,* an awareness of the responsibilities and obligations she owed England and its people. That attribute was clearly revealed in the two situations bearing directly on the line of succession to the throne after the death of George V. Each time Mary refused to allow her emotions to subvert her austere attitude toward duty.

During the crisis leading to the abdication of Edward VIII, Mary had to make an agonizing choice between love for her favorite son and devotion to the dignity of the crown. Every natural impulse prompted her to intercede with Prime Minister Stanley Baldwin and the Archbishop of Canterbury on Edward's behalf. By remaining in the background and refraining from using her influence, Mary gave tacit approval to the inner council's demand that Edward relinquish the throne.

Mary also opposed the last royal wedding she lived to see, the marriage in 1947 of Princess Elizabeth, then the Heiress Presumptive, to Prince Philip of Greece. Again she subordinated her family loyalty to the will of the people. She realized that the handsome, virile Philip, a welcome relief from the effete nincompoops cluttering up the *Almanach de Gotha* and *Burke's Peerage,* was extremely popular with the British public. In fairness to Philip, he has proved to be a devoted husband to Elizabeth II and a conscientious consort. Mary had nothing against him personally. She disapproved of Philip because he was a Battenberg and, above all, the nephew of Earl Mountbatten of Burma. It was as though Mary had overheard a bold prediction Mountbatten made to me before Elizabeth was born.

In 1924 I visited Mountbatten and his wife, Edwina, at Brook House, their home in London. The walls of Mountbatten's study were decorated with an unusual panorama showing the navies of the world dispersed in battle formation. In commenting on the mural, I made a reference to the illustrious naval tradition of the Mountbatten family. I could have bitten my tongue out a moment later. Unwittingly, I had touched a sore spot that has been rankling Mountbatten for forty years.

At the outbreak of World War I, Mountbatten's father, Prince Louis of Battenberg, was first sea lord of the Admiralty, the top post in the British Navy. Prince Louis immediately changed his family name from Battenberg to Mountbatten, the Anglicized equivalent. (The British royal family, officially the House of Saxe-Coburg, did not adopt the name of Windsor until 1917.) There was absolutely no reason to doubt Prince Louis's loyalty to England, but Tory aristocrats forced him to resign because of his German descent. A decade later, Mountbatten openly expressed to me, a comparative stranger, his bitter resentment of the treatment his father had been given.

"I'll make them pay some day for what they did to my father," he said. "Someday a member of my family will be on the throne or close to it."

It took Mountbatten nearly a quarter of a century to make

good on his prediction, but he is a tough-minded, persevering man. He supervised the education of Philip, the son of his sister, Alice of Battenberg, and of Prince Andrew of Greece, to groom his nephew for the role. He sponsored Philip in the smart, young Mayfair set. It was an open secret that he engineered the romance between Philip and Princess Elizabeth. Throughout his flanking movement on the throne, Mountbatten served England with a distinction few men can equal. He organized the Commandos early in World War II, then became the British counterpart of General Douglas MacArthur as the Supreme Allied Commander for Southeast Asia. After the war, he was Viceroy and Governor General of India. As this is written, he is commander in chief of the NATO Mediterranean fleet.

Despite his brilliant record, Mountbatten and his wife, a magnetic couple, have not been accepted socially by the palace guard. Both have been victims of racial discrimination, Mountbatten for his German blood, Edwina for her Jewish ancestry. Her grandfather was Sir Ernest Cassel, a wealthy banker who bailed Edward VII out of gambling jams and made China, Egypt and the Argentine outposts of Britain's financial empire. Something more than stupid prejudice, however, is behind antagonism to the Mountbattens.

Old-line aristocrats distrust Mountbatten's liberal political views and the influence he may exert on Philip. Philip recently was designated by law to supersede Princess Margaret as regent in the event Queen Elizabeth dies before Prince Charles, the heir apparent, reaches the age of eighteen. Philip or his son will be the next sovereign of England — and both are Battenbergs.

The course of history has been accelerated in this age of

jet propulsion. The House of Battenberg's original title lapsed in 1314 and was not restored until 1851 by the Grand Duke of Hesse. In little more than a century, the Battenbergs have risen from the obscurity of a tiny duchy to the portal of the world's loftiest throne.

Chapter 12

THE upheaval that swept a half-dozen monarchs under the rug after World War I coincided with the emergence of a new species of royalty — the nobles of Hollywood. The movie colony's weather was better, its favorites were prettier and its panjandrums were surrounded by larger retinues of sycophants. Otherwise, there was little difference between the social atmosphere of Hollywood and a European court. The people and the protocol were as rigid in both spheres.

I first went to Hollywood in the spring of 1932, through the customary combination of crazy circumstances that seemed to be the only entree to the movie capital in those days. A few months earlier, after I returned from Europe, David O. Selznick had come to me with a proposition to edit a new magazine for the carriage trade he was planning to publish. Everything went along famously until someone with the semblance of a brain in his head threw a monkey wrench into the works. The carriage trade, he reminded us, was eating its horses to keep body and soul together. He further observed that mental institutions were crowded with inmates who had been committed for lesser aberrations than launching a magazine for the elite during a depression.

While we were giving the project a hasty burial, Selznick

asked me what I intended to do next. I said I was thinking of going to California to see my mother, then stopping off in Hollywood to look for some sort of work to pay for my return fare to New York.

"Don't go to Hollywood unless you have a definite job lined up," Selznick said. "That's my old stamping ground" (his father, Lewis Selznick, was a pioneer in the movie industry) "and I know the runaround you'll get if you go out there cold. You won't get past the front gate of a studio. Wait a minute. Didn't you tell me you could get Somerset Maugham to write for the magazine?"

"Sure. Willie Maugham and I are old friends," I said. "I've known him for twenty years."

"Are you familiar with Maugham's early writing?"

"I've read every line he's ever written."

"You're just the gal I'm looking for," Selznick said. "The next picture I'm producing is *Our Betters*, a play by Maugham set in the prewar period. How would you like to be the consultant on the clothes and the general tone of the picture? I'll give you a thousand a week."

The sum of one thousand dollars a week was approximately ten times more than anyone in his right mind ever had paid me. I accepted Selznick's offer before he could be seized by a spasm of sanity.

My first night in Hollywood was splendid conditioning for the squirrel cage. Dorothy di Frasso had arranged for me to stay with Gary Cooper in the house he rented from Greta Garbo. Cooper was away on location when I arrived, but twenty minutes later he had visitors. As I was unpacking in a bedroom over the driveway, there was a sudden outbreak of frightful, bloodcurdling screaming and howling, as though all the demons in Southern California had their tails caught in wringers. I looked out of the window and saw a sight that would have raised the hackles of a gargoyle. There were about twenty mature women in the driveway yowling like lovesick cats. Some were making horrible mewing noises and clawing frantically at the walls of the house.

"What in the world is going on?" I asked the housekeeper.

"Oh, they're just Mr. Cooper's fans," she said. "They think he's home because they saw the lights go on in the bedroom. You get used to them after a while."

"Can't you call the police to drive them away?"

"They always come back as soon as the cops leave," the housekeeper said glumly.

"How about throwing old shoes or something at them?"

"There will be a hundred dopey women out there if you do that. They'll think Mr. Cooper is giving them personal souvenirs."

"What about dousing them with water?"

"That won't do any good, either. They hang around all night during the rainy season."

The next morning I was initiated into another strange rite of Never-Never Land — the story conference. I had heard how the plots of novels and plays were distorted beyond all recognition in movie adaptations, but I never really believed it until I sat in on a brain-washing session. Selznick's synopsis of the scenario for *Our Betters* began auspiciously. He identified the characters correctly. Thereafter, his outline of the movie treatment bore as much resemblance to Maugham's play as did *Abie's Irish Rose.*

Maugham's original version was a biter exposé of the rich American expatriates and the vicious British snobs who dominated society in prewar London. It was common gossip that the leading character, Lady Grayston, was a true-to-life portrait of Lady Emerald Cunard, my old enemy. The movie conflicted with the mood and the motivation of the play at every essential point. The scathing attack on the reactionary British aristocracy was diluted into a sophisticated comedy of manners. The role of Lady Grayston, played on the screen by Constance Bennett, was reversed so completely that it was a portrayal of the noblest female since Florence Nightingale. In the play, Lady Grayston, who was having an affair with a gigolo, callously sacrificed her young sister to protect her own reputation. In the movie, the sister set up light housekeeping with the gigolo and Lady Grayston tried to save her from scandal by appearing to be involved with the bounder. Through a contrivance too improbable to recount, Lady Grayston retained her virtue and Lord Grayston reaffirmed his everlasting love for her in an ending that was happy only because it finally brought down the curtain on the dreary rigamarole.

Selznick finished his recital and leaned back overcome by the stark dramatic impact of the fadeout. His covey of yes men nodded solemnly, lost in admiration of the boss's genius. George Cukor, the director of the picture, had the baffled look of a man who has missed the punch line of a joke.

"What do you think?" Selznick asked.

"I think I'm going to be sick," I said. The yes men blanched. "It's nauseating what you've done to the play. Why did you pay a lot of money for the screen rights if you intended to cut out the heart and guts of Maugham's idea?"

"You can't have a big star like Connie Bennett play the part of a bitch," Selznick said patiently. "You've got to make her sympathetic. Lady Grayston must be a living doll and her kid sister has got to take the rap."

"Why don't you keep the original script and let Bennett play the sister?"

Selznick smiled at me indulgently. "The part isn't big enough for Bennett. You don't understand the mass market."

They say no one ever went broke in Hollywood underestimating the intelligence of the public, but Selznick blazed a new trail with *Our Betters*. The imposing egg the picture laid taught him a lesson that eventually was worth a fortune to him. He quit tinkering with plots and made several outstanding adaptations of good novels, notably *Rebecca* and *Gone With the Wind*, the biggest money-maker in the history of the movies.

There were many things in Hollywood I didn't understand, including the one province in which I was qualified as an expert — the social life. I had gone there expecting to see parties that reflected the stock-in-trade of the movies — glamour. Instead, I found the same attitude toward parties that European peasants had for baths. It was something to be done methodically every Saturday night, the only time during the week anyone entertained at home.

A valid reason limited the Hollywood hierarchy's social engagements to that one night. The business of making faces at a camera is hard, exhausting work, and production schedules were so heavy in the pretelevision era that performers, executives and technicians had to be at the studios early every morning except Sunday. But there was no earthly excuse for the stultifying routine that made one party indistinguishable from every other mob scene.

The same people usually turned up at every dinner party — all four hundred of them. I am not exaggerating the number or using it as a symbol of the elite. There were approximately four hundred people — counting married couples and free lances of both sexes playing the field — jockeying for top billing in the industry and they appeared on every guest list as a matter of protocol and self-preservation. One never knew who would be in a position to crack the whip the day after tomorrow. To avoid conflicts on the one night all the current and potential bigwigs were available, hostesses tacitly respected claims to dates staked out months in advance and waited in line to feed and water the herd. As a result, there was only one place to go on any given Saturday night and everyone went there like so many prisoners released on a twenty-four-hour parole.

There was nothing different or spontaneous from one party to the next. In my time, I had attended parties where enough liquor was lapped up to float the Eiffel Tower, but the drinking in Hollywood far exceeded anything I ever had seen. People didn't get mellow or pleasantly tight. They started out with the fixed intention of drinking themselves into stupors, and the compulsion that drove them to the bar was obvious. It was to escape from the cultural vacuum in which they existed.

A recent arrival from Outer Space who attempted to discuss politics, the arts, personalities in the news or business unrelated to the movies wound up talking to himself. No effort was made to cultivate the eminent writers and musicians — men of the caliber of Heifetz, Rubinstein, and Stravinsky — who were next-door neighbors. Getting a series of images on strips of film was a single-tracked obsession that blotted out all other mental activity.

Sex was the other common escape from boredom in Hollywood. Again, I had seen dissolute behavior among Europe's decadent aristocracy, but the movie colony's utter lack of inhibitions revolted me. Actors who were instantly recognizable on every street in America openly picked up waitresses and young girls. The women had no more discrimination than the men. They took lovers for diversion as casually as they played bridge or golf. Stars who were paid fabulous salaries for the allure they projected from the screen didn't even have the sense or the self-respect to maintain a pretense of respectability. They publicly paraded lovers like exhibits at a livestock show.

Please remember I am referring now to conditions I saw on my first trip to Hollywood in 1932, conditions which no longer prevail. I also want to make it clear that there were many people in the movie industry whose moral standards were above reproach. One more amendment must be made. I said Hollywood was a cultural vacuum in the early thirties. Just as there is no perfect vacuum in nature, there could be no cultural vacuum in a community that included Charlie Chaplin.

Chaplin has been discredited, deservedly, for parroting Communist propaganda, and by the sordid aspects of his private life, but it must be conceded that he is the one true genius developed by the movies. His home was Hollywood's only salon in the European tradition, and he was the most brilliant, stimulating host I ever have known. He entertained all the intellectuals and artists who visited Hollywood, but Chaplin himself was the prime attraction. He could hold a group fascinated for hours with his extemporaneous flights of imagination.

The first time I saw Chaplin, he gave an unforgettable one-man show at Biarritz in 1928. Jean Patou had hired a fleet of motorboats to take a party of guests to a bullfight at Bayonne, but the excursion was canceled by a violent hurricane that blew up suddenly. The storm knocked out the electric lights and several women showed signs of panic as the wind and the rain mounted in fury. Patou's house was on the water and everyone was wondering apprehensively whether it was safe to remain, until Chaplin took charge of the situation.

"It's nonsense to sit around like this," Chaplin said to me. "Let's amuse ourselves. Play something from *Carmen* and I'll take it from there."

With absolutely no preparation, Chaplin proceeded to give an enthralling pantomime of a bullfight in the flickering candlelight. He impersonated, in turn, a frenzied spectator, the bull, a picador, a gored horse, and the matador. Each characterization was so perfect and the continuity had such dramatic purity that there was a collective gasp when he made the matador's final thrust at the bull. With a subtle shrug, Chaplin abruptly changed the mood and improvised a tragic triangle in which a husband murdered his wife and her lover, then committed suicide. Chaplin's artistry held us spellbound for three hours, by the watch. It was not until he finished that we realized the hurricane had long since subsided.

No one could compete with Chaplin as a host, so I did the next best thing. I gave parties with all-star casts providing impromptu entertainment. I thought it was absurd that the abundant talent in Hollywood was going to waste at moribund social affairs that needed shots of adrenalin and I decided to show the movie stars how to enjoy themselves. All theatrical people are extroverts; their craving for attention impels them to choose acting as a career in the first place. They are happiest when they are "on," holding the center of the stage, but until I came along no one ever had asked the stars to perform at private gatherings.

My innovation, which hardly was a stroke of inspiration, was introduced soon after I got my first pay check from Selznick. I moved out of Gary Cooper's home and rented a small house on Schuyler Road in Beverly Hills. Fanny Brice, who had a passion for decorating houses, helped me to fix up the place and I invited about twenty people to drop in on a weekday night.

Noel Coward, who knew how I ran parties, was in Hollywood and didn't have to be coaxed to light the first firecracker under the gathering. He, too, was ready to blow his top for want of social stimulation. People were sitting around and, as usual, talking of box-office receipts in Omaha and who had run off to Mexico with whom for the week end. Noel casually strolled to the piano and sang a song he had just composed. My guests stared at him in embarrassment, as though he had committed a frightful faux pas.

Marlene Dietrich, another European refugee homesick for *Gemütlichkeit*, immediately caught on to what Noel and I were trying to do and she sang the number she had introduced in *The Blue Angel*. That broke the ice; before Marlene was finished, the others were clamoring for a chance to contribute to the fun. Douglas Fairbanks, Jr., did a satirical take-off on Hitler. Reginald Gardner did his night-club act. Fanny Brice revived one of her old comedy turns from the *Ziegfeld Follies*, and an unknown girl named Mary Martin sang a little tune. I can't remember the entire program, but I do know that everyone had such a good time that the gathering didn't break up until four o'clock in the morning.

That party was the simplest one I had given since learning the technique of stalling off a Parisian concierge on rent day. The only refreshments were soft drinks and pretzels. I deliberately served no liquor, because I didn't like being gouged by bootleggers — this was during Prohibition — and, more pertinently, I wanted to prove to the movie crowd that it was more fun staying sober than getting blind drunk.

My twenty guests spread such enthusiastic reports of the party through the grapevine that I was bombarded with requests to stage similar affairs for other hostesses. I tried to tell them the only trick in giving good parties was to invite interesting people, but they wouldn't believe it until they saw the formula work in their own homes. It always did, of course, with a slight change in ground rules. I made the piano, not the bar, the center of activity. Through the years, I've given or staged for friends more than a hundred parties in Hollywood, and only once did excessive drinking lead to an untoward incident. The occasion was a costume ball I put on for Dorothy di Frasso in 1938.

A few months earlier, I had used an ingenious gimmick for a formal dance at the Waldorf-Astoria Hotel in New York. It was a prosaic affair until one o'clock in the morning, when I pulled my surprise. The men and women were told to separate and go behind screens set up on opposite sides of the Starlight Roof. They were flabbergasted to find a staff of dressers waiting to help them change into fancy eighteenth-century paper costumes made especially for me by the Butterick Pattern Company. I also had paper accessories to carry out the Louis XIV motif — white wigs, lorgnettes for the women and swords for the men. It sounds very elaborate, but the outfits cost only a dollar apiece. While the guests were putting on the costumes, the décor of the ballroom was changed by moving in artificial trees and shrubbery to simulate the formal gardens at Versailles. The big idea, of course, was to have a brand new party after the transformation, and it was such a huge success that Dorothy di Frasso asked me to bring the costumes to Hollywood for a clambake she was giving.

Dorothy's party was proceeding in orderly fashion until a predictable complication popped up. A well-known actress reached her alcoholic saturation point, whereupon she sat down in the middle of the dance floor and screamed at the top of her well-developed lungs. Her escort was prepared for the inevitable emergency and put a knockout pill in a glass of champagne. She had had a lot of experience spotting Mickey Finns, and the butler was told to maneuver a tray full of drinks so that she would take the one meant for her. The butler, a tactful and resourceful fellow, said he understood perfectly, as indeed he did. The actress had been a guest in Dorothy's home before.

While the butler was threading across the crowded dance floor, he passed Leslie Howard and Merle Oberon, who were madly infatuated with each other. Howard, caught up in the ineffable rapture of the moment, grabbed the glass intended for the victim and drained it before the horrified butler could stop him. The actress had built up such an immunity to Mickeys that the dose required to put her out was strong enough to subdue a horse. It had an instantaneous effect on Howard. He collapsed to the floor in sections with the glass at his lips. He was carried to an upstairs bedroom and another potion was whipped up for the actress. That one was delivered safely and she was deposited in the room next to Howard.

"The joint looks like a funeral parlor with those two stiffs laid out," la Comtessa di Frasso thoughtfully observed. "Anybody else who feels like getting loaded better make arrangements now to have the body taken to the next of kin."

The year 1938 was a memorable milestone in Hollywood history. It was proved conclusively that the motion picture had gained sufficient stature as an art form to survive what could have been an irreparable setback. I became a movie actress at the age of fifty-five. I compounded the felony by getting under false pretenses the sum of $80,000 for making two full-length features and three shorts.

The five epics were advertised as comedies, but the biggest laugh was how my movie career was launched. I was staying with Constance Bennett after finishing a lecture tour when the Duchess of Westminster arrived in Los Angeles to attend the unveiling of Gainsborough's famous painting "The Blue Boy," which her husband had just sold to the Huntington Museum. The duchess was about to be divorced from the duke, but she had such a strong sentimental attachment for the painting that she wanted to see it installed in the museum. I was the only one in town the duchess knew and since I had no facilities for entertaining her myself, I asked Connie to invite her to stay with us. Connie was glad to put her up and gave a party to welcome the duchess.

Among the guests were the Darryl Zanucks, whom I never

had met. I was making the usual chit-chat with Zanuck, whom I thought the most dynamic man I had met in Hollywood. Out of nowhere, Zanuck said: "You have a warm personality that will project well on the screen. How about making a picture for me?"

"Who in heaven's name wants to see me make a spectacle of myself?" I scoffed. "I'll clear a theater faster than a fire alarm."

"I'm utterly serious about it," Zanuck said. "I'll give you twenty-five thousand dollars to help with a script and appear in the picture."

"For that kind of money I can be as serious as a Supreme Court judge," I answered. "When do we start?"

Much to my astonishment, the first feature, *Elsa Maxwell's Hotel for Women,* wasn't too bad, although it was chiefly distinguished for introducing Linda Darnell and Ann Sothern. My next vehicle, *Public Deb Number One,* proved the soundness of the old gambling dictum, "Quit when you're ahead." It was a real flop and the only sop to my aesthetic sensitivity is that I did not work on the script. It was a moot question whether anyone did. I think it was put together from scraps dug out of a wastebasket. The story began as a travesty on social climbers and, in some inexplicable manner, ended with a scene showing a dog raising its leg on a copy of Karl Marx's *Das Kapital.* The only significance to be drawn from that bit of symbolism was that the dog had more critical judgment than anyone associated with the picture.

My best movie opus — relatively speaking, of course — was the first of three shorts I made for Jack Warner at $10,000 apiece. It was a satire on my week end in the British hunting

set thirty years before, and was very successful at the box
office. Then I did a two-reeler with Maxie Rosenbloom in
which I played an old maid who inherited a prize fighter, an
idea that was funnier on paper than it came up on film. The
last short was so awful that I cannot — or refuse to — remember it. A clear-cut case of protective amnesia.

I never thought I'd see the day that making $80,000 would
be a bore, but I hated the monotonous "Cut! Take! Cut!
Take!" routine of shooting movies. I imagined my inept acting was the cause of the constant retakes, until I was assured
it was standard operating procedure to slog through the grind
eight hours a day to get two minutes of actual playing time on
the screen. All newcomers are staggered by the money and the
painstaking craftsmanship expended on the technical quality
of pictures. Even the little gems of nonsense I helped to per-
petrate had the slick polish that is Hollywood's hallmark.

My second visit to Hollywood was an eye opener in another
respect. Although only five years had elapsed since my previous
visit, there were striking evidences of more mature attitudes at
every turn. Drinking had been curbed drastically and studios
were cracking down on stars whose immorality and irresponsible escapades brought damaging publicity to the industry.
The marked improvement in the moral climate was only one
indication of the new trend. "Message" and "problem" pictures invariably are commercial failures, but the major studios
were disregarding the box office with increasing frequency in
an effort to raise the cultural level of the medium. The standard of living, formerly pegged to vulgar extravagance, no longer
was flagrantly out of line with any other group in the same income bracket. Hollywood was growing up, with a few excep-

tions, and one of the most conspicuous of them was the movies' most glamorous star of all time — Greta Garbo.

Garbo has been called an enigma, but the wall she has built around herself has been transparent to me for a long time. It's not that I know her especially well; no one does. I just happened to see, purely by accident, her secret frustration nakedly revealed.

Garbo's shyness is not a pose. She genuinely wants to be alone in a dream world that is a refuge from one reality every living soul must accept. Garbo is haunted by the fear of growing old. Like a child, she associates age with ugliness, and the dread of losing her beauty has warped her entire personality.

Anyone who has a nodding acquaintance with Garbo can relate an experience similar to mine when I ran into her at Maxim's in Paris in the spring of 1951. She looked like the caricature second-rate comediennes have been portraying for two decades. She was wearing a loose polo coat and a shapeless slouch hat and her divine face was disfigured by an expression of stark despair. Garbo is so introverted that it is impossible to carry on a conversation with her beyond the trite amenities, so I asked her whether she was glad to be back in Europe.

"What is happiness?" she said hollowly. "I never have known it."

"There is no excellent beauty that hath not some strangeness in the proportion," Sir Francis Bacon wrote. Garbo, the most radiant actress in the movies, retired in 1941 because she thought her beauty had faded. I realize this is an extreme statement in view of the fact that Garbo is not regarded as a vain woman.

On the contrary, her appearance is drab to the point of

eccentricity. Some women try to turn back the clock by dyeing their hair or reverting to giddy mannerisms. Garbo's austere clothes and personal life can be interpreted, I believe, as telltales of her desire to perpetuate an illusion.

Garbo seldom wears in public the smart clothes designed for her by Valentina, one of New York's top couturiers. She affects unbecoming, severely tailored suits and dresses to prove — as she did in her heyday — that she can look more luminous in a gunny sack than current belles bedecked in sables.

Although she has not had any problem with her weight since her first Hollywood picture, Garbo has been a fanatic on dieting for a quarter of a century. Why? When she arrived from Sweden in the mid-1920's, she was considered too heavy for the American audience and was ordered to reduce. The flat, angular figure then in vogue (the "boyish" look) was modified long ago by the trend toward rounder, more natural contours. But Garbo continues to diet rigorously to demonstrate that her magnetism transcends sensual attraction.

Garbo clings for security to older people who remember her as she was. Most of the men in her life are hand-kissing opportunists who have been using her for years to promote their own schemes. I'm sure she is aware of it but, like Barbara Hutton, she wants men to be dependent on her. Barbara dominates them with money, Garbo with the memory of her legendary beauty and reputation. It is significant that her few friends date back to her early career. Even when she was younger, the only social invitations she accepted were from people such as Cole Porter, Clifton Webb and George Cukor, who knew her in Europe.

Everyone realizes now that Garbo never will make another

picture. I predicted it in my newspaper column in 1941, before her last film, *Two-Faced Woman,* was released. The source of my information was Garbo herself, although she did not speak a word of her intention to retire. She didn't have to tell me. She divulged, unwittingly, her secret at a small party the Cole Porters gave for Clark Gable and Carole Lombard, who had recently been married. Garbo was uncommunicative, as usual, and no one noticed that she slipped out of the room after dinner. I went to the powder room, opened the door and stood there transfixed with embarrassment.

Garbo was staring so intently in the mirror that she did not hear me enter. I have no idea how long she had been studying her reflection, but she shuddered suddenly and buried her head in her arms. Only she could have found a flaw in that exquisite face. Only a woman with a morbid fear of aging could have failed to see that time would enhance the beauty of her classic features and magnificent bone structure. Garbo was thirty-five, and all she could see were middle-aged roles in her future. Then, as now, she would not mature gracefully — and she never will.

Since 1939, I have been returning annually to Hollywood for extended visits of a nonprofessional nature. I hasten to add I have not made a dime directly from the movies since tarnishing the reputations of Messrs. Zanuck and Warner as shrewd showmen. What with television and rising production costs, the movies have enough trouble without me casting a blight on the box office. Other business takes me to Hollywood. It is an important stop on my newspaper beat for reporting the activities of celebrities, artists and prominent socialites.

That's right. I said socialites, and Hollywood is one of the few remaining places in the United States where they are worthy of attention. What is known, for want of a better term, as High Society is moribund in America today. It is decayed and decadent. It has reneged on the obligations owed by people with money, leisure and position. Society, with a capital S, has two responsibilities: (1) To support cultural programs; (2) To take the initiative in sponsoring attitudes and projects that contribute to the general welfare. Society is infested with dry rot in America and Europe because it has forfeited leadership in the second function, which is the chief excuse for its continued existence.

Any social or economic class must participate vigorously in the main stream of life to survive. Few Americans of great wealth have the courage to stand out as individuals. The great majority huddle together in frightened groups feeding like parasites on inherited money,

The Bible of the bluebloods is the Social Register, a stud book of mediocrities. There are not a dozen women in it of the caliber of Mrs. O. H. P. Belmont and Mrs. Harry Payne Whitney, the most distinguished sculptress of her time.

For each philanthropic Rockefeller, there are fifty enormously rich families that have no more social consciousness than chipmunks. I know the old argument; the countless millions the Rockefellers have given away are a manifestation of the guilt complex that is their legacy from old John D. At least, the Rockefellers have a conscience. That is more than can be said for a motley assortment of insipid nonentities my lawyer will not permit me to enumerate. Unfortunately, the truth is not an iron-clad defense in libel actions.

I have seen at close range three generations of American and

European society and each one has deteriorated successively. Yes, I'm past seventy and crotchety old fogeys always deplore the decline of manners and morals, but there is daily evidence of it in the newspapers.

Once upon a time, the staples of society news in America were weddings and charity affairs. Today, society's springboards to the headlines are divorces, scandals and drunken brawls. The complete abandonment of dignity by youngsters who have had the alleged advantages of good breeding is disgusting. The girls who pass out in gaudy saloons are sick mentally and spiritually. Years ago, John D. Rockefeller engaged Ivy Lee, a public-relations consultant, to keep references to his family out of the newspapers. Now, debutants lend themselves to cheap publicity stunts concocted by press agents who are hired to get their names in gossip columns. High-powered attorneys are retained to keep heirs to fortunes out of jail on charges ranging from disorderly conduct to pandering — and the efforts are not always successful.

These youngsters are the second generation of Café Society, an expression coined some twenty years ago by the late Maury Paul, a veteran society reporter. It was a necessary invention to define the changing scope of his work. Paul and others assigned to the same beat would have been out of jobs had they continued to rely on functions in private homes as sources of news. The art of gracious entertaining was obsolescent among hostesses too lazy to plan parties and hosts too apathetic to provide any stimulation that did not come in bottles. It was much easier to invite guests to saloons thinly disguised as night clubs and let former bootleggers, the new arbiters of so-called Café Society, take care of the bothersome details.

It would be pointless to mention that few socially prominent people entertain at home nowadays if it were not symptomatic of something more basic — the distintegration of those homes. There is a strong sense of family unity among the lower and middle classes in the United States, and thank God for it. That feeling has been destroyed among the rich by divorces and neglectful treatment of children.

Primitive tribes stone parents who fail to instruct their children in the mores and taboos of the group. In our civilization, wealthy parents suffer no punishment for abandoning their off-spring to the haphazard guidance of servants, boarding-school teachers, psychiatrists and, eventually, courts established to preserve ethical codes. You know how impressionable kids are. They see their parents exchange bedmates as casually as partners are switched in a square dance. They see excessive drinking and self-indulgence and they follow the pattern. Each repetition compounds the damage to the structure of the family.

The one admirable aspect of European society today is its strong feeling for family ties. Homes rarely are disrupted by divorce, a circumstance that can be attributed in part only to the fact that the continental aristocracy is predominantly Catholic. The divorce rate among Protestants and Jews of social standing in Europe is far below the figure for those groups in America. Religious or moral scruples have nothing to do with the case. It's an old, and true, story that infidelity is more prevalent abroad than it is in this country. The majority of men in upper European circles keep mistresses, and I'd hate to make an estimate of the women who have had extramarital affairs. Marriage vows may be broken, but homes are kept intact for the sake of the children involved. I once thought it was the height of hypocrisy when a father interrupted a holiday with his mistress and returned home to celebrate a child's birthday. I since have learned to regard it as a sincere effort to retain identity with the family.

Amorality, not immorality, has undermined European society. A shameful percentage of the nobility collaborated actively with the Germans during the war, especially in France and Italy. Europe has been keeping the world in a turmoil for centuries with its saber-rattling and bleating of national honor. But when wealthy aristocrats were confronted with a choice between integrity and treachery, entirely too many took the easy way out to save their miserable skins.

England was the only country that was not disgraced by its upper class. It is possible that England would have been contaminated with collaborationists had it been occupied by the Nazis, but I doubt it. The British are the hungriest, most luxury-starved people in Western Europe, yet not one showed up at the elaborate ball given in Paris in the spring of 1953 by Oswald Mosley, the former leader of the Fascistic Black Shirts. The place was crawling with termites of all nationalities, but Mosley's countrymen had not forgiven his defection.

A cynical, what's-in-it-for-me? attitude permeates the upper crust on the continent today. Anyone with enough money to furnish free food and liquor for all comers can be a social lion overnight in Paris, Rome and on the Riviera. It makes no difference whether the money is polluted by the stench of the Nazis. Bearers of once-proud names lead the parade of collaborationists, grifters, graduated streetwalkers and black marketeers attracted to it like vultures flocking to carrion.

In 1953 I made the mistake of going to a large dinner party given in Cannes by an American acquaintance who had handed out invitations indiscriminately all over the Riviera. Among the guests were a wealthy French industrialist and his wife, who had been an official hostess to Nazi generals and diplomats during the occupation. Another repulsive creature was a bleached blonde whose head had been shaved after the liberation for making her bedroom an annex of the German army barracks. I felt obliged to apologize to Odette Massigli, the wife of the French Ambassador in London, for our American hostess's unintentional blunder in exposing them to such corrupt company. A Frenchman whose own war record was unimpeachable overheard me.

"Why do you insist in keeping alive a dead issue?" he said impatiently. "We've forgotten the war and the split among ourselves. Why don't you?"

"I'm a foreigner and maybe it's none of my business, but I can't forget it," I answered.

"You don't speak for all of us," Odette told the man. "I feel cleaner for holding myself aloof from the swine."

To avoid a scene, Odette and I left the party. We never were missed. I imagine everyone felt more comfortable after we had gone.

Much as I dislike to mention the indelicate subject, I cannot gloss over the shocking increase in homosexuality as further evidence of decadence in the top levels of American and European society. Thirty years ago, Lesbians and sash boys — a euphemism for commoner terms I prefer not to use — were almost unknown in America. There were homosexuals in theatrical and artistic circles, of course, and guarded references were made to effeminate men in certain fields such as interior decoration and fashion designing. But the average American rarely, if ever, encountered a sexually maladjusted person. Perhaps I was näive, but I never saw a woman who was an obvious Lesbian until I went to Europe.

The incidence of homosexuality always has been higher in Europe, especially of sash boys in England. It can be attributed in some measure to the general custom of sending upper-class British boys to boarding schools at an early age and keeping them confined in an unnatural environment during adolescence. The chief contributing factor, I'm convinced though, is sheer boredom, the by-product of too much money and indolent leisure. Only those who have earned leisure know how to use it profitably. I have seen scores of thoroughly normal men and women turn to perversion in their forties, and even their fifties, simply because they were jaded and searching for new thrills. That sort of eroticism is not unusual in Europe, where fortunes have been passed on over long periods, and it is cropping up in the third and fourth generations of wealthy American families.

Rich women of my generation also are carriers of the germ of homosexuality, even though they never have practiced it themselves. As they grow older and lose their attractiveness, they seek "safe" young men to dance attendance on them and flatter their vanity. Sash boys, with their feminine sensitivity and graceful manners, make agreeable companions, in sharp contrast to Lesbians, who are coarsened and rendered awkward by the affectation of masculinity. Older women, trying to fill their empty lives by coddling sash boys, are partially responsible for the effete, lavender tone of society today.

In 1889, Ward McAllister, a stuffy New York socialite, said only four hundred people had the necessary qualifications for admittance to his exclusive set. In 1889, too, Nellie Bly, an American newspaperwoman, circumnavigated the earth in seventy-two days, a new record. The world has shrunk considerably since that time. The globe can be circled in a little more than seventy-two hours. And the Four Hundred is an archaic figure of speech in New York and any other social center. It is a fairly accurate census of the combined elite on the face of the earth.

Chapter 13

"THE lights are going out over Europe," Sir Edward Grey, the British Foreign Minister, said on the eve of World War I. Twenty-five years later, I literally saw the lights go out again. The most dreadful calamity that could have happened to humanity nullified the most wonderful thing that ever happened to me. The night another war darkened Europe, I was entertaining 200 dinner guests in a house given to me in perpetuity by Eleanor Loder, the wife of Major Eric Loder, one of my oldest friends. I have not occupied the house, or even seen it, since September 1, 1939. It is associated with too many poignant memories I would like to forget.

I had returned to the Riviera that summer loaded with my Hollywood loot, able to afford luxury for the first, and last, time in my life. I brought two cars and a chauffeur from America, and gave lavish parties all over the Côte d'Azur. My extravagance alarmed the Loders, who remembered when a thousand francs made me feel like a plutocrat.

Eric and I have been friends since 1912, when he was the handsomest Rolls-Royce salesman in London and I was the plumpest song writer. There are certain compensations for overweight women. Men do not suspect them and other women do not fear them as competition. Some wives resent their husbands' former friends, but I saw more of Eric after he married Eleanor, the widow of Sir Mortimer Davis, a fabulously wealthy Canadian. In fact, Eleanor Loder has been my one real friend, with the exceptions of Millicent Hearst and Dickie Gordon, for a quarter century. I don't know how it is with other single women, but my married friends worry about me incessantly. Eleanor had been harping on my extravagance all summer and one day she gave me another lecture during lunch at her estate, Les Glieula, in the hills above Cannes.

"Invest some of your money in a house before you squander it all," Eleanor said. (She is a financial genius and reads the *Wall Street Journal* as if it were authored by Mickey Spillane.) "If you don't, you'll be at loose ends again after this silly spending spree. You're as irresponsible as a child."

"You ought to know by this time how I feel about owning things," I replied. "I don't want to be burdened with property. I like being free as a bird."

"I thought that would be your answer, so I'm going to force you to act sensibly and put your money into something worthwhile," Eleanor said. "There's a nice little place on the estate about a half mile from here that hasn't been lived in for years. I'm giving it to you for life. It's in perfect condition but you'll have to refurnish it. The house is yours, free and clear, as long as you live. Now fix it up and have something to show for your money."

"Wait a minute," I protested. "Nobody gives away a house just like that. Besides, I don't want to be tied down and . . ."

"There's a lovely terrace overlooking the coast," Eleanor said blandly. "It's big enough to give parties for more than a hundred people."

"That's a dirty trick. You know darn well that's one temptation I can't resist. All right. The housewarming is a week from tonight."

"You're out of your mind," Eleanor cried. "The house has been vacant for at least twenty years. It will take a couple of weeks just to put it in order."

"The housewarming is a week from tonight," I repeated. "Wear your dancing shoes. There's going to be a big time at the Maxwell ménage."

It is all too easy to remember the date Eleanor gave me Lou Paradou. It was Thursday, August 24, 1939 — the day after Communist Russia and Nazi Germany signed the nonaggression treaty that left Hitler free to attack the democracies on one front without danger of retaliation by Stalin. Announcement of the unholy alliance brought the paralyzing realization that war was inevitable. But it was 1914 all over again. People tried to dissemble their fears in the trivialities of normalcy.

I was glad to be preoccupied with the house; anything was better than waiting for the time bomb to explode. I engaged a staff of eight servants and led a broom-and-bucket brigade that scoured Lou Paradou from attic to cellar. I ran myself ragged buying furniture and accessories; Eleanor's "nice little place" had five master bedrooms and three acres of ground. I invited Millicent Hearst and a half-dozen other house guests to stay with me, and they moved in with a platoon of carpenters, painters, decorators and caterers preparing for the party. The confusion helped to muffle the approaching tread of marching feet and the clamor of armor that reverberated louder and louder with every newspaper edition and radio broadcast.

On Thursday, August 31, the day of the party, the uncertainty became intolerable. I sent a telegram to my friend Paul Reynaud, the French prime minister, asking for his appraisal of the situation. Reynaud's answer was prompt and terse: "Allez vous en (get out)." Signed "Paul." I was in no mood for a silly party and I didn't believe anyone else was, so I didn't bother to call it off. In times of great emotional stress, however, people herd together for protection and morale. I had invited 200 guests and everyone showed up, producing the one incident that raised a wry laugh. When Eleanor Loder was ready to leave her house for the party, she told Eric to call the chauffeur.

"I'm afraid you'll have to walk, darling," he replied. "The road is impassable."

"That's ridiculous," Eleanor cried. "We've just spent a lot of money to have it resurfaced."

"The road is fine, but it's blocked by cars bound for Elsa's party," Eric said.

Everyone at the party was seething with conflicting rumors. My telegram from Reynaud was the most authoritative word anyone had, but it had been sent at noon and there might have been more recent developments in the crisis. I decided to call Joe Kennedy, the American Ambassador to England, for advice. Kennedy owed me a favor for an unofficial job I had done at his request the previous spring when Italy denied Arturo Toscanini a visa to return to the United States after he refused to play the Fascist anthem at a concert in Bologna. Kennedy asked me to use whatever influence I had to get the visa for Toscanini. The State Department, Kennedy explained, could not intervene because Toscanini was an Italian citizen.

I called Count Ciano in Rome and gave him a song-and-dance to the effect that good will would be created for Italy in America if Toscanini were permitted to keep his concert commitments. Maybe it was sheer coincidence, but Toscanini was granted a visa shortly after.

I put in a call to Kennedy at the American Embassy in London and, incredible as it may sound to anyone who ever has struggled with the French telephone system, the connection was made immediately. I didn't have to ask Kennedy any questions. He knew the purpose of my call.

"Where are you now?" he asked. I told him. "I would leave if I were you. All Americans should go home immediately. The news is getting grimmer by the hour."

As I hung up the receiver, someone called from the terrace: "Something strange is going on. I wonder what it means?"

We went out on the terrace, which commanded a wonderful view of the coast. To the west, a black carpet was rolling over Cannes, smothering street and house lights. Directly below, two giant hands suddenly blotted out Juan-les-Pins and Golfe Juan. To the east, the glow in the sky marking Nice, France's fifth-largest city, began to fade. Each labored breath seemed to blow out another block of lights until nothing was left to be extinguished. The Riviera was shrouded in darkness and silence.

The French government, alerted that Hitler was massing panzer divisions and planes on the Polish border, had ordered a blackout in anticipation of an air raid. Armageddon had come again.

Upon returning to the United States in September, 1939, I put frivolity, but not gaiety, behind me for the duration.

Laughter is the best therapy for despair when reason and sanity seem to have disappeared from the face of the earth. In the next six years I gave, and helped to arrange, innumerable parties and balls, but only one — to celebrate the liberation of Paris — was purely a social affair. All the others were for American, British and French war-relief organizations. Although millions of dollars were raised, I like to think I made a more valuable contribution to the war effort.

The late William Allen White, the distinguished editor of the Emporia, Kansas, *Gazette*, Herbert Bayard Swope, and I, teamed up on extensive lecture tours urging active support of the Allies long before America was drawn into the war. We stumped the country warning that America would be the next target of totalitarianism if the European democracies were permitted to fall. Hostile audiences incited by America Firsters and Communist hecklers hooted us when we argued that providing England with arms and ships was vital to our own defense. I don't know what effect we exerted on public opinion, but our mission was accomplished if we were vaguely instrumental in influencing one congressman. It was by the perilously thin margin of one vote that the Selective Service Act was extended by the House of Representatives less than four months before Pearl Harbor.

I was so vehement in pleading for all-out aid to the Allies and American participation in the war that I talked and wrote myself out of a job. In 1940, I was signed by the Hearst syndicate to write a daily column about celebrities and socialites, but as the war progressed I began to inject political opinions into the column. William Randolph Hearst sent one of his famous memos from San Simeon ordering me to lay off politics and stick to the beat I was hired to cover. I ignored the warning and continued to express views that conflicted with the policy of the Hearst papers. When Hearst told his editors to kill political columns, I quit and went over to Dorothy Schiff's New York *Post* early in 1942.

Phony pressure groups bleated shrilly about freedom of the press and tried to use me as a *cause célèbre* for attacking Hearst. I refused to have anything to do with them. Freedom of the press was not involved in my differences with Hearst. He had a perfect right to restrict and censor my copy. I had been hired for a specific job and I failed to perform the function for which I was getting paid. It was as though I insisted on chasing fire engines when I was assigned to write school news. Freedom of the press is a two-way street. It is a publisher's privilege to adopt any editorial policy he chooses and he is justified in expecting employees to conform to it as long as they accept salaries from him.

I loved the *Post* because Dorothy Schiff was as ardent as I was in rallying support for General Charle De Gaulle as the spearhead of French resistance to the Nazi conquerors. De Gaulle later disillusioned his American — and French — admirers with his obstinacy and dictatorial complex, but during the war he symbolized the patriotism and pride France needed desperately.

I spent eight enjoyable years on the *Post*, but after the death of Hearst his son, Bill, Junior, made me an offer I could not refuse. I hope to remain with the Hearst organization until I am the oldest working newspaper gal in the history of American journalism. I don't know of a more satisfying or fascinating career.

During the war, I was a headache to a second employer due to another rooted predilection — my fondness for eating regularly and plentifully. I was paid the cushy sum of $750 a week for a fifteen-minute interview with celebrities on a radio program sponsored by Ry-Krisp, a low-calorie substitute for bread. The imposing array of guest stars I was able to deliver was of incidental interest to the agency handling the account. I was selected because I could serve as a living, breathing before-and-after advertisement for the product. Some unknown genius conceived of the idea of having me weigh in before each show on a scale in full view of the studio audience. According to the script, I was to go on a diet and my subsequent loss of weight from week to week would be a glowing testimonial to Ry-Krisp. The whole thing was a first-class example of wishful thinking.

The first week I weighed in at 193 pounds. For the next seven days I ate Ry-Krisp until I crackled when I walked and I grimly stuck to a diet that for me was one step removed from starvation. Came the second show. I got on the scale, and the indicator took off like a rocket. As it shot purposefully toward the 193-pound mark, the announcer rushed in front of the scale and, running his hand across his mouth, mumbled triumphantly, "One hundred and erty-farf pounds! Splendid!" I really had eaten my meal ticket conscientiously, but the stuff agreed with me so well that I continued to gain for several weeks. Eventually, I did lose a little weight, but I'm afraid the Ry-Krisp people paid me more for each pound than the Aga Khan receives from his followers.

Washington's outstanding hostess in the 'forties was Mrs. Evelyn Walsh McLean, whose selective dinner parties were a good deal more than social affairs. Allied diplomats and staff officers needed a clubhouse where, unhampered by protocol, they could meet to compare notes and exchange off-the-record opinions. Mrs. McLean's home, "Friendship," served that important function. I think it's safe to say that more high-level policies were discussed and formulated there than any other place except 1600 Pennsylvania Avenue and 10 Downing Street. During the course of one week, I saw Mrs. McLean entertain Vice-President Truman, five cabinet members, three Supreme Court justices and thirty-eight senators. There were a dozen ambassadors and their wives at an important dinner one night with Lord Halifax (the British Ambassador) on her right and Monsieur Henri Bonnet (the French Ambassador) on her left. She placed a tiny radio in front of her empty plate (she rarely ate at dinner) and listened intently, completely ignoring her guests. Suddenly she clapped her hands for silence to announce what she had just heard — the first news of our invasion of North Africa by troops under General Mark Clark — 3000 ships and not one lost. I screamed the news to all her distinguished guests, who threw down their napkins, and the dinner became a complete riot. Mrs. McLean was delighted. She adored the unexpected and was thrilled at watching her guests dash to their various posts without even a thank you or good night.

It is a pity that Mrs. McLean was known to the public only as the owner of the Hope Diamond — a singularly ugly stone — and as a bit of an eccentric on criminology. Although she was a remarkably perceptive woman in many areas, she was a pushover for any cock-and-bull story relating to crime. She offered $100,000 reward for the return of the kidnapped

Lindbergh baby and unhesitantly gave the money to Gaston Means, a notorious confidence man, on nothing more than his say-so that he had made contact with the culprits. Mrs. McLean also went for a tidy bundle trying to solve the murder of Sir Harry Oakes in Nassau. She did not know the victim or any of the suspects; she simply was fascinated by mysteries. (Private investigators convinced Mrs. McLean that a voodoo cult murdered Oakes for seducing a native woman.)

Mrs. McLean was a tremendously vital, warmhearted woman with a great love for people. When the Bonus Army marched on Washington in 1931, she fed the veterans in a camp set up on her estate and converted Friendship House into a huge nursery to take care of their babies. She, who had received all the political celebrities worth knowing, was as twittery as a bobby-soxer at the anticipation of meeting the movie stars when I went with her to Hollywood in 1943. Mrs. McLean loved pompous, arbitrary John L. Lewis, which took a lot of doing. When Lewis secluded himself after the death of his wife, Mrs. McLean went to his home in Virginia and roused him out of his lethargy by reminding him of the responsibilities he owed to the members of his union.

After Mrs. McLean died and Mrs. Mesta was appointed Minister to Luxembourg — where, to give her her proper due, she did a first-rate job of creating good will for America — several women tried to grab the spotlight as Washington's Number One hostess. Mrs. Gwen Cafritz, the Hungarian bombshell with a wet fuse, sputtered briefly, then was put on the shelf by parties that were fiascoes, when the Republicans came in.

The jockeying and wire-pulling for the leadership of Washington society that attended the Republicans' return to power in 1952 were exercises in futility. There was only one possible heiress apparent. She was, of course, Mrs. Alice Longworth, the daughter of Theodore Roosevelt. No upstart dared to contest Mrs. Longworth's right to the honor of receiving the guests at President Eisenhower's Inaugural Ball, the distinction traditionally awarded to the capital's ranking hostess. Ever since she was married in the White House in 1906, Mrs. Longworth has been holding the fort of dignity and good taste against Republican and Democratic carpetbaggers who have debased the social tone of Washington.

Will you excuse me for a moment, please, while I rummage through old clippings and calendars? I want to document three predictions which no one with a healthy streak of skepticism will accept at face value. It probably is incorrect to label them predictions; that implies forecasts based on reasoning power. They were, rather, inexplicable hunches about a dramatic event of the war and the last two successions to the Presidency of the United States.

On July 27, 1944, while the Allied armies still were fighting in the hedgerows of Normandy, I sent out invitations for a party in Hollywood on September 9, to celebrate the liberation of Paris. The Allies then were 150 miles from Paris and rival columnists had a field day ridiculing me as a military expert. I was wrong — but on the side of the angels. A Free French armored division entered Paris on August 25, fifteen days before the date I selected. I borrowed Dorothy di Frasso's home for the party, and the talent that performed was worthy of the occasion commemorated. The program was opened by Alicia Markova and Anton Dolin dancing to Chopin's *Sylphides* played by Artur Rubinstein at the piano. Lauritz Melchior, Judy Garland, Frank Sinatra and Danny Kaye sang, in that order, numbers with Parisian themes. Edgar Bergen did a French routine with Charlie McCarthy. For the stirring finale, my 130 guests joined Charles Boyer in singing the *Marseillaise*.

On January 19, 1945, the day before Franklin D. Roosevelt's fourth inauguration, I was invited to a buffet luncheon in the White House. Roosevelt sat alone near a window, with a tray on his lap and Fala at his side, and each guest was brought to him separately for a brief audience. When my turn came, I said: "I hope you do well at Yalta, Mr. President." He was leaving shortly for his historic conference with Churchill and Stalin.

"I'm sure we'll agree on the important issues now that victory is assured," he answered. He added a few more words, but I didn't comprehend them.

At that moment, a dreadful premonition struck me with the impact of a numbing blow. The sunlight streaming through the window seemed to penetrate the President's once ruggedly handsome head. It was like looking at a skull.

I tried to throw off a frightening sense of impending tragedy, but it surged back more acutely than ever the next time I went to Washington, to have lunch with Evelyn McLean on April 8, 1945. The President was at Warm Springs, Georgia. Vice-President Truman and Mrs. Truman were also lunching at Mrs. McLean's. I asked Mr. Truman whether he would be in San Francisco for the opening of the first conference on April 25 to write the Charter of the United Nations.

"Oh, no," laughed Truman. "That's the President's baby. I'd love to go, but the President will welcome the delegates."

An impulse I could not control made me turn to Mrs. Truman. "A great calamity will occur," I said. "Your husband will be the President before the conference opens."

Mrs. Truman gasped and recoiled a few steps. Senator Arthur Vandenberg, who was at her side, stepped between us and said sharply: "Don't talk like that. Don't ever say that again."

Four days later, the President was dead.

The same day, I phoned Mrs. Truman to wish her and her husband Godspeed in their new responsibilities. "I can't forget what you told me on Sunday," she said. "How did you know this would happen so soon?"

"I can't explain it," I answered truthfully. "I just had an overpowering feeling it was coming."

The first time I met Harry Truman, at Mrs. McLean's Friendship House early in the war, I had a bone to pick with him. He then was head of the Senate Investigation Committee cracking down, among other abuses, on phony commissions granted by the armed forces to people with political influence. One of Truman's chief targets for criticism was Darryl Zanuck, who was a colonel attached to a photographic unit taking documentary films of the North African invasion.

I asked Mrs. McLean to seat me next to Truman at dinner, and practically the first words I said to him were: "Senator, they tell me you're a fair man, but you're doing a grave injustice to a friend of mine."

"Who's that?" he demanded.

"Darryl Zanuck. He didn't get his rank by pull, as you've charged. He's been a reserve officer in the army since the First World War, just like you. He earned his commission."

"I didn't know that," Truman said. He seemed genuinely upset. "I would like to make amends."

"Why don't you write him a letter that you were misinformed in his case?"

"I can't do that. If the letter is released for publication it will look as though the committee is giving him and the movies a special boost."

"I promise you the letter never will be divulged by Zanuck. I think you owe him that small courtesy."

Several months later Mr. Zanuck told me he had received a nice letter from the Senator, and he never has let it out of his personal files.

Truman had to make two agonizing decisions which required moral and political courage — the use of the atomic bomb and the intervention in Korea. He further served the cause of democracy well by firmly supporting the Marshall Plan, military aid to Greece and Turkey, the recognition of Israel and the Berlin airlift. I admire him, but the feeling is not exactly mutual. I committed the one unpardonable offense he can neither condone or forget. I criticized his daughter Margaret's singing. I did it in eight cryptic words, but they were enough to put me on the Truman blacklist.

A few nights after Margaret gave her first recital in Carnegie Hall, I appeared as a regular member of the panel on a radio quiz show, "Who Said That?" I had answered a question unrelated to music when Bob Trout, the moderator, casually asked me whether I had attended the recital. I said I was there. Then Trout, the scoundrel, lowered the boom without warning.

"What did you think of Miss Truman's singing?" he asked.

"I went to the concert," I repeated cagily, wishing Trout

would drop dead, but he insisted on a direct answer. I heard myself say, as far as I remember:

"There was no singing at Miss Truman's recital."

This unfortunate remark was relayed to President Truman, but Mrs. Truman, whom I have always respected and liked enormously, felt I had every right to express my opinion of Margaret's voice. I've always thought Margaret is a clever, charming and attractive young woman who deserves infinite credit for breaking away from the social-butterfly life of Washington to try to make a career for herself, which she has certainly done. But I do wish she had listened to Helen Traubel, the great Wagnerian soprano who was coaching her, and studied for a few more years before she made her professional debut.

My third hunch is the easiest to document. Early in July, 1947, a few days after I arrived on the Riviera, Francis Rico, a feature writer for the Paris *Presse* and Nice *Matin,* dropped in for his annual interview with me. Rico usually pumps me for inconsequential social notes about the international set, but on that occasion our conversation drifted into more serious channels. The Marshall Plan had been proposed a month earlier and the French, as major beneficiaries, were intensely interested in the attitudes of leading American politicians. Rico asked me who would be elected President in 1948.

"I haven't the slightest idea," I replied, "but I do know who the president will be after the 1952 election." I pulled from a desk drawer an autographed picture of which I was as proud as a little girl with her first pair of high heels.

"General Eisenhower!" Rico said incredulously.

The picture had been given to me in May, 1947. I had asked

General Eisenhower if I could have an autographed picture for my autobiography, if it would be published, and the very next day he sent it to me with an inscription I did not deserve but which I naturally treasure: *For Miss Elsa Maxwell — who has remained a most charming lady while becoming a contemporary American Institution.*

The Nice *Matin* ran the story under a big headline on July 12, 1947, fully six months before the Republicans and Democrats tried to draft Eisenhower as their candidate.

For the life of me, I can't explain why I picked Ike's name out of thin air. I idolized him as the commander of the armies that liberated France, but at that time I had met him only twice. The first occasion was in 1945 at Freedom House, in New York, when he was awarded the organization's annual award for his diplomatic and military achievements. I was introduced to an elderly woman standing with Edith Willkie. It developed that she came from Abilene, Kansas, and remembered Ike as a barefoot boy who rattled her picket fence with a stick whenever he passed her house. I took her over to Ike and made her repeat the story. He promptly captivated her with his charm.

"I hope I wasn't a pest to you," he laughed. "I always wondered who lived in that house. It was the grandest place in town. I always wanted to see the inside."

"If you'll visit us, General, the house will be yours," the woman said fervently.

Ike remembered the woman who had come halfway across the continent to witness a ten-minute ceremony in his honor. On his next trip to Abilene, he made a point of stopping at the house to pay his respects to her.

I have a more personal reason for recalling my second meeting with Ike. In 1947, Mrs. Robert Lowe Bacon, one of the grand women of Washington society, gave with Madame Bonnet, wife of the French Ambassador, a charity ball for the rehabilitation of Saint-Lô, the French town that was destroyed in the decisive battle of the Normandy campaign. The crowd was so noisy and unruly that Mrs. Lowe could not introduce Jarmilla Novotna, the Metropolitan Opera soprano whom I had brought down from New York.

"May I help?" Ike asked. "Turn out the lights for a moment and the racket will die abruptly. It's an old trick that always works."

At Ike's direction, we took our places on the stage while the lights were out, and when they went on again Madame Novotna sang her aria to an attentive audience. Afterwards, I thanked Ike for his suggestion.

"It's the least I could do for a lodge brother," he said, nodding at a tiny red ribbon sewed on my dress, the badge of the greatest distinction ever conferred on me. That same afternoon, I had been awarded the Legion of Honor by Ambassador Henri Bonnet at the French Embassy. I was wearing the ribbon for the first time — and Ike was the only one who noticed it. I knew then that he was a cinch to win the women's vote.

If there was a prize for reading the future, it would have to be given posthumously to Mrs. O. H. P. Belmont for her uncanny prophecy concerning Clare Boothe. Earlier, I related what Mrs. Belmont told me in 1920 when Clare was only seventeen: "If she gets half the advantages she deserves, you'll be proud to know her twenty-five years from now."

Mrs. Belmont did not trust to capricious luck to fulfill the girl's rare combination of brains, beauty and talent. She was the stage manager of Clare's marriage to George Brokaw, a wealthy socialite, in 1923, the first of three turning points in her life. The second was her marriage to Henry Luce, founder of the *Time-Life-Fortune* publishing empire, an event in which I had a hand. The third turning point was a tragedy.

For many years, I wondered what Mrs. Belmont saw so clearly in an unknown girl. Each new phase of Clare's meteoric career brought the answer into sharper focus. Mrs. Belmont was one of the most progressive women of her time and she recognized a similar capacity for growth in Clare. From editing a fashion magazine Clare progressed to plays written with a shrewd insight of human nature. She progressed from politics to diplomacy, from conservatism to liberalism. Above all, she progressed as a compassionate woman.

In the early 'thirties, Clare was putting a high, but superficial, polish on Mrs. Belmont's prediction. Within four years after her divorce from Brokaw in 1929 she had risen to the managing editorship of *Vanity Fair*, a society magazine dying of pernicious anemia. Clare was the prototype of the glamorous career woman; she was beautiful, clever, acidly witty — and aggressively ambitious. She seemed to be searching in a hyperthyroid sort of way for a stabilizing influence, and she found it at a ball I gave in 1933 to celebrate Cole Porter's latest show, *The Gay Divorcee.*

Condé Nast, the publisher of *Vanity Fair*, invited some of my guests to a dinner party before the ball. Clare was there and so was Henry Luce, who seldom attended social affairs. Luce said parties bored him, but Nast persuaded him to go along with the rest of the crowd, "just for an hour," to the ball on the Starlight Roof of the Waldorf-Astoria. Soon after we arrived I was rather surprised to see Clare and Luce engrossed in conversation in a far corner of the room. According to the grapevine, there was a feeling of antipathy between them, but I was too busy to wonder about the tête à tête. But at four o'clock in the morning they still were at the same table deeply absorbed in each other. When I told them the party was breaking up, they looked around in bewilderment, as though they were coming out of a trance. Still, I didn't think anything of it. Luce, the son of missionaries to China, was married and had two sons.

That was the beginning of something more serious than anyone suspected. Luce fell in love with Clare and, a year later, decided to marry her. When I sailed for the Riviera in the spring of 1935, Clare was on the same boat with her ten-year-old daughter, Ann Brokaw. She was going to Europe to avoid publicity until Luce's divorce was granted. Clare took a house on Cap Ferrat, but she held herself aloof from the social whirl of the Riviera and left Ann with a governess while she toured the continent. Ann remained in Europe when Clare returned home for her marriage to Luce in November, 1935

For the next seven years Clare was busy setting off a series of brilliant skyrockets. She bowled over Broadway with three plays that were smash hits in successive seasons — *The Women* (1937), *Kiss the Boys Goodbye* (1938) and *Margin for Error* (1939). She wrote movies and articles. After the outbreak of war she plunged into politics and twice was elected to Congress by Connecticut.

But while Clare was piling success on success, Ann was approaching maturity a stranger to her. Then Clare discovered her daughter and tried to make up for the lost years by lavishing affection and companionship on her. On January 11, 1944, Clare went to San Francisco to spend a few hours with Ann, a student at Stanford University. That night, on the way back to college, Ann was killed in a motor accident.

Clare's life stopped and she went into a complete collapse verging on melancholia, and nothing relieved it until she turned to the Catholic Church. Clare took religious instructions from Monsignor, now Bishop, Fulton J. Sheen, and was given a new purpose in life by her conversion. The experience also effected a transformation in Clare's personality. She became gentle and patient, considerate, affectionate — qualities she never had possessed.

After finishing her second term in Congress in 1947, Clare left public life, but she had too much ability to remain in permanent retirement. President Eisenhower appointed her Ambassador to Italy, where, laboring under two handicaps not of her own making, she got off to an inauspicious start. The Italians always have resented women holding high office. They further were antagonized when Clare, in her first press conference, urged the government to implement its program of land reform, the root of the country's economic and social unrest. Clare was blasted for interfering in Italy's affairs, but the criticism was thoroughly unjustified. She was ordered by the State Department to talk cold turkey to the reactionary elements that are the Communists' best propagandists among the oppressed lower classes. There was loose talk that the Italians would demand Clare's recall, but after the furore died down she won their approval with her sympathetic understanding of their problems.

What does the future hold for Clare, who has just turned fifty? She will continue to succeed, but her achievements will bring her a deeper, more enduring gratification because they will be built on stronger foundations — including a truer understanding of herself.

Chapter 14

FORTY–FIVE years after my blighted romance in San Francisco, my old home town finally married off its most determined spinster. Friends always said my wedding would be a red-letter day, and they called the turn correctly. My marriage was announced in a San Francisco newspaper on April 25, 1945, the day the first United Nations conference opened. I was Madame Vyacheslav Mikhailovich Molotov for one edition of the paper, which was just about as long as the honeymoon lasted among the forty-six countries represented at the conference.

Some women are wooed by tender words, sweet music or the soft rustle of folding money. My phantom courtship began with a peal of raucous laughter. It burst from the gallery at the dedication of the UN when Molotov, the head of the Soviet delegation, entered the Opera House surrounded by a phalanx of muscular Russian secret police wearing suits that looked as though the creases had been tailored to their muscles. Molotov, realizing belatedly that a bodyguard hardly was in keeping with the spirit of the occasion, dispensed with his strong-arm squad when he left the hall for the first recess. A covey of reporters pursued him down the aisle bombarding him with questions.

Although I had to give away cumbersome handicaps in weight and age to the field, I broke fast from the barrier. I must have been the first news hound to overtake Molotov, for a picture was snapped showing me practically talking into his ear. When the photo editor got the print, he was rushing to get it into the paper for an extra and there was no time to identify the people in the picture. He assumed a woman as chummy with Molotov as I appeared to be was his wife, and that's how I was labeled in the caption.

There have been unkissed brides, but I was an untalked-to bride. Molotov did not speak a word to me as we hurried down the aisle together. That night I tried to get an interview with my elusive groom in his suite on the eighth floor of the St. Francis Hotel. I waved the picture and smiled winsomely at the secret police on guard. They waved their machine guns, trained on the elevator door. I fled like a German infantryman. The only San Franciscans to whom the Russians endeared themselves were the haberdashers. They bought up all the ties customarily unloaded on color-blind customers at Christmas.

During the conference I gave a dinner for all the delegations. Each country's table was decorated by a product historically associated with it, a chore that took a good deal of ingenuity. Saudi Arabia had me stumped until I borrowed two exquisite miniature Arabian horses which I found in an antique shop. Prince Faisal Al-Saud, the brother of King Ibn Saud, was attended by a chamberlain who admired the horses so extravagantly that I knew he was trying to wheedle them as a gift, but I couldn't give away something I didn't own. After the dinner, one of the horses disappeared — and it cost me $250 to make good with the antique shop. I wouldn't vouch for it, but I think that was the first time I ever entertained a horse-thief.

Somehow, an abortive marriage and horse-stealing seemed to epitomize the first United Nations conference. The principals were letter perfect in rehearsals promising to honor and obey the precepts of Franklin D. Roosevelt's visionary union, but all the while they were plotting raids on the other fellows' preserves. The UN became an impotent instrument of collective security the instant the Russians insisted on writing the veto power into the charter, and everyone with a knowledge of history was aware of it. The refusal to surrender national sovereignty to an international authority presaged the dreary deadlocks that had reduced the League of Nations to a feeble debating society.

After World War I, people did not learn for several years that their hopes for peace had been betrayed by the secret covenants of the Versailles Treaty. In World War II, they were disillusioned before the end of hostilities by the open, bitter controversies that split the UN from the start. The Russians' sabotage of the UN cast a pall of pessimism over the world, and nowhere was it more apparent than in France.

When I returned to Europe in December, 1946, for the first time in more than seven years, France already was infected with the futility that has made it the sickest country on the continent. The proud French had thrown up a smoke-screen of cynicism to hide the humiliation of the German occupation and their prostration until they were rescued by the Americans and British. France suffered frightful losses in World War I, but its national honor never was higher. A generation later,

France was disgraced by its Nazi collaborationists and disrupted by its Communists. Patriotic Frenchmen were sucked into a political vacuum created by the collapse of the UN, and they have not yet pulled themselves out of it.

I love France, my second home, but there is no country after my own that I admire more than England. I didn't see the British during the war, in what Winston Churchill has called "their finest hour," but I did see them meet an equally grave challenge with character, courage and humor. In 1946, England was the bleakest and, paradoxically, the brightest spot in Western Europe. It was broke, but it was not morally bankrupt. Although England had a poorer standard of living than its former enemies, there were fewer black marketeers, Fascists, Communists or demagogues than in any other country.

The British, masters of the world for more than three centuries, knew they were finished as a first-ranking power. Yet they did not evade the responsibilities of leadership that meant the continuation of wartime sacrifices and crippling taxes. There was widespread economic and social unrest, yet the British did not lose confidence in their democratic institutions.

With my usual luck, I met the brilliant Sir Hartley Shawcross, the youngest attorney general in the history of the United Kingdom, before going abroad in 1946. Sir Hartley, who had been England's chief prosecutor at the Nuremberg war-criminal trials, was in New York for the conference of the Big Four foreign ministers drafting peace treaties with Hitler's satellites. I entertained Sir Hartley at several small dinners and he said he would reciprocate by having the Labor cabinet give me a luncheon in the House of Commons when I arrived in

England. I refrained from telling him that twenty years before I had been denounced twice in Commons for escapades that brought unfavorable publicity to peers of His Majesty's realm.

Several months earlier I had booked passage on the *Queen Mary* for the scheduled sailing from New York on December 13th. On the twelfth the Big Four meeting ended, enabling the British, French and Russian delegations to catch the ship. Sir Hartley introduced me to Ernest Bevin, the foreign minister, and other prominent members of the government who were fine newspaper copy for me. I noticed, however, that titled Britishers on the ship whom I had known for many years were giving me the cold shoulder. When I asked them what the trouble was, they tore into me for fraternizing with "that dreadful Labor rabble." They were Tories, of course, and they gave me an idea for a little surprise party.

Two nights before the *Queen Mary* docked at Southampton, I invited Mr. and Mrs. Bevin, Sir Hartley and several Labor bigwigs to a dinner. I also invited the most rabid and articulate Tories on the ship, a bit of a Machiavellian trick, to be sure, but one that was not dreamed up as a mischievous whim. My attitude toward the political situation in England was, I think, typically American. Emotionally, I felt that Winston Churchill had been treated shabbily by being turned out of office immediately after the war — a war he, more than any other man, had won with his eloquence and sheer guts. Rationally, though, I could understand why the British elected a party that supported a more liberal social program than the Conservatives endorsed. I wanted to hear both sides of the issue, and bringing together the champions of the rival camps promised a lively and informative evening.

Dinner was a strained, chilly affair until the coffee and brandy were served. I rose holding a box of Havana cigars I had intended to give Mr. Churchill. "I'm offering this as a prize in a debate," I announced. My guests winced, probably wondering how I had made a reputation as an amusing hostess. "The proposition is: Resolved that the Labor Party is better qualified to govern England than the Conservative Party."

The British generally presented a united front to outsiders, but among themselves they scrap like Kilkenny cats. The forensic fur began to fly in eighteen different directions, with Sir Hartley, the leading legal light of the Empire, hard pressed to beat off the attacks of the choleric Tories. At one point the argument got so hot that Bevin slipped away from the table and took a walk around the deck to compose himself. I never did decide which side won the debate. I was afraid the losers would throw me overboard.

The following day, when I filled out my customs declaration, I regretted the hard time I had given Sir Hartley. I needed someone with a lot of influence to get me out of a jam. I was bringing about $1000 worth of food as gifts to friends in England, and until that moment I had not given a thought to the duty that would have to be paid on the stuff. I nearly passed out when I looked at the tax schedule. It added up to almost as much as the food had cost. I went to Sir Hartley and asked him to help me.

"I can't possibly pay the duty," I said. "I've got just enough money to see me through the trip. You're the chief law-enforcement officer of England and I demand justice." I was getting more indignant by the minute. "All this food is for your hungry people and it will be an outrage if it's confiscated or impounded or something just because of a stupid, outdated law."

"Take it easy," Sir Hartley laughed. "I've had enough of your debates to last me a long while. Calm down. I'll get your gifts through customs without payment of duty."

"Oh, that's wonderful," I gushed. "I'll send you and Lady Shawcross some tinned hams and turkeys and . . . "

"Good Lord, that will make me an accomplice!" Sir Hartley said. "Don't dare give me a scrap of food. Besides, I ate extremely well in your country for six weeks. Give the food to people who have been trying to exist on our austerity rations for six years. It will be a Godsend to them."

I whisked through customs without a hitch, but when I checked into Claridge's Hotel in London the manager told me there were a dozen gentlemen waiting to see me. He motioned to a grim group standing in the lobby. The voice of conscience whispered that they were detectives ready to haul me to Old Bailey on charges of smuggling. They came toward me lugubriously and, to my relief, introduced themselves as British newspapermen. The spokesman explained that they had married Russian girls while they were on assignments in Moscow but had not been permitted to bring their wives with them when they were recalled home. The majority had children they had not seen in several years.

"We're appealing to you as a colleague to intercede with Molotov and ask him to let our families join us in England," he said.

"I sympathize with you, but what makes you think I have any influence with Molotov?" I asked, mystified by the whole thing.

"Since you will be his house guest . . . "

"I'll what!" I exclaimed.

"There was a dispatch in the papers yesterday reporting that you're going to visit Russia and stay with Molotov as his personal guest," the man said. "Here's the clipping."

I told the group, as gently as possible, that the story was a pure fabrication — and I made a mental note to strangle a Russian named Pavlov the next time I saw him. Coming over on the *Queen Mary*, I had passed the time of day with Pavlov, the Russian's official interpreter at international conferences. Pavlov, a bland young man dubbed "The Angel" by the press corps, urged me to go to Russia and tell "the truth" about the Soviet Union to the American public.

"Commissar Molotov has delegated me to invite you," Pavlov continued, "on the condition that you do not stay with your ambassador, but with Madame Molotov and himself in Moscow. You will then see *everything*."

I doubted that Pavlov was authorized to make such an astonishing offer, so I laughed and said, "It may be embarrassing to Madame Molotov to have a rival under the same roof." Pavlov smiled wanly at the reference to the photo caption in the San Francisco paper linking me with Molotov. I assumed that was the end of it, but Pavlov evidently told the Tass News Agency I had accepted. I can't imagine what his motive was, except, perhaps, to present Molotov in a human-interest light in the western press. I have no regrets that I didn't take the chance to see Russia — assuming the bid was genuine. I would have seen only what the Russians wanted to show me and, besides, I would have missed the luncheon in the House of Commons promised me by Sir Hartley.

Foreign Secretary Bevin was the host at the luncheon, an

honor previously conferred only on bona fide V.I.P.'s, a category in which I certainly did not belong. Just to indulge in name-dropping, the other cabinet members present in addition to Mr. Bevin and Sir Hartley were Emanuel Shinwell (Fuel and Power), Hector McNeil (State), Chuter Ede (Home Office), John Strachey (Food) and Harold Wilson (Board of Trade).

The first course on the austerity menu was a thin, watery soup that was palatable only because it was hot and the dining room was frigid. Food was the least of the attractions the occasion held for me, but I could not help bridling with surprise, then growing revulsion, when we were served thick, juicy steaks. The British were rationed to something like four ounces of meat a week, and here were the top members of the government about to gorge themselves on a month's meat allowance at one sitting.

For more than seventy years I have yielded to none in vast enthusiasm for food, but the sight of those delectable steaks made me nauseated. Everyone was looking at me, waiting for me to commence eating. Strachey, the Minister of Food, was watching me with an intensity that would have been embarrassing under ordinary circumstances, but I was too mad to care what anyone thought. I pointedly folded my napkin and leaned back from the table.

"What's the matter, Elsa?" Bevin asked. "Eat your steak. You're not a vegetarian, are you?"

"You'll have to excuse me, Ernie, but I've lost my appetite," I replied. "Much as I appreciate your hospitality, I think this lunch is a disgrace. The people who voted for you would sell their souls for a meal like this. I expected you and your government to set a more admirable example."

Bevin was singularly unperturbed by my outburst. "Go on, eat your steak," he said.

To avoid further unpleasantness, I took a mouthful — and grabbed frantically for my napkin. The steak had such a horrible, fishy taste that I gagged on it.

Bevin roared. "That's whale steak you've just eaten. We're planning to introduce it to augment the meat ration. It's very cheap and the experts tell us it's highly nutritious. You're our first guinea pig. Now it's my turn to have a go at it." He, too, shuddered at the taste of the whale meat. "This could cost us a general election." He sighed wistfully. "There's no substitute for a good, thick cut of beef."

Ernest Bevin, a former truck driver who rose to second-highest position his country could offer, was a shining example of England's genius for developing leaders. Politics are an honorable profession in England, unlike other countries, because the tradition of public service attracts — and rewards — its best men regardless of social rank. The British have had their share of mediocre statesmen, yet even the hidebound reactionaries and the appeasers were men of integrity. Bevin was an implacable enemy of Tories and aristocrats, but he fought his own party to champion Conservatives whose ability he respected.

In 1947, on my second postwar trip to England, I again had lunch with Bevin in the House of Commons. There were rumors to the effect that my old friend the late Alfred Duff Cooper, later Viscount Norwich, would be relieved as ambassador to France, and I asked Bevin point-blank if they were true.

"I'm afraid they are," he answered. "For more than two years I've resisted the heaviest pressure from my own party to give the post to one of our members. Cooper is the best ambassador to France we've ever had, and it will be impossible to replace him. I'm giving in only because his appointment threatens to disrupt the party unity we need for more important issues. It's a great mistake to let Cooper go. My generation has produced few men of higher caliber."

It is a comfort to recall Bevin's tribute on this cold, drab day early in January, 1954, a day made more depressing by the news of Alfred Duff Cooper's death. He was another type of man, the versatile, vigorous intellectual, from whom England has derived strength and stability. Duff Cooper was a soldier decorated for gallantry in action (D.S.O.) in World War I, an aesthete and a literary man (two fine biographies and his own memoirs), a member of five cabinets and, above all, a man of unshakable principles.

In 1937, he was condemned as a "disgraceful scaremonger" for urging Britain to rearm against Hitler. The following year, he resigned as First Lord of the Admiralty in protest against Neville Chamberlain's appeasement of Hitler at Munich. "I have ruined, perhaps, my political career," he said. "But that is a little matter. I can still walk about the world with my head erect."

It was a walk relieved of loneliness by the companionship of his wife, the former Lady Diana Manners, one of the most beautiful women I ever saw. Their marriage in 1919, a sensation in European and American society, was violently opposed by Lady Diana's father, the Duke of Rutland, who had more ambitious plans for her. Duff Cooper then was an untitled, penniless war veteran, and the land-poor duke hoped to marry his daughter to the heir to a throne or, at least, a great fortune. There is little doubt that such a match could have been made.

Diana was an unbelievable vision of blond loveliness. New Yorkers stormed the box office just to stare at her when she portrayed the Madonna in Max Reinhardt's spectacle *The Miracle* in 1924. British aristocrats looked down their noses at Lady Diana's unseemly, "bohemian" behavior, but she was too independent and intelligent to give a hoot for the stuffy conventions of her world. In 1913, she appeared in one of the first ballet films ever made, and as a young girl she broke away from the stifling cocoon of a social butterfly to find stimulation among artists and musicians. Had Diana been interested in money or a title, she could have had her pick of the most eligible bachelors on both sides of the Atlantic, but she was twenty-seven when she married Duff Cooper. He was a man well worth waiting for. I never have known a happier couple.

I especially treasure the memory of Duff Cooper for one of those moments that have enriched my life. Back in the early 1920's, Duff and I were in a gondola floating down the Grand Canal in Venice reciting to each other the poetry we had written. Most young ladies of my generation went through a poetic phase and, inspired by Duff's creative efforts and the romantic surroundings, I made an excursion into the past. I recited the last six lines of a sonnet I had composed many years before in San Francisco:

> Art thou joy
> That I could cherish as some jeweled toy and lightly wear,
> Or art thou but weird, fantastic melancholy
> That holds me within its shadowed spell,
> Or art thou sin
> That honies and stains eternity.

A quarter of a century later, the first time I had seen Duff since the war, he greeted me with "Art thou joy that I could cherish as some jeweled toy . . . "

Duff Cooper, a constructive man, was penalized for alerting his country to dangers of war he foresaw so clearly. It is ironic that his most vicious critic, Lord Beaverbrook, a disruptive force in England, continues to thrive on many defeats. "Wrong-Horse Max," the Canadian-born tycoon of British journalism, has been backing spurious candidates and causes for thirty years, but he has cleverly fostered a legend of political influence far beyond his capability to exert it.

Beaverbrook is a pompous martinet who seems to invite ridicule even by his friends. For years, he was the butt for practical jokes pulled by Freddie Lonsdale, the playwright, Valentine Castlerosse, Captain "Mike" Wardell and Lord (Perry) Brownlow, a quartet united in deflating him although they liked him. Once, during a water shortage in Cannes, Castlerosse had 800 bottles of mineral water put on The Beaver's bill at the Carleton Hotel just to hear him squeal indignantly when the manager explained that a member of his entourage had bathed in it. Another time Lonsdale bribed a shopworn cocotte to fake a tearful reunion with The Beaver in the crowded gambling casino at Cannes and loudly remind him of an old affair. The Beaver nearly had apoplexy before Lonsdale told him it was a put-up job.

Beaverbrook's sense of responsibility is on a par with his sense of humor. Although he professes to be a Conservative, he split his own party so badly in 1929 that Ramsey MacDonald's Labor coalition was swept into office, with disastrous results for the country. He flirted with Marxism by supporting Aneurin Bevan, who since has turned so many political flip-flops that he now is called "the Bollinger bolshevik" by his own party. (Bollinger is a popular brand of champagne in England.) The Beaver might have impeded rearmament during the crisis leading to World War II by assuring his readers there would be no war.

The Beaver's worst defeat was his attempt to form a King's Party to keep Edward VIII on the throne after his marriage to Wallis Simpson. In that incredible campaign Beaverbrook had such strange allies as Sir Oswald Mosley, the Fascist, and Willie Gallacher, the lone Communist M.P. Beaverbrook made a fortune copying some of the techniques of American journalism, but he never has understood the temperament or the basic character of the British. Millions buy his papers but, fortunately for England, few read his editorials.

In accordance with journalistic ethics, I must serve notice that in this forthcoming passage I will be a volunteer propagandist for Prince Aly Khan. I can't be objective about Aly and I might as well admit it right off the bat. To me, Aly is *un homme fatal* —an opinion shared by a great many women who will thank me to keep a discreet tongue in my head. Aly has been maligned and misrepresented in the press ever since his divorce from Rita Hayworth, and I feel a sense of responsibility for it because I brought them together at one of my parties.

This, too, is a labor of love on behalf of Aly's father, the Aga Khan, who has been caught in the backwash of his son's notoriety. It has been my privilege to call many famous people my friends, but none is a more distinguished figure than the Aga. The Occident knows him mainly as an enormously wealthy man who receives his weight in rare gems from his followers on certain ceremonial occasions. It does not know that the Aga returns the tribute to his people for charitable and educational purposes. Nor is it aware that the Aga has been playing a leading role in global affairs longer than any other contemporary statesman.

For half a century the Aga has been the Islamic world's chief spokesman in the West — and, conversely, the West's staunchest advocate among his coreligionists. In 1924, India nominated the Aga for the Nobel Peace Prize for his skillful diplomacy in helping to end a bloody war between Greece and Turkey. He was the prime mover in the unprecedented exchange of several hundred thousand Greeks and Turks living as aliens in the belligerent countries, a tremendous repatriation project that eliminated an age-old powder keg in the Balkans.

The Aga is an astonishingly liberal man considering that he has been an Oriental potentate for seventy years. Since 1885, when he was eight years old, the Aga has been the spiritual leader of fifteen million Moslems of the Ismaili sect who venerate him as the direct descendant of Fatimah, the daughter of the Prophet Mohammed. Perhaps the most surprising side of the Aga's personality is his cultural sensitivity. He long has been a generous, well-informed patron of the arts in Europe and Asia and in 1910 he founded Aligarh University in India, an outstanding center of Moslem learning today.

Aly cannot compare with his father in mental attainments. He has a good, quick mind, but it is preoccupied with one special field of inquiry. He disagrees with Alexander Pope, who suggested that the proper study of mankind is man. In Aly's lexicon, women are the most intriguing subject on earth. I don't want to sound naïve, but I honestly believe that Aly's love of women is basically more aesthetic than physical.

Every facet of women delights him. He loves the way they

dress, walk, speak, think and react emotionally. When he is with a woman, he makes her feel no other person exists for him. He is completely absorbed in her, to the exclusion of all distractions. He talks to her with breathless excitement. His eyes burn her intently, as though she is an enchanting discovery. He dances with her slowly and rapturously, as though it is the last time he ever will hold her in his arms. His mood and manner never vary, whether he is with an eighteen-year-old girl, a beauty in full bloom or a grandmother. He even acts that way with me, for heaven's sake.

A fascinating footnote to history can be attributed to Aly's romantic allure. Edward VIII might still be on the throne of England today if not for Aly. In 1934 Lady Thelma Furness, for years the then Prince of Wales's favorite companion, fell in love with Aly, who was only twenty-three, and followed him to America when he came to this country on business connected with his racing stable. During Lady Thelma's absence, Wallis Simpson moved into the orbit of Edward's serious attention and affections, as the saying goes.

Aly's amatory activities have given him a reputation as a playboy which, I suppose, he deserves. It is more truth than propaganda, however, to report that he works harder than any man of his wealth and position I have known. He spends three months a year visiting his father's followers, who are scattered throughout Asia, Africa and South America. Aly once confided that he trains for these pilgrimages as seriously as a fighter preparing to defend his championship. Wherever he goes, he is mobbed by devout Ismailis, who worship him. On the trips he puts in a fourteen-hour day conducting religious ceremonies.

On the temporal level, Aly manages the famous racing stable

and nine stud farms he and the Aga own in partnership. They have millions invested in horses, and Aly, who closely supervises the entire operation, earns his share of the handsome profits they return. A few years ago Tulyar, their English Derby winner, was sold to the Irish National Stud for $750,000, the highest price ever paid for a horse. A half-dozen other horses bred by the Aga and Aly have been bought for more than a quarter of a million dollars.

Aly himself has won more than a hundred races as a gentleman jockey. Most people may regard that as a small accomplishment, but he has one medal that is a memento of something more than a pleasant pastime. Aly was awarded the Bronze Star by the U.S. Army for gallantry in the field during the Allied invasion of southern France and the campaign in Alsace-Lorraine. Aly saw the war coming and joined the French Foreign Legion early in 1939. When it erupted, he transferred to the British Army and was in uniform for six years.

A good deal of Aly's magnetism for women stems, I believe, from his animal vitality. I'm convinced he was born with a built-in benzedrine plant that impels him to find an outlet for the stupefying energy he generates. I've never seen him sit still for ten consecutive minutes except at dinner and the bridge table. At his age — he was forty-three in June, 1954 — he should not be risking his neck in strenuous sports, but he seems to have a strange affinity for danger. I'll do anything in the world for Aly except get into a car when he is at the wheel. His normal cruising speed in traffic is eighty miles an hour and he has been known to hit 120 in his Alfa-Romeo. Once, to keep a rendezvous in Paris, he set out from Cannes, and drove nearly 600 miles in eight hours.

I suspect Aly's recklessness is a compulsion to prove his physical toughness as a counterbalance for his soft sentimentality. Aly sometimes embarrasses himself with his demonstrative displays of affection, especially for his two grown sons by Joan Yarde-Buller, his first wife. Although he has been separated from Joan for fifteen years, Aly has maintained a very close relationship with his boys, Khanim and Amyn, and has them spend half their school vacations with him. He contested Rita Hayworth's divorce solely because he wanted partial custody of their daughter Yasmin, the first girl in his family for 200 years. Aly responds to affection as impulsively as a bird on the wing to a mating call. When he tells a woman he loves her, he sincerely means it at the moment. The trouble is that a moment passes so quickly.

When I first met Aly in New York in 1947, I was interested in him only because he had just bought Maxine Elliott's house on the Riviera which I knew so well. He was charming, of course, but like most strangers I dismissed him as a playboy and did not see him again until the summer of 1948. I gave a dinner for the late Admiral Forrest P. Sherman at the Palm Beach Casino in Cannes, and I invited Aly, quite frankly, to dress up the party. Knowing that he was fond of beautiful women, I tried to round up as many as I could. I like pretty girls, too, at parties; they're cheaper and more decorative than flowers. The most attractive unattached prospect in sight was Rita Hayworth, who was living at the Cap d'Antibes waiting for her final divorce decree from Orson Welles.

Rita was in the doldrums — she still was in love with Orson — and tried to beg off coming to the party, saying she had nothing appropriate to wear. I gave her the address of a good shop in Cannes and talked her into accepting the invitation. "Dinner is at nine-thirty, but I want you to be late," I said. "Make a grand entrance. It'll be good for your morale."

On the night of the party I was chatting with Aly, who was sitting next to me at the table, when he suddenly stiffened and pointed like a bird dog. "My God, who is that?" he exclaimed.

Rita was standing in the doorway of the room wearing an exquisite white bouffant dress and looking more beautiful than the law should allow. "That's your dinner partner," I answered.

"My partner?" he said incredulously.

"Yes, I asked her especially for you."

Aly was captivated by Rita, and after dinner took her to the Californie, a night club high above Cannes, "to look at the stars." I'm positive nothing more happened that evening, because Aly flew to Ireland shortly after midnight to attend an important race. The following morning I called Rita and asked her what she thought of Aly. "A nice little fellow," she said carelessly.

Three weeks later I went to Aly's for lunch. Rita was there too, but that was no cause for speculation. Aly keeps open house for all comers and, besides, he did not lavish attention on Rita as he usually does when he is infatuated. A few days later Aly went to America for the yearling sales at Saratoga and I assumed that was the end of his romantic interest, if any, in Rita. I didn't think anything serious was in the wind when Aly went to Hollywood and was reported as Rita's constant escort. Legally, Aly still was married to his first wife, the daughter of Lord and Lady Churston. When he and Joan separated amicably, Aly gave her a settlement of three million dollars, with one string attached. Knowing his weakness for women, Aly asked Joan not to get a divorce until he requested it. That was his safety net against plunging into a rash marriage, and he decided to remove the obstacle after courting Rita for four months in Mexico, Cuba, Ireland and Switzerland. They were married on May 27, 1949.

Aly was ecstatically happy in the following months, but Rita seemed morose and ill at ease. I ascribed her general depression to the fact that her baby was on the way, but she was not in better spirits after Yasmin was born. Aly persuaded Rita to accompany him on a trip to Africa to visit his followers, but in the middle of it Rita said she was going to Paris to buy clothes. The next thing Aly knew, she was back in America with Yasmin, announcing she had left him. It was the first time a woman ever had walked out on Aly and his pride was piqued. He followed her to Hollywood and made a reconciliation with Rita. It didn't last long. Rita returned to Paris with Aly, but a week later she told the press that their break was final.

The trouble with Aly's marriage to Rita is quite simple to explain. Rita did not have Aly's social flair, just as she did not have the intellectual interests of Orson Welles, her previous husband. Rita basically is a nice, simple girl. There was nothing in her background to prepare her for the role of a princess, and she cannot be blamed on that score. But she can be arraigned for statements about Aly which might affect his succession to his father's title.

The Aga Khan was very fond of Rita and blamed Aly for their breakup. The Aga once set a pretty fast pace on the social merry-go-round himself, but he always has been strait-laced in maintaining the respectability of family relationships.

It is taken for granted that Aly, the oldest son, is the nominal heir to the Aga's fortune and spiritual leadership of the Ismailis

— but it is a thoroughly false assumption. The Aga can disinherit Aly and name as his successor one of his two other sons. The Aga, furious after the unpleasant publicity attendant on Aly's second divorce asked me last summer to tell him, then romantically entangled with Gene Tierney, that he disapproved of Gene as a daughter-in-law. This was an unpleasant task for me to perform, for I adore Aly. But I obeyed the Aga's request after assuring him that Gene has much more intelligence and stability than Rita. But the Aga was adamant.

"I cannot sanction his marriage to another actress," the Aga said. "I have nothing against Miss Tierney personally. It is essentially a matter of Aly respecting the religious obligations he owes his people. The purity of my family's lineage has been of deep symbolic significance to my people for thirteen centuries and I will not permit Aly to destroy it with indiscriminate marriages. I have told him this repeatedly but he does not seem to realize his responsibilities. Perhaps he will listen to you."

I carried the Aga's message to Aly, who listened and showed obvious distress. But he continued to see Gene until she returned to America at Christmas, and then he made a special trip to California to see her. For Aly's sake, I hope he does not marry again during his father's lifetime. Aly, a gentle Romeo, loves women too much to remain faithful to a wife. I once asked him to explain his romantic urge.

"When I'm in love," he answered, "I think only of the woman's pleasure."

Chapter 15

THE most exalted throne on earth was renounced for love
in our time by Edward VIII, King of Great Britain, Ireland
and the British Dominions beyond the seas, Defender of the
Faith and Emperor of India. Today, nearly a generation later,
an event that was as controversial as it was dramatic has lost
none of its original impact. There are those who, paraphrasing the most distinguished Briton of the twentieth century,
maintain that never before did one man give up so much for
so little. They are balanced by romanticists who still are captivated by a story that has few counterparts in classical literature.

Until I withdrew from their intimate circle a few years ago,
I had ample opportunity to appraise the characters of the Duke
and Duchess of Windsor. Despite the duke's defections, I respect him for his unswerving devotion to the wife who prompted
his agonizing decision, and for the good grace with which he has
accepted his reduced station. The duchess, frankly, alternately
fascinates and baffles me with her behavior and attitudes.

I never really knew the duke until 1946 — and I wish I had
never gotten to know him better. I would prefer to have retained my illusions and remember him as he was the first time
I saw him, in 1922, at a party in Mrs. Cucco Belleville's house
in Manchester Square, London. He was a gay, debonair Prince

Charming, the most famous celebrity in the world, and he projected an aura of glamour that was as unmistakable as it was authentic. Illusions are notoriously perishable. The Prince of Wales's pedestal began to show telltale streaks of clay the next time I saw him and had an opportunity to talk to him. In 1927, on a short visit to London, I borrowed Lady Milbanks's house at 20 Talbot Square to give a cabaret party. About sixty people were invited but, at Sheila's suggestion, no royalty was included. The Marquis of Cambridge, Queen Mary's brother, had just died, and the royal family was in mourning.

Before the party, which was called for eleven o'clock, Lady Louis Mountbatten gave a dinner for some of my guests. We were on the last course at ten-thirty when I was called to the phone. Captain Alastair MacIntosh, a young man-about-town, was on the other end of the line.

"I'm in a bit of a jam, Elsa, and you've got to help me out," he said. "Joe Schenck, the American movie mogul, is with me and he's dying to meet the Prince of Wales. It may mean a first-rate job for me if I can arrange it. May I bring Schenck to your party tonight?"

"Of course, but what has that got to do with the Prince of Wales?" I asked. "He won't be there."

MacIntosh laughed. "That's what you think. The P. of W. and two of his brothers already are at the Milbanks's house waiting for the fun to begin."

"What!" I cried incredulously. "That's impossible! I didn't invite them."

"Royalty needs no invitation," MacIntosh answered. "You'd better fly to your party. It's a bit thick, you know, keeping their Royal Highnesses waiting."

We rushed from Claridge's to Sheila's house and, sure enough, there was a fleet of Daimlers in the driveway festooned with the royal coat of arms. The Prince of Wales and his brother, Prince George, had discovered the bar, but the Duke and Duchess of York, who were to ascend the throne after the abdication, were sitting together in the drawing room.

"They've got to be separated," the Duchess of Sutherland said to me, motioning toward the royal couple. "No man should sit with his own wife even if he is the Duke of York. You're the only one who can do it. They'll think you're just an ignorant American, but ask them to circulate among the guests. They're absolute darlings, but it will be a frightful bore if we have to go through formal presentations. I'm sure they won't mind."

To save the evening from the deep freeze that threatened to envelop it, I told the duke and duchess that only Hollywood movie stars were permitted to sit side by side at parties. "They appear together in public so infrequently that it's their way of announcing they're still married," I explained laughingly.

The duke smiled and wandered off, leaving me with the duchess. The band was blaring a hot number and the duchess, who had recently returned from a good-will tour of the South Seas with her husband, remarked that the dancing in London was more primitive than anything she had seen on the trip. To illustrate the point, the future queen rose and did a charming, impromptu native dance, waving her arms and swaying her shoulders gracefully.

When supper was served, MacIntosh told me that the Prince of Wales requested me to join him at the bar. The prince, who had been drinking steadily, was sitting alone at a small table and seemed to be bored. For want of something to say, I commented on the styles he had introduced in men's fashions — the Windsor tie, the backless waistcoat for evening wear, the boater hat.

"It's depressing to think that's all I'm to be known for," he muttered. "Such trivial things."

He stared morosely at his glass, then blurted: "I don't want to be king. I wouldn't be a good one."

It was an astonishing statement to make to a total stranger, but I learned later that it was characteristic of him. He was anxious to shirk the responsibilities of his heritage long before he assumed them.

I reminded the duke of this remark to me three years ago when he was dining at La Tour d'Argent in Paris. He looked surprised. He had obviously forgotten. Then, with that strange prescience he sometimes unexpectedly possesses, he said, "Elsa, what do you think of me?"

"Well, sir," I replied, "at the moment I am wondering why Your Royal Highness is so attracted to rich people when you yourself are a wealthy man."

The duke looked startled, then asked whom I meant.

I started to catalogue his consistent companions without implying any criticism of them, for some were also friends of mine: Mr. Robert F. Young, Mrs. George F. Baker, Mr. Charles Wrightsman, Mr. Charles Munn, Mrs. Joe Davies, Mrs. Jessie Donahue, Mrs. Margaret Biddle, Mr. and Mrs. Byron Foy . . .

The duke did not seem to resent my question, but he offered no explanation.

But back to my story. I did not see him again until I caught a glimpse of him in Vienna in 1936. By that time he was Edward VIII. And by that time, also, his friendship with Mrs. Wallis Simpson was so well known that the British press had to abandon a gentleman's agreement to maintain a discreet silence about His Majesty's infatuation with a twice-married American.

Edward was indifferent to the scandalous implications of the liaison. In August, 1936, seven months after he ascended the throne, Edward chartered the Nahlin, a sumptuous yacht, for a Mediterranean cruise with Mrs. Simpson, who had not yet instituted divorce proceedings against her second husband.

The king studiously paid formal calls on four dictators within range of the Nahlin's itinerary. He visited Kemal Ataturk in Turkey, Joannes Metaxas in Greece, Admiral Horthy in Hungary and Prince Paul of Yugoslavia. Only the plea of Anthony Eden, his foreign secretary, dissuaded him from stopping off in Fascist Italy. Two years earlier, England had imposed economic sanctions against Italy for its attack on Ethiopia.

After socializing with Admiral Horthy in Budapest, the king then brought his party to Vienna, his favorite city in Europe. I happened to be there and one night there was a great to-do in the lobby of the Bristol Hotel where I was staying. The clicking of heels by the manager and his staff sounded like castanets and a crew of porters scurried through the door with mountains of luggage. Then the king's entourage entered, led by a small, beautifully dressed woman. Her sullen expression and the purposeful way she walked gave me the impression that she would brush aside anyone who had the temerity to get in her path. I took a second, startled look at her when I saw the king following a few paces behind. I never had seen Mrs. Simpson, but from pictures of her it was no feat of deduction to guess her identity. Just to make sure, though, I stopped Lord Perry Brownlow, who brought up the rear of the procession.

He was surprised by the question. "Why, that's Wallis Simpson." Then he added cryptically, "I thought everyone knew her."

It was difficult to believe that this was the woman who was creating such a turmoil throughout the British Empire. Yet a few nights later, when I saw the king's look of adoration as he danced with the woman he was to marry, I knew he was utterly in love with her — as he still is today.

Forgetting sentiment and looking at the king's abdication realistically, it was an extraordinary stroke of luck for the British Empire and its wartime allies. Edward simply did not have the strength of character or the *noblesse oblige* of King George VI and Queen Elizabeth, his successors, who gave their subjects such a tremendous psychological lift during the blitz and threatened Nazi invasion of England.

The reign of Edward VIII lasted less than eleven months, but the most conclusive evidence of his inability to rule as a constitutional monarch was his struggle to make Mrs. Simpson the Queen of England. It is incomprehensible that a man forty-two years old, who had been trained from infancy to uphold the tradition he inherited, had absolutely no concept of his subjects' reverence for the crown or its symbolic significance. Edward did not realize — or he refused to recognize — that an accident of birth had made him merely the curator of a symbol that unifies people with a common culture and aspirations on the six continents of the globe. Maintaining the dignity and purity of that symbol is the paramount duty of the monarch temporarily entrusted with it. For that symbol has been England's greatest asset in two world wars.

It is essential to clarify one point, the heart of the matter, for a proper perspective of Edward's abdication. Mrs. Simpson was not repudiated by the British people, the cabinet or the Anglican Church because she was an American or a commoner. She was unacceptable as a queen because she was a divorced woman, and the social stigma attached to divorce would have defiled the purity of the crown.

A few years ago, when we still were on friendly terms, the duke confessed to me that his chief mistake was believing he could ride out the storm of protest and impose his will on the British. It was not until an angry mob stoned Mrs. Simpson's house in Cumberland Terrace, forcing her to flee to France for safety, that the king finally realized he was the servant, not the master, of his people.

Even Mrs. Simpson knew Edward overplayed his hand. She once told me she telephoned him from Evreux when she arrived in France and begged him not to abdicate — and the story was confirmed by Lord Brownlow, who accompanied her on the flight.

It is important to keep in mind another salient point. Edward VIII was not forced to abdicate. He could have remained the sovereign by abandoning the idea of marrying Mrs. Simpson. Maybe it is true that he never wanted to be king, but, in the final analysis, he gave up the throne for the woman he loved.

Like everyone, I was full of curiosity about a woman who had inspired such a fateful decision, but I did not have a chance to satisfy it until the winter of 1946. Shortly after the

Windsors moved into a suite a few floors above mine in the Waldorf Astoria Tower Apartments in New York, a curious message was delivered over the phone by Mrs. Charles Suydam Cutting.

"The Duke of Windsor would like you to have tea with him tomorrow afternoon at five in his apartment," she said. "He's anxious to see an old friend again after all these years."

The invitation was a surprise on two counts — the tea, a new habit cultivated by the duke, and the "old friend" reference. As I have said, I had met the duke only a few times years before when he was the Prince of Wales. Further, I had been anything but friendly to him and the duchess in a number of critical articles I had written.

I had taken the Windsors over the coals for visiting Hitler at Berchtesgaden while on their honeymoon and again for their intimate relationship with Charles Bedaux, at whose French château they were married. He was the same Charles Bedaux who committed suicide in a Miami jail on February 8, 1944, while awaiting investigation by a Federal grand jury on charges of conspiring with the Nazis and the Vichy government against the United States. In the 1930's Bedaux devised a point system of wage payment that was bitterly denounced by unions as a cutthroat speed-up scheme to exploit labor. When the Windsors announced in 1937 that they were coming to America as guests of Bedaux, New York dock workers threatened to boycott their ship. It was only after the British Foreign Office explained the facts of life to the duke that he changed his plans. During the war I had criticized the duke for his frivolous administration of the Bahamas while he was governor general and the duchess for flying models and fitters from New York to Nassau to replenish her wardrobe.

Those blasts ran through my mind as I weighed the duke's invitation. "Will the duchess be there?" I asked Mrs. Cutting.

"Yes, of course," she answered. "They're inseparable."

The prospect of meeting the woman who had rocked an empire was too good to pass up. "Please tell the duke I'm delighted to accept his invitation," I said.

The duke could not have been more cordial the following afternoon. We chatted for a few minutes about mutual acquaintances, and then a maid wheeled in a teacart. The duke guessed what I was thinking.

"Yes, it's actually tea, Elsa," he said with a smile.

I waited for the entrance of the duchess, which, I knew, would be made at precisely the right moment — not too soon to dull the edge of my anticipation and not too late to make me resent the delay. Sure enough, as we were finishing our tea, the duchess swept on stage beautifully dressed, and coiffured as meticulously as a wax model in the window of a hairdresser. I recall that I was struck by her diminutiveness and her remarkably blue eyes.

"I simply had to meet the famous Elsa Maxwell," she said.

I murmured an appropriate compliment and after a pleasant half hour I left. I didn't quite know what to make of this tiny, rather ordinary woman who had climbed from a middle-class home in Baltimore to the threshold of Buckingham Palace. She had assurance and poise; her clothes were perfect. But I could detect none of the strong physical attraction she obviously held for the duke.

Yet I did sense a terrific drive in the duchess, a drive comparable to the vibration you feel constantly on an ocean liner. The source or the nature of the force that made the duchess tick intrigued me more than ever.

The Windsors were to be in New York only a week or so before leaving for Antibes on the Riviera, where they rented the Château de Croe from Lady Pomeroy-Burton, widow of a Hearst executive. I saw the duchess twice again during that week, the first time at a benefit luncheon for the American Women's Voluntary Service arranged by Mrs. George F. Baker, a mutual friend. I was at the microphone introducing speakers when there was a buzz of excitement. The duchess entered the ballroom wearing a handsomely tailored black suit and a single string of pearls. As she was ushered to the dais, I said, "Duchess, will you please speak a few words to the audience?"

Unintentionally, I put the duchess on the spot. She was nervous and unaccustomed to public speaking, but the thousand women at the luncheon were fascinated by her.

A few nights later I saw the duchess in a more natural habitat, a small dinner party given by the Byron Foys. On that occasion I was impressed by what appeared to be her candor and sense of humor, two things I've always admired in people. A good many anecdotes about the duchess that sounded apocryphal were floating around, and I asked her whether they were authentic.

"What did you hear?" she asked.

Well, that after the abdication, someone said:

"Duchess, how would you feel if the royal crown were placed on your head?"

"Just like a forced landing," she was supposed to have said.

I asked her if that one was true. She laughed and admitted the soft impeachment.

Then there was the time she was playing bridge as William Somerset Maugham's partner. Maugham dealt and opened the bidding with one no-trump. The player on his left and the duchess passed, but the other opponent bid two spades. Willy went to two no-trump, and there were three passes, ending the bidding. When the duchess laid down her hand, it showed three kings. Maugham, who stammers when he is excited, looked at the dummy and said reproachfully:

"D – D – Duchess, why d – d – didn't you s – s – support me with three k – k – kings in your hand?"

"My kings don't take tricks. They only abdicate," she retorted.

Again she laughed. "I'm afraid that's true, too," she told me.

Since she was in a confidential mood, I asked her a question that would make good reading for my column. She had just been voted the best-dressed woman in the world for the sixth or seventh consecutive year.

"Why should you, who married a king, devote so much time and attention to clothes?" I said. "It seems such a frivolous pursuit for a woman who has so many other responsibilities."

"My husband gave up everything for me," the duchess answered. "I'm not a beautiful woman. I'm nothing to look at, so the only thing I can do is dress better than anyone else. If everyone looks at me when I enter a room, my husband can feel proud of me. That's my chief responsibility."

The duchess has impeccable taste and she spends more money on her wardrobe than any woman I've ever known. Her clothes are beautiful and chic, but though she invests them with elegance, she wears them with a certain rigidity which destroys the impression of ease or casualness.

I did not see the Windsors for some months, until I returned to the Riviera in the summer of 1947 for my first prolonged visit since the war. A few days after I moved in with Dickie Gordon at her farmhouse in Auribeau, the duchess invited me to dinner at the Château de Croe. I was eager to go because I had heard so much about her reputation as a hostess. The reports were not exaggerated.

I found the duchess had an unusual flair for making a home highly attractive. She is as skillful as a Japanese professional in arranging flowers; her food is superb; and she knows how to make the most of furnishings and decorations. After dinner, she took a group of us on a tour of the château, which featured, among other things, a gold bathtub. The most interesting exhibit for me was a dressing table in her bedroom decorated with mementos of her courtship by the duke. The top of the table was painted with the first formal invitation she received from the then Prince of Wales, fragments of a letter, a bouquet of flowers with a card bearing the royal crest, a pair of white evening gloves, a fan and a pair of golf socks evidently worn by the duke on a week end in the country.

Downstairs in the drawing room, tables were set up for bridge and gin rummy, but everyone was feeling too gay for cards.

"Won't you play the piano for us, Miss Maxwell?" the duchess asked. "The duke adores popular music. I think we can get him to sing 'The Surrey with the Fringe on Top' if you'll play it."

The duke, wearing a kilt with a blue and white tartan I

never had seen before, sang the number from *Oklahoma* with a Western twang just as it was done in the show. He had no voice at all, but it was so amusing that everyone clustered around the piano singing until one o'clock in the morning. It was a thoroughly enjoyable evening and when I left the duchess said I must come back soon, including Dickie Gordon in the invitation. I was evasive about Dickie because she is an unreconstructed Scottish rebel who regards all English kings after the House of Stewart as German upstarts. When I returned to the farm after the party I told Dickie of the duchess's invitation.

"I'll never sit at the same table with Hanoverians," she said indignantly, drawing herself up to her full height of five feet, ten inches without heels. "I don't see how you can associate with Germans who usurped the throne."

"It's too late to go through that song and dance again," I said. Then, to give her a needle, I added, "You'll like the duke. He was wearing a tartan tonight."

"A *tartan!*" Dickie blazed. "It wasn't green and black, was it?" That is the tartan of the Gordon clan.

"No, it was blue and white," I said.

Dickie snorted. "There is no blue and white tartan. He made it up!"

"Don't be silly. He couldn't invent a tartan. I'm sure it's genuine. Come and see for yourself."

Dickie maintained that she wanted no part of the Windsors, except, maybe, their heads on a medieval pike. She refused to come to a dinner I gave for the Windsors and the Darryl Zanucks in Cannes, but curiosity got the better of her and she at last accepted an invitation to the Château de Croe. I felt

Dickie bridle with anger when she saw some of the guests drop a curtsy to the duchess, a gesture of respect accorded royalty which she did not merit. The duchess was clever. Sensing Dickie's antagonism, she stepped forward quickly and put out her hand in greeting, indicating she did not expect a curtsy from her. The duke was again wearing his blue and white tartan and Dickie began to mutter under her breath ominously. To settle the matter once and for all I drew the duke into a corner.

"Sir, what is the tartan you're wearing?" I asked.

"It's the Lord of the Isles," he said. "Only the Prince of Wales is supposed to wear it."

My critical Scottish friend went to the party prepared to dislike the Windsors, but she succumbed to the duke's charm immediately.

"What do you think of him now?" I asked *sotto voce*.

"Charming," said Dickie grudgingly.

The duchess did not conquer her so easily, but after we saw the Windsors a few more times that summer, Dickie broke down and confessed that they were much nicer than she had imagined.

Although I can blame no one but myself on going overboard for the Windsors, Dickie's conversion was a factor in my changing attitude toward them. Dickie's approval checked with my own appraisal and I decided to present the Windsors in a favorable light to counteract the damaging attacks being made on them in newspapers and books. The duke's entire life revolved around his wife, and I wanted to help preserve his illusions, as well as mine. My judgment was wrong, but I still believe my motive was right.

While the duke was preparing his autobiography, A *King's Story* — a job he took very seriously, he often worked late into the night with his collaborator. The duchess became bored with the project and started to go out with a much younger, faster crowd. Her frequent appearances in night clubs with young escorts gave rise to a good deal of loose talk that was damaging to both the Windsors. On the night of the ANTA ball at the Plaza Hotel I insisted that the duke come as a member of my party and take at least one turn around the dance floor with the duchess. The duke said he was tired and tried to beg off, but I was so insistent that he finally took my advice. The resultant pictures of the Windsors dancing together promptly stifled overwhelming rumors of their impending separation.

Since we're playing truth and consequence, I must admit the friendship of the Windsors was a valuable asset. I am a newspaperwoman, and it was extremely advantageous having this contact with a couple who were in the forefront of the news. They were great "copy." The duke still is, but the duchess has lost somewhat of her original news value. Also, I was more intrigued than ever by a woman who had the colossal determination to ride roughshod over all obstacles in her pursuit of her ambition.

In his autobiography A *King's Story*, the duke unwittingly described the calculated cleverness of Mrs. Simpson's strategy in their first meeting. It was at a fox hunt at Melton Mowbray in 1931. For some unexplained reason the then Prince of Wales, an enthusiastic horseman, did not ride with the chase that day. Mrs. Simpson, a guest with her second husband in the same house, also stayed behind to nurse a bad cold. The prince commiserated with Mrs. Simpson and asked whether she missed America's central heating. The following dialogue is quoted from A *King's Story:*

"I am sorry, sir," she said. "But you have disappointed me."

"In what way?"

"Every American woman who comes to your country is always asked the same question. I had hoped for something more original from the Prince of Wales."

The Duke concluded the incident with this admission: "I moved away to talk with the other guests, but the echoes of the passage lingered."

Mrs. Simpson's gambit obviously was a reversal of the usual approach. The Prince of Wales was accustomed to deference. Mrs. Simpson brought him up short with a caustic, provocative crack — and it worked. "I moved away . . . but the echoes of the passage lingered."

Having put the prince on the defensive, Mrs. Simpson kept the initiative. She took a flyer on a long shot and it paid off at fantastic odds.

During 1950 I was in Palm Beach for a short visit with Millicent Hearst. The night before I returned to New York, Mrs. Hearst gave a dinner party for a number of people, including the Windsors. Millicent likes to amuse her women guests with a fortune teller and she was fretting over her failure to find one in Palm Beach.

"If you don't give me away, I'll be your fortune teller," I said.

"How can you?" Millicent asked. "You know all the women intimately."

"That will make it all the more fun. Don't worry. I'll carry it off all right. You just play it straight."

For props I bought cheap incense, a long black veil and some cheap jangling ornaments that gypsies wear. We put a dim light in a cloak room off the foyer and fixed it up with two chairs and a table. After dinner, I left the party on some pretext and ducked into the cloak room. I popped two pieces of cork inside my cheeks, an old trick to disguise the voice, put on my trappings and was ready for business.

Beautiful Audrey Emery, once married to the Grand Duke Dmitri, was the first customer. Using what I fondly believed to be an authentic Romanian accent, I recalled a few innocuous incidents that sent her out raving about the remarkable gypsy who had read her past so accurately.

The duchess was skeptical. "She's a plant. Millicent has told her enough about us to make a couple of lucky guesses."

"How did the woman know who I was?" Audrey asked. "The room is too dark to recognize faces, and, besides, any one of us might have gone in first."

"That's true," the duchess conceded. "I'll try her."

She walked into the cloak room and sat down defiantly.

"Haf you any qvestion you vant to ask, Lady?" I inquired.

"No. You're paid to tell *me*, not I you," she said brusquely.

"Oh, Lady, you are very strong, too strong for a lady," I said in my phony accent. "I see you are mixed up with history." I mumbled something in gibberish. "You have changed history. This is dangerous. You have been married one — two — three times. Your husband is sailor, soldier, admiral, general, prince — king!"

She straightened stiffly in her chair.

"You have great responsibilities, Lady," I droned.

"Never mind that," she said tersely. "Tell me the worst. I can take it. I can take it."

"Oh, there is no worst, Lady, because your husband loves you. All will be well if you return his love. If you do not, I see trouble. Big trouble."

The duchess sat motionless for a long moment. Then she said, "You are quite good," and left the room.

Outside, the other women pounced on her and asked what she thought of the gypsy.

"She's marvelous," the duchess answered.

The duchess's fortune was the last I told. When I faced them with the imposture later, they were amazed.

I continued for two years to invite the duchess to the annual balls I put on for charitable organizations in Paris. The duchess, a most hospitable hostess, gave dinners for a number of my guests before the parties — but she never appeared herself before one o'clock in the morning. She would stay for fifteen minutes or so before taking off for the night clubs.

The breach between the duchess and myself was widened by society columnists who seized upon an incident without knowing the details and blew it up into a so-called feud. In December, 1952, Mrs. Lytle Hull asked me to stage a benefit for her pet charity, the Hospitalized Veterans of the Musicians Emergency Service. I thought it would be a splendid ticket-selling and publicity gimmick to have the duchess lend her name to the affair and participate in a fashion show. On the night of the ball, just as I was going up to the microphone to express my gratitude to everyone who had contributed to the success of the event, the duchess said to me, "Please don't mention my name to the audience." I can't imagine why she made the request, but I obeyed it. Some people thought the omission of the duchess's name was a deliberate snub on my part, and a number of silly stories were written commenting on it. The duchess made no attempt to put the record straight.

The final straw came just before I again aided Mrs. Hull's charity a year later. My original plan, which subsequently was changed, was to have a costume ball sponsored by four duchesses representing distinguished houses of their respective countries. The friends I selected were the Duchess of Argyle (England), the Duchess de Brissac (France), the Duchess of Alba (Spain) and the Duchess di Sera (Italy). When society reporters asked the former Wallis Warfield what she thought of my choices, she said:

"It would take four ordinary duchesses to make one Duchess of Windsor."

When I read that quote in the papers, a sharp feeling of revulsion swept over me, for I thought the duchess was too hard, too possessive, with a destructive quality within, to be a friend. There are chemical reactions between people that cause a friendship to endure or wither on the vine. I suddenly resolved to cut all my ties with the duchess. Maybe the decision was superfluous. It is entirely possible that the duchess had made the same resolve long before I reached it.

My only regret was the loss of the duke's friendship. Since the duke and I usually were among the first to leave parties, he frequently gave me a lift back to my hotel, and on those rides I got to know this lonely man who tries hard to be a regular good fellow. On one occasion our car stopped for a traffic light and a car with two pretty girls drew up alongside. They instantly recognized the duke and he smiled back at them in acknowledging their attention.

"Look, Elsa, they know who I am," he said in astonishment. "Isn't it nice that people are so friendly?"

Another time the duke again dropped me off at a party in New York given by the Josh Logans to honor Emlyn Williams, the British actor who was giving readings of Dickens in a local theater.

"Why don't you come in, sir?" I said. "They would be so happy to have you."

He replied: "No, I'm tired. I must go home. But tell me, Elsa. Does that man fill a theater just by giving readings?"

"Oh, yes," I said. "He's a great success."

He went on: "It's a wonderful way to earn a living. I gave a reading once in Vienna just after the abdication when I went to stay with the Eugene de Rothschilds. The British minister had phoned me that they would like me to read the lesson at the English church. I was very nervous but accepted, and strangely enough when I got in the pulpit to read from one of the gospels, a great peace came over me, and I felt comforted." He laughed wryly. "These things can happen, you know."

For five years I was the Windsors' most ardent champion in America, but I finally seceded from a circle that held a good deal of charm and glamour because I could not stand by and witness the dissolution of a legend. It would indeed be tragic if the duchess, by some perverseness in her character, utterly destroyed the greatest love story of all time.

Chapter 16

THIS book, and the eighth decade of my life, began with a party. This book never would have been published, though, if the sum of my seventy years merely added up to a superficial round of social events. What significance — a formidable word — is there in the story of a woman who parlayed a small talent for the piano and a great capacity for gaiety into a unique career?

Maybe it demonstrates in this age of cynicism that fairy tales still come true for the most improbable Cinderellas. Perhaps it suggests that inconsequential, but sincere, pursuits do as much good in the long run as events which appeared to be far more important at the moment. Giving parties is a trivial avocation, but it pays the dues for my union card in humanity. My parties have raised countless millions for charity and have given happiness to the donors as well as the recipients. Creating good will that impels people to give gaily to a charity is far more important to me than dunning people into donations.

I never have been apologetic about my reputation as a party-giver, and I have no intention of adopting a defensive attitude at this late date. The ultimate perfection is happiness, and my parties helped to achieve it. That is ample justification for any activity or ambition. To me, the laughter of my guests is a sweeter sound than the unheard voice of posterity. Janet Flanner once wrote of me: "She is not a social promoter. She is an evangelist under crystal chandeliers whose shout of 'Isn't this divine?' is the hilarious hallelujah of the saved." No one has had more fun than I have at my parties, and few people ever have derived more satisfying rewards from the pursuit of happiness.

It is a source of never-ending astonishment and delight to find myself a celebrity. I loved riding around the world on a donkey last year when a news photo was taken of me dressed as Sancho Panza at the Marquis de Cuevas's gala in Biarritz. An Indian diplomat told me that the picture was reprinted more widely in India than that of Madame Vijaya Pandit, who was elected president of the United Nations General Assembly a week later. I loved impersonating Mae West at Baron de Cabrol's fête in Paris for the homeless children of France, and inadvertently stealing the show when I tumbled off a stepladder. I loved going on Edward R. Murrow's TV program "Person to Person" for a fifteen-minute interview and getting 4000 letters from listeners who were inspired by a brief reference to my father's philosophy. I love having to hire a secretary when I'm in New York just to acknowledge requests for my participation in charity affairs. And I love being able to pitch in and call a friend like Gianni Agnelli and get him to donate a $10,000 Fiat car to a raffle for the benefit of the blind babies of the New York Lighthouse.

But most of all, I love the cheerful shouts of "Hi, Elsa!" from strangers on the street, and getting into confidential conversations with taxi drivers, chambermaids, and store clerks. The people of my class, the ordinary, common people who struggle with uncommon valor to pay their bills and educate their children and observe the rules of decent behavior, are not fooled by my chi-chi façade and fantastic activities. I have been earning my living for nearly fifty years, and it is gratifying to be recognized by working people as one of them. Their warm friendliness is, I like to think, a reflection of their secret amusement that I, of all people, hobnob with notables of talent, position and wealth without possessing any of their attributes or advantages.

I'm proud of the niche I have created for myself, and why shouldn't I be? I made it the hard way — through my own efforts, without asking or receiving favors from anyone except a few intimate friends. I reached for the moon and made it by refusing to accept easy compromises with mediocrity. I demanded the best when I was in no position to demand anything. I preferred to have nothing rather than take shoddy substitutes for top quality. When I gave parties in the old days, I starved for weeks and wore the same clothes for years to make mine the best parties. When I couldn't afford first-class travel and hotel accommodations, I stayed home in a grubby room and ground out songs, wrote magazine articles or wracked my brains learning the tricks of new trades until I had enough money to live in the style to which I was unaccustomed.

Intolerance of mediocrity has been the main prop of my independence, but I must confess that it has been a fault as well as a virtue. I regret that I was not always as kind or considerate to some people as I should have been. I was a social bulldozer so intent on leveling obstacles to my objectives that I left behind old friends who did not keep pace with me. Yet "old friends" always has seemed a contradiction to me.

Age cannot wither nor custom stale the infinite variety of friends who, as long as you know them, remain as vibrant and stimulating as the day you first met them. They march along with you, maturing and mellowing with you, sharing your expanding scope of interests. It has been said that a person is fortunate to have one good friend. If that is true, I am lucky, indeed, beyond all reasonable expectations. Although the attrition of time is becoming increasingly harsh, I still have a number of friends I have known for more than forty years. But I don't consider them old friends. I think of them as my best friends, because the passing years have strengthened our accord.

The only fear I ever have had is the dread of boredom, and as I grow older it is almost a phobia. It's the best of all possible neuroses and I cherish it. Authorities in geriatrics, the branch of medicine concerned with the diseases and emotional problems of old age, confirm what is suspected by everyone as the years rush by with dismaying speed. The most malignant diseases of the aged are boredom and apathy induced by the feeling that they no longer serve a useful purpose.

This old gal is more alive and kicking harder than ever. The past year has been the busiest of my life — except the one coming up — and I love every minute of it. I can't remember a year I worked on more charity committees, arranged more parties and dinners, met more people, saw more shows, read more books and wrote more special articles. The other day I posed for publicity pictures and made a recording for the Heart Fund in the morning. In the afternoon I went through the same routine for the March of Dimes, then went home and dashed off a column before going to the theater and a supper party afterward. Of course, my bones ached by the time I fell into bed, but I'd rather be dead tired than dead, period.

One of the most satisfying aspects of my life is the fascinating variety of people I know and meet. At a party given by Anita Loos in April, 1954, shortly before I sailed for Europe, there was Aldous Huxley, the distinguished British author and an outstandingly refreshing spirit of our time. As I turned away from chatting with him, I ran smack into Audrey Hepburn, whom I can only describe as a delightful creature. Looking over her shoulder I saw Constance Collier, who took me back thirty years to a dismal day at Sunning Hill Park in Surrey. Constance, the greatest Shakespearean actress of her day, was being carried out of the house dying of diabetes. As a last resort Maxine Elliott was sending her to a sanatorium in Switzerland, where, as an experiment, she was to be one of the first diabetics treated with insulin. Only a woman my age can appreciate what a tonic it was to see Constance immortally young and full of fun. And only a professional collector of personalities like me could fully appreciate a prime specimen at the party such as Fleur Cowles.

Mrs. Cowles is one of those women who yearns to be beautiful, but nature has been lavish in endowing her with other attributes. She is a born organizer and an opportunist who can take any situation in her ambitious life in stride and turn it to her advantage. She is not a good housekeeper — I often have gone away hungry from one of her dinner parties — yet by sheer energy she has gained something of a reputation as a hostess. Fleur's chief charm for me is her boundless enthusiasm. Through her husband, Gardner Cowles, the publisher, she has met many outstanding celebrities in recent years, yet she still regards them with the starry-eyed delight of Cinderella examining her pumpkin coach. She invests all her heroes and heroines with a wonder and a glamour they probably do not possess — but I understand her fervor because I had it myself when I was her age. In many respects I feel that Fleur is like me in this book. As the pages are turned, "the suspense of the author becomes unbearable."

I'm still a little girl on Christmas Eve lost in the delicious anticipation of the treasures piled around the tree for me. When I wrote this in the spring of 1954, I even found myself hoping the clock and the earth would turn faster because I could hardly wait for the new experiences in store last summer. It was singularly gratifying to have been the only American invited to appear at the Scholar Theatre in London in a play for the benefit of the Invalid Children's Aid Association, a charity sponsored by Queen Mother Elizabeth. My social calendar never was so crowded with banner dates in Rome, Lisbon, Paris, London, the Riviera and Venice. And a summer never carried the promise of such a glittering climax as a trip to Greece as the personal guest of King Paul and Queen Frederika.

I have lived by my wits all my life and I thank the Lord they still are in one, whole piece. I don't need glasses, benzedrine or a psychiatrist. I can play the score of any standard opera and I know the lyrics of every popular song hit from "She's Only a Bird in a Gilded Cage" down to Cole Porter's tunes in *Can-Can*. I can answer a city editor's four-alarm emergency and knock off a feature story or a series in time to catch a deadline. I haven't missed one yet in fifteen years of newspaper work.

The days are too short for all the things I want to do. But on the way to dinner with the King and Queen of Greece last winter, I did have time to remember I promised to send a bottle of Joy perfume to a taxi driver who had told me wistfully that he never could buy such an elegant gift for his wife. Money means nothing to me, but I was glad at that moment I could afford to spend $45 to give happiness to a woman I never had seen.

Any period since the dawn of history was a good time to have been alive, but I can't imagine a time that would have brought me more satisfaction for having reached the Biblical span of threescore and ten than September, 1953. Princess Dorothy of Liechtenstein, the tiny principality tucked between Switzerland and Austria, invited me to spend a few days with her. Princess "Dumpy" formerly was the daughter-in-law of Theresa Fair Oelrichs — the Theresa Fair whose family did not consider the Maxwells good enough to ask to her party in San Francisco in 1895.

The wheel had turned full circle.

Index